The Defence of French

MULTILINGUAL MATTERS SERIES
Series Editor: Professor John Edwards,
St Francis Xavier University, Antigonish, Nova Scotia, Canada

Other Books in the Series
Language and Society in a Changing Italy
  Arturo Tosi
The Other Languages of Europe
  Guus Extra and Durk Gorter (eds)
Motivation in Language Planning and Language Policy
  Dennis Ager
Multilingualism in Spain
  M. Teresa Turell (ed.)
A Dynamic Model of Multilingualism
  Philip Herdina and Ulrike Jessner
Beyond Boundaries: Language and Identity in Contemporary Europe
  Paul Gubbins and Mike Holt (eds)
Bilingualism: Beyond Basic Principles
  Jean-Marc Dewaele, Alex Housen and Li Wei (eds)
Ideology and Image: Britain and Language
  Dennis Ager
Where East Looks West: Success in English in Goa and on the Konkan Coast
  Dennis Kurzon
English in Africa: After the Cold War
  Alamin M. Mazrui
Politeness in Europe
  Leo Hickey and Miranda Stewart (eds)
Language in Jewish Society: Towards a New Understanding
  John Myhill
Maintaining a Minority Language
  John Gibbons and Elizabeth Ramirez
Urban Multilingualism in Europe
  Guus Extra and Kutlay Yagmur (eds)
Cultural and Linguistic Policy Abroad: The Italian Experience
  Mariella Totaro-Genevois
Language Decline and Death in Africa: Causes, Consequences and Challenges
  Herman M. Batibo
Directions in Applied Linguistics
  Paul Bruthiaux, Dwight Atkinson, William G. Eggington, William Grabe and Vaidehi Ramanathan (eds)
Language Diversity in the Pacific: Endangerment and Survival
  Denis Cunningham, D.E. Ingram and Kenneth Sumbuk (eds)
Multilingualism in European Bilingual Contexts: Language Use and Attitudes
  David Lasagabaster and Ángel Huguet (eds)
Linguistic Landscapes: A Comparative Study of Urban Multilingualism in Tokyo
  Peter Backhaus

For more details of these or any other of our publications, please contact:
Multilingual Matters, Frankfurt Lodge, Clevedon Hall,
Victoria Road, Clevedon BS21 7HH, England
http://www.multilingual-matters.com

MULTILINGUAL MATTERS 137
Series Editor: John Edwards

The Defence of French
A Language in Crisis?

Robin Adamson

MULTILINGUAL MATTERS LTD
Clevedon • Buffalo • Toronto

Library of Congress Cataloging in Publication Data
Adamson, Robin.
The Defence of French: A Language in Crisis?/Robin Adamson.
Multilingual Matters: 137
Includes bibliographical references and index.
1. French language. I. Title.
PC2073.A32 2007
440–dc22   2006022560

British Library Cataloguing in Publication Data
A catalogue entry for this book is available from the British Library.

EAN-13: 978-1-85359-949-1 (hbk)

Multilingual Matters Ltd
UK: Frankfurt Lodge, Clevedon Hall, Victoria Road, Clevedon BS21 7HH.
USA: UTP, 2250 Military Road, Tonawanda, NY 14150, USA.
Canada: UTP, 5201 Dufferin Street, North York, Ontario M3H 5T8, Canada.

The policy of Multilingual Matters/Channel View Publications is to use papers that are natural, renewable and recyclable products, made from wood grown in sustainable forests. In the manufacturing process of our books, and to further support our policy, preference is given to printers that have FSC and PEFC Chain of Custody certification. The FSC and/or PEFC logos will appear on those books where full certification has been granted to the printer concerned.

Typeset by Archetype-IT Ltd (http://www.archetype-it.com).
Printed and bound in Great Britain by MPG Books Ltd.

Contents

List of Tables vii

List of Abbreviations viii

Preface xi

Introduction xiii

1   Defending French: A Story of Love and Power 1
      Creating Classical French 1
      Enlightenment and Revolution: The 18th Century 6
      Education and the Defence of French: The 19th Century 9
      – Responses to the Modern World: The 20th and 21st Centuries . . 11

**2   The Dynamics of Defence: Some Contemporary
      Themes and Trends** 20
      French-speaking Professional Groups 20
      The Legal Response 24
      On the Fringe? Regional and Minority Languages 29
      Beyond the Fringe: Europe 34
      – Technology and the Defence of French: The Internet 45

3   Official Agencies: The Language of Power 50
      L'Académie française: The Grandmother of Them All 50
      L'Alliance française: The Friendly Face of French 55
      La Délégation générale à la langue française: Official Action 60
      La Francophonie: Commonwealth and Common Wealth? 67
      – Foreign Affairs: The French Government and Language 74

4   Language and Politics: Inseparable Partners 82
      Rois, Révolution, Républiques 82
      Dependence or independence? The Separatist Parties 90
      A Slippery Slope 98

5   **Languages in Europe: How Does France Compare?** 107
    An Overview 107
    Germany: The Old Enemy, the New Ally 112
    Italy: Romance Neighbour .118
    Spain: Another Romance 124
    The United Kingdom and English: *vieux compagnons de route*. 132
    Conclusions. 138

6   **Problems and Paradoxes; Interference and Interaction.** 143
    Cross Currents in the Resistance Movement 143
    Tradition and Modernity 147
    Political Ambiguities. 150
    Language and Identity 153

7   **Conclusion** 161

Notes. 176
Bibliography 181
Index. 196

List of Tables

Table 1.1   Non-government Defence of French. 18
Table 2.1   Professional Groups 21
Table 3.1   History of the DGLFLF 61
Table 3.2   Ministry of Culture and Communication (2006) 61
Table 3.3   Structure of the DGLFLF 63
Table 3.4   *La Francophonie*: Administrative Structure 68
Table 3.5   Francophone Summits 69
Table 3.6   Ministry of Foreign Affairs (2006) 75
Table 3.7   Selected Reports – Cultural and Language Policy 78
Table 4.1   Movements allied to the *Alliance souverainiste* 102
Table 5.1   Languages with an Official Organisation 108
Table 5.2   Language Protection and Promotion in Europe 139
Table 7.1   The Defence of French – Government Agencies 162
Table 7.2   The Defence of French – Non-government Actions 166

List of Abbreviations

ACCT   *Agence de coopération culturelle et technique*
(Agency for Cultural and Technical Cooperation)

AFAA   *Association française d'action artistique*
(French Association for Artistic Action)

AFAL   *Association francophone d'amitié et de liaison*
(French Association for Friendship and Networking)

AFP   *Agence France Presse*
(French Press Agency)

AIF   *Agence intergouvernementale de la Francophonie*
(Intergovernmental Agency for Francophonia)

AIMF   *Association internationale des maires francophones*
(International Association of French-speaking Mayors)

ALF   *Avenir de la langue française*
(Future of the French Language)

APF   *Association internationale des parlementaires de langue française*
(International Association of French-speaking Members of Parliament)

APROBI   *Association des professionnels de la traduction des brevets d'invention*
(Association of Professional Translators of Patents)

ASSELAF   *Association pour la sauvegarde et l'expansion de la langue française*
(Association for the protection and expansion of the French Language)

AUF   *Association des universités partiellement ou entièrement de langue française*
(Association of Universities Partially or Entirely [using the] French Language)

CLIC   *Centro di consulenza sulla lingua italiana contemporanea*
(Centre for Consultancy on the Contemporary Italian Language)

CSA   *Conseil supérieur de l'audiovisuel*
(Higher Council for Audiovisual Media)

CSLF   *Conseil supérieur de la langue française*
(Higher Council for the French Language)

DCCF   *Direction de la coopération culturelle et du français*
(Directorate for Cultural Cooperation and French)

DGCCRF *Direction générale de la concurrence, de la consommation et de la répression des fraudes*
(General Directorate for Competition, Consumer Affairs and the Repression of Fraud)

DGCID *Direction générale de la coopération internationale et du développement*
(Directorate General for International Cooperation and Development)

DGLF(LF) *Délégation générale à la langue française (et aux langues de France)*
(General Delegation for the French Language (& the Languages of France))

DLF *Défense de la langue française*
(Defence of the French Language)

DWB *Deutsches Wörterbuch*
(German Dictionary)

ECML European Centre for Modern Languages

EFNIL European Federation of National Institutions for Language

FFI *Forces françaises de l'intérieur*
(French Interior Forces)
Forum francophone international
(International Francophone Forum)

INED *Institut national des études démographiques*
(National Institute for Demographic Studies)

INSEE *Institut national de la statistique et études économiques*
(National -Institute for Statistics and Economic Studies)

MAE *Ministère des affaires étrangères*
(Ministry of Foreign Affairs)

MCC *Ministère de la culture et de la communication*
(Ministry of Culture and Communication)

MEN *Ministère de l'éducation nationale*
(Ministry of National Education)

OIF *Organisation international de la Francophonie*
(International Organisation for Francophonia)

OVF *Office du vocabulaire français*
(Office for French Vocabulary)

RIF *Rassemblement pour l'indépendance et la souveraineté de la France*
(Assembly for French Independence and Sovereignty)

UN United Nations Organisation

UNESCO United Nations Educational, Scientific and Cultural Organisation

UPF *Union internationale de la presse francophone*
(International Union of the French-speaking Press)

Preface

For a foreigner, and an *anglophone* at that, to write a book about the defence of French may need some justification. All those who have learned French as a foreign language, particularly teachers of French, probably have the necessary credentials for the job. In my own case, apart from *une longue liaison amoureuse* with the language, the country and its people, there are two biographical details that perhaps explain why I felt the need to study this topic.

In the 1980s, when I was teaching at the University of Dundee, the university, guided by the Thatcherian principles then in vogue, decided to discontinue the teaching of modern languages. With the support of enlightened colleagues, I managed to convince the executive that French at least should be saved. Thus the citation for my *Palmes académiques* (*Officier*, 1989) refers, among other things, to the *défense de la langue française*.

In 1997, in Paris for a sabbatical term, I was in St Germain des Prés with my mathematician husband looking for the tomb of Descartes. Our search, quite by chance, also revealed the tombs of two Scottish Douglases (Archibald Tyneman de Douglas, *Duc de Touraine* and his son James) who had died at Verneuil on 17 August 1424 – *pour la défense de la France*. Since these two Douglases and I share a common ancestry, I am encouraged to involve myself in the defence of the French language, always with the hope that today's struggles will be more successful than the French and the Scots were at Verneuil!

The University of Western Australia and its remarkable Reid Library have once again provided a delightful environment for research. Colleagues in European Languages and Studies have been consistently supportive and helpful. The comparisons between France and other European countries benefited from the expertise of John Kinder and Marinella Caruso (Italy), Alexandra Ludewig (Germany), Linda Hartley (Spain) and Angus Ross (UK). Any remaining errors are mine.

Stéphane Le Fur (*Attaché linguistique*, Education Department of Western Australia) shared his expertise on *la Francophonie* and helped to organise meetings and interviews in Paris. Hélène Becker and Hubert Sévin

(*Directeurs, Alliance française de Perth*), Bertrand Calmy (*Attaché culturel, Ambassade de France,* Canberra) and Jean Harzic (former General Secretary of the *Alliance française*) provided help with the section on the *Alliance française* and fruitful contacts in Paris.

For memorable visits to the legendary bastion of the French language, the *Académie française,* I thank Jean-Claude Pasqualini and Monsieur Personne. The complexities of the *Délégation générale à la langue française et aux langues de France* (DGLFLF) were unravelled for me by Pierre Janin, and Laurence Lalatonne and Alain Villechalanne provided invaluable insights at the *Alliance française de Paris.* Albert Salon, doyen of the defensive associations, willingly and entertainingly contributed his unique knowledge of this important area.

Many other people have supported and encouraged me with warmth and friendship in this labour of love as I explored the myriad aspects of the defence of French. To all of them, and particularly to Iain who, as usual, bore the brunt of it all and still came up smiling, *grand merci !*

Introduction

The defence of French arouses passionate discussion, both in France and elsewhere. The language used ranges over the emotional spectrum and is marked notably by metaphors of love and war. Some external commentators treat the topic with barely concealed derision while others admire the strong stand taken by the French. Nevertheless there is general agreement that the question of language defence is taken with greater seriousness in France than in most other countries. This book is an attempt to explain rather than judge the attitude of the French towards their language.

Many French people, whether they feel themselves involved in the 'battle' or not, speak of their language with love. Their education, their history, their very identity are all bound up in the language they have been explicitly taught to revere. A long history of centralised political power and of standardised education means that they have, until very recently, shared to a greater extent than those in many other countries basic ideas on identity. They have all been taught, particularly in the two centuries since the Revolution, that their beloved language is an essential element of the Republic and of their identity. Their intense involvement with their language has a long and passionate history.

This partly explains why some of the more vocal of the defenders of French, the *résistants*, feel that war has been declared on their language and thus that their duty of resistance is no less imperative than it was for the *Résistance* in the Second World War. The language of the new war is deliberately designed to make this analogy explicit: from terms such as *guerre* (war), *lutte* (struggle), *combat, offensive, défense, résistance* to the description of the 'enemy' as the *Empire*, and its policies as *impérialistes, totalitaires, colonialistes, hégémoniques*, the discourse of the *résistants*, its vocabulary, its metaphors, its rallying cries show clearly that they consider themselves to be at war.

Who are the defenders of French? There are two main, and dramatically different, camps: the private groups and individuals (*les résistants*) whose reasons for engaging in the battle are often emotional, and the hugely powerful government agencies whose linguistic battles are part of a much more extensive political agenda. The contrasts between the two groups could hardly be greater. The private and semi-private associations and lobby groups are small and impoverished. They have to fight to make their voice heard, often against the might of the government whose policies and spokespeople frequently disappoint and enrage them. They make speeches, hold rallies, write books and articles, appeal for funds, lobby government. Their work is almost always confined to the national stage and they labour under the same difficulties as other small privately organised associations.

The official government agencies on the other hand, based in powerful ministries such as foreign affairs and culture, employ large staffs of specialists and receive funds for publications, publicity and travel. Their activities in favour of French are not confined to metropolitan France, but cover the countries of the European Union, all the countries associated with *la Francophonie*, and other political arenas throughout the world – the United Nations (UN) and the United Nations Educational, Scientific and Cultural Organisation (UNESCO) for example. The extent of official support for action in favour of French bears witness to the primary importance attached in successive French governments to the political potential of the national language.

But the distinction between the two very unequal groups of language defenders is less clear than might at first appear. Three of the private associations receive government funding and thus with it specific responsibilities, notably in connection with the application of the 1994 *Loi Toubon*. Boundaries are blurred and lines of demarcation constantly changing and this must be taken into consideration when studying the work of language defence in France. In an attempt to analyse and compare the activities of the many agencies involved in language defence in France, I have used tools developed by Cooper (1989) and Spolsky (2004). To the three types of planning policy identified by Cooper: status, corpus and acquisition policies (1989: 99–163), I add Spolsky's concept of diffusion policy (2004: 71). The distinctions between these types of language policy are far from clear, particularly in the French case, where an enormous and multi-faceted state apparatus is in operation.

Cooper (1989: 98) suggests the use of a grid based on eight questions for classifying actions taken in the implementation of language policies. This provides a very useful framework that was more fully developed by Ager (1996). Using the adapted grid as a comparative tool, it is possible to summarise the activities of the various defensive groups. The grid also allows us to highlight the main differences between, for example, the private and the governmental agencies and to observe the areas where their activities overlap. Tables 7.1 and 7.2 in the Conclusion, based on Cooper's eight basic questions, give a description of the differences between the two main sets of language defenders.

Much has been written about the defence of French, particularly in histories of the language but also in books devoted specifically to the topic which is characterised by a number of two-way, polarising conflicts. Some commentators (mainly linguists), both inside and outside France, see the situation as a classic example of inevitable language change and possible decline. Others interpret what is happening to French as a blatant case of American imperialism, sometimes claiming to find evidence of an American plot to produce an English-only world. The French–English opposition is just one of many polarities resulting in the use of a discourse of war, in the drawing up of linguistic battle lines. For example, confrontations between linguists and more conservative groups, many of whom are happy to be described as purists, are standard features of the linguistic landscape in France – as they are in many countries.

A number of other differences of view inside France polarise opinions about language. Frequently the older generation and young people find themselves ranged on opposite sides. Related to this opposition is the growing gap between the written and the spoken language, identified by generations of linguists as a concomitant of the long-standing normative linguistic policies characteristic of France. The French government sometimes meets opposition to its francophone policies from French intellectuals and cultural leaders. It is itself torn between policies of linguistic *dirigisme* and *liberté*. Its desire to maintain a considerable degree of the traditional French centralisation of power, including power over the language, runs counter to the need to respond to the growing demand for political decentralisation in France. Political and constitutional arguments rage over the need to protect the national language and the apparently conflicting claims of the regional and minority languages. In this area, France may find itself opposed to its European partners rather than enjoying its more usual role of unquestioned leadership in European construction. And the old problem of the relationship between the élite and the *peuple* in the country of the *Déclaration des droits de l'homme* is more obvious than ever in discussions about language issues.

So what is the diagnosis at the beginning of the 21st century? Is French really in crisis? There are some voices, particularly among the private *résistants* (among others Decaux, 2002; Mignot, 2002a, 2002b; Salon, 2003), telling us that, because French is used less and less often as a working language for international diplomacy, that in the European Union, at the UN and in UNESCO, the language is in crisis and is seriously threatened. The same arguments, however, may be heard from some government sources. French, they remind us, is no longer the language of learned con-

xvi   The Defence of French

ferences, even those held in France, and French researchers have to present their research in English if they are to have an international audience.

What is even worse according to the leading private defenders is the 'betrayal' of the language by those in power, so that even in France itself French is being replaced by English (of a kind). In many French firms, not only those owned by multi-nationals, English is used routinely. Even in the Ministry of Defence English is used for some purposes. Advertising and the media continually use English words and phrases. The modern forms of the French language are, according to some of its defenders, degenerate and unworthy of the purity and precision of classical French. All this, they argue, is to the detriment of French and the disadvantage of French citizens. It is a crisis that threatens the very existence of the Republic and private citizens must act if the government is unwilling or unable to stem the tide of decline.

On the other hand, there are those who offer another diagnosis – Bengtsson (1968), Calvet (1999), Cerquiglini (2003) and Hagège (2002b, 2002c) for example. They and other linguists find that the patient is in good health. French is more widely spoken throughout the world now than at any other time. There are growing numbers of learners of French as a second or foreign language and the language itself is adapting well to the demands of the modern world. These views do not make them any friends among the defenders. But we cannot dismiss the views of the linguists as left-wing utopianism any more than we can disregard the opinions of the defenders as right-wing rants or republican posturing.

For the French, their language defines and shapes both personal and national identity; it has been lovingly and deliberately crafted over centuries by kings, by the Revolution, by emperors and by the Republic as an instrument of political unity, the force that binds many disparate elements into one proud identity, a confident monolingual people. As the stresses of the globalised world oblige the French, like the citizens of every other nation, to re-examine some of their basic certainties, that identity and that confidence are under increasing strain. The unique role of the French language in shaping the nation and its citizens, the almost mythic stature its speakers attach to it, have forced it on to the front line of language defence where it is now the European standard-bearer, the symbol of the determination of the French people not to succumb to the inimical globalising forces that seem to be attacking them on many fronts: economic, political, cultural and linguistic.

Like most Europeans, the French live with a daily consciousness of their history and, like all languages, French reveals – in its vocabulary and its structures – the history of those who speak it. So, in addition to love and war, there is yet another metaphor for how they feel about their language.

It seems to them that they are in danger of losing their *disque dur* (hard disc) (Védrine, quoted by Decaux, 2002). The contents of the disc, the history of French and the heritage of the nation, are of great importance to the private linguistic resistance groups, and they frequently exploit events and places that resonate within the French national consciousness in an attempt to mobilise national feelings and national pride.

Thus the group FFI (*Forum francophone international* (International Francophone Forum)), a semi-private umbrella group for 52 existing associations both inside and outside France, set up to defend French on 3 July 2001, chose initials that would powerfully recall, at least for older French people, the bravery and courage of the *Forces françaises de l'intérieur* (French Internal Forces) during the Second World War. It may be going too far to recall that the date chosen for the creation of the FFI is also the date of the coronation of Hugues Capet in 987, but he was the first king to speak the language that subsequently became French (web site, *Université Laval*, History). It is also the date of remembered Anglo-Saxon perfidy at Mers-El-Kebir in 1940. The *Comité Valmy* chose for itself the name of the battle, known to all French schoolchildren, where the foreign invader was repulsed by the small but determined French revolutionary army in 1792. The *Comité*'s declaration on 7 December 2001, the *Appel de Villers-Cotterêts* (Villers-Cotterêts Appeal), reminds French people of the historic *Ordonnance de Villers-Cotterêts* (Villers-Cotterêts Proclamation), where François 1er in 1539 issued the first edict to promote the use of French. Other terms, notably *Résistance* and *résistants*, recalling proud moments in French history, are similarly exploited to 'mobilise the troops'.

As we observe, with varying degrees of sympathy perhaps, the growing anxiety and stridency of some of those who want to defend their language, we may wonder at the lack of a historical perspective on language change characteristic of some of their published pronouncements. To read some of what has been written by private *résistants* in recent years, we might suppose that some of them consider what they see as the deliberate destruction of French by the all-powerful speakers of English as the first example of a shift in language dominance. This is of course far from being the case. French is, for example, one of a number of languages formed as the dominance of Latin throughout the western world diminished. In Western Europe Latin itself, because of the power of the Roman empire, had been the powerful survivor from among a number of Indo-European languages. These had probably in earlier times gradually come to dominate the Finno-Ugric languages. In all such cases of language domination, it is reasonable to suppose that there was anguish among the speakers of the disappearing languages as new political realities encouraged the dominance of foreign tongues. Similar situations arose in the

French colonies. While many colonised people came to love French, even today hostile reactions to the dominance of the language of the coloniser are still apparent.

The world dominance of English is just the most recent example of this tendency to adopt the language of the politically, economically and culturally powerful. What makes the present situation different is the fact of globalisation. More languages will be destroyed by the dominance of English than has been the case in previous examples of language shift, and this is of increasing concern to professional linguists who write with deep concern of the death of languages. French is not one of the languages threatened with imminent death, but the French are so sensitive where their language is concerned that they are already on full alert. For the *résistants*, forewarned is fore-armed.

It is impossible in a book of this size to cover all the elements of the battle for French. The situation in Quebec, where the struggle for French is particularly heated, has been left unexplored. Other French-speaking countries and regions have similarly had to be excluded. In comparing French with other languages (Chapter 5), the book limits itself to the situation in Europe. For English, for example, it has only been possible to refer in passing to the increasingly bitter language confrontations taking place in the United States and the discussion of Spanish is restricted to Spain itself although there are more speakers of Spanish in the Americas than in Europe. In addition to English and Spanish, French has been compared with German and Italian but Portuguese and other European languages have not been included.

Inevitably many tempting byways have appeared during the research. There is, for example, a very full literature on the decline and death of languages (Crystal, 1997, 2000; Fishman, 1991; Hagège, 2002a; Janse & Tol, 2003; Nettle & Romaine, 2000 for example) and on the sociology of language, including theories on languages and the market economy (Ball, 1997; Bourdieu, 1982; Downes, 1988; Fishman, 1972; Sanders, 1993). It is only possible to make passing reference to these and many other fields related to our topic. Rather than trying to unravel the detail, I have concentrated on regional at the expense of minority and immigrant languages. Although polemic abounds and temperatures are constantly raised over the thorny questions of spelling reform and the feminisation of professional and job titles, in trying to draw a broad picture of language defence and resistance in France, these two important areas have been left largely unexplored.

Another area that clearly merits close study is the discourse of the defensive movement, a discourse marked by invention and the highly polemical. The pronouncements of the *résistants* include:

- demonisations of Americans: *'l'Empire-vampire'* (the vampire empire) (*Comité Valmy*, 2003);
- attacks on English speakers (*les Anglo-saxons*) and their language: *'langue de la super-puissance américaine'* (the language of the American super-power) (Buffon, 2003);
- outraged reactions to what is seen as the imperialism of the Americans: *'[les] volontés hégémoniques anglo-saxonnes'* ([the] Anglo-Saxon desire for world dominance) (Mignot, 2002a); *'oligarchies technocratiques qui veulent imposer une langue unique'* (technocratic oligarchies wanting to enforce the use of a single language) (FFI, *Appel de Villers-Cotterêts*, 2001);
- accusations of collusion in this process by French government officials who, it seems, have: *'pris l'initiative, en toute illégalité, d'agir pour éliminer la langue française en France même'* (initiated action, operating completely outside the law, to eliminate the French language in France itself) (Griesmar, 2001);
- criticisms of the European Union *'majoritairement vassalisée par l'empire américain'* (most members of which have been 'vassalised' by the American empire) (*Comité Valmy*, 2003).

This book attempts to explain the passionate engagement of the French with their language, to discuss the historical and political background to attitudes to French today and to consider the challenges the language and the policy-makers face in the 21st century. As well as taking into account various histories of the language (Lodge, 1993; Price, 1971; Rickard, 1989, for example), the book is based on literature on language policy in general (Ager, 1997; Cooper, 1989; Spolsky, 2004; Spolsky & Shohamy, 2000; Wardhaugh, 1987) and language policy in France (notably Ager, 1996, 1999; but also, among others, Saint Robert, 2000; Sanders, 1993; Salhi, 2002). However, because the book aims to see the language from the perspective of those who speak it, it tends to rely more heavily on books, commentaries and articles by French authors: histories of the language (Bruneau, 1955; Chaurand, 1999; Hagège, 1987), discussions of language policy (Certeau *et al.*, 1975; Citron, 1991; Kessler, 1999) and analyses of the defence of French (Bengtsson, 1968; Hagège, 1996; Laurent, 1988; Walter, 1988).

The research for this book also demonstrates some of the advantages for researchers and readers of the constantly growing opportunities now offered by the Internet. Information can often be more up to date than in printed sources. The full texts of essential primary documents such as laws, discussions in parliament and government documents can be quickly accessed and, through the inclusion of an extensive list of web sites in the

Bibliography, readers are able to consult them as they read. Reading a book based on such readily available sources is a potentially interactive experience. It encourages further research and allows the reader to follow lines of enquiry suggested by the text. A wide variety of primary and other source documents on the Internet has been consulted for this book where the use of the Internet by government and private defensive organisations engaged in the defence of French is also examined. New research methods and reading skills are required by this approach: documents available on the Internet may not have been subjected to the careful editing process normally required for a printed book or article. The statements of government and other agencies and individuals cannot always be taken at face value and the impossibility of tracing the authorship or publication date of a promising document may preclude its inclusion. Nevertheless the Internet opens up new research possibilities for both author and reader.

The book covers the history of the defence of French (Chapter 1), the main contemporary trends (Chapter 2) and the role of the government in language defence (Chapter 3). Chapter 4 looks more closely at aspects of politics before the comparisons with other languages in Chapter 5. Chapter 6 considers the relationship between identity and language. Finally, Chapter 7, the Conclusion, tries to assess the necessity for the multiplicity of defensive actions, to estimate their chances of success and to evaluate their effectiveness (Cooper's 8th question). It analyses the differences and similarities between private and official defensive agencies, and makes a prognosis based on an interpretation of what is happening to the French language today. It looks to the future and makes some suggestions about how best to ensure that it will still be possible for those who come after us to experience the wonder and the richness of a language that has carried so many important messages for the world.

This is a celebration of one of the languages of humanity and a salute to its future in a multi-lingual and multi-cultural world. Rather than focusing on a putative crisis or on external threats it looks to the French to take back the initiative, to illustrate rather than defend their language (Dargent, 2004b: 61; Du Bellay, 1549). Accepting the existence of a rich variety of languages in France and arguing that national and personal identity are multi-faceted, evolving, dynamic and intertwined (Touraine, 2003), it attempts to show how the future of French might be assured by policies encouraging the acceptance and management of linguistic diversity (Calvet, 1999: 43).

Chapter 1

Defending French: A Story of Love and Power

Creating Classical French

Most native speakers of English have never felt the need to defend their language. They simply take it for granted. Many of us are only too happy to assume that, because our language has, through an accident of history, acquired a dominant position in the world, it is superior to others. This can give rise to a misplaced and inappropriate linguistic arrogance on the part of English-speakers – whom the French call, with varying degrees of affection, scorn or bitterness, *les Anglo-saxons*.

This introduction is an abbreviated account of a long, involved and fascinating history, and provides the background for the analysis of the present-day situation in later chapters. A full history of the defence of French is also a history of France, of the creation of the nation and its values, of the construction of French identity, and of labyrinthine political developments from the 16th century to the present. Chaurand (1999), Hagège (1987, 1996) and Lodge (1993) give good introductions to the historical and linguistic intricacies of the subject, while Ball (1997), Gordon (1978) and Grillo (1989) cover some of the sociolinguistic intricacies associated with the defence of the language. The University of Laval web site provides a perceptive and objective overview of the wider aspects of the history of the French language while *l'ABC de la langue française* has a very comprehensive chronology. The various official sites of the French government and the *Académie française* give the government perspective.

Because English has not on the whole aroused fiercely defensive attitudes, it may surprise speakers of English to find that official and public concern with the defence of French began at least as early as the 16th century – even earlier according to some commentators (for example, Citron, 1991; Judge, 1993: 9; Walter, 1988: 95). As Bernard Cerquiglini (2003), the *Délégué général à la langue française et aux langues de France* said when he took office in May 2003: '*Les noces de l'État et de la langue dans notre pays sont anciennes.'* (The close ties between the State and language in our country are very old.) It was in August 1539 that François 1er (1515–1547) issued, from his hunting castle at Villers-Cotterêts, an edict now known as the *Ordonnance de Villers-Cotterêts*. This imposed the use of French instead of Latin in legal judgments. The stated purpose of the *Ordonnance* was to avoid the problems caused by the ambiguities in various legal documents written in a kind of low Latin, *le plus souvent « macaronique »* (usually a clownish jumble) (University of Pennsylvania web site, 2005).

The castle at Villers-Cotterêts has become virtually a sacred site for modern associations for the defence of French who declare that they are following in the footsteps of François 1er. Citron (1991: 231) reports that the date of the *Ordonnance* became in the 1990s a *date-repère* (historical signpost) for the teaching of French history in schools. It is clear in any case that the purposes of the *Ordonnance* were very different from those of 21st century defenders of the language. If we speak of François 1er defending the language, defending must be understood not as resisting attack, but as supporting or promoting. The king was apparently motivated, not by a wish to protect his language against Latin, but by legal and political considerations: Article 110 : 'So that there should be no cause of doubt about the meaning of the said decrees, and we command that they be drawn up and written so clearly that there should not be, nor could be any ambiguity or lack of clarity.'[1] As the *Académie française* web site puts it: 'Thus the public life of the country was indissolubly linked with the scrupulous use of "the native French language"' (Article 111)[2]. This early and unbreakable link between power and the court version of one of the languages of France, the *langue d'oïl*, set the tone for a great deal of what was to follow.

Ten years later, the poet du Bellay (1522–1560), together with Ronsard (1524–1585) and other poets of the group known as *la Pléiade*, published their poetic manifesto, the *La deffence et illustration de la langue francoyse* (Defence and Illustration of the French Language) (Du Bellay, 1549), associating the word *deffence* with the language for the first time. Like François 1er, du Bellay was using the word in a pro-active sense. He wanted to extend the uses of French and to develop it, as well as resisting a perceived threat from Latin. French was at this time considered by many to be an undeveloped, impoverished language, suitable perhaps for use in legal and political documents, but incapable of expressing the ambitious and elaborate nuances required, for example, by poetry.

By insisting that it was not only possible but desirable that poetry be written in the *langage maternel français* (native French language), du Bellay added a new motivation to those of François 1er for extending the use of French: its suitability as a literary language. This 16th century identification of the defence of French with its use as a literary language was accepted unquestioningly by successive French educational establishments and underlies much of the teaching of French in schools to this day. Ronsard, du Bellay and their fellow poets left as their legacy the conviction that French is innately suited to express the highest thoughts and passions of which humans are capable. The *Deffence* provoked spirited attacks on du Bellay and his friends and their refutations were no less vigorous, the first example of the lively polemic, or, as Calvet (2002b: 33) calls it *hystérie* (hysteria), which continues to characterise the defence of the language in France today.

Although he is not as important a figure for the defence of the language as du Bellay, Henri Estienne (1528?–1598) seems to have been the first to 'defend' French in the sense of combatting a perceived threat to the language. His 'Two dialogues in the new italianised, and otherwise disfigured, French, mainly between the courtiers of the present time'[3] (1578), and his 1579 publication, *Essai sur la precellence du langage françois* (Essay on the Superiority of the French Tongue), prepared at the request of the king (Walter, 2001b), ridicule people who spoke the fashionable Italianised French of the period. The role played in the history of French by fashion, and the French are perhaps particularly sensitive to changing trends, is far from insignificant. The fact that it is now fashionable to speak English, just as it was to speak Italian in the 16th century, is one of the factors that infuriate those who today battle against the dominance of English.

As the 16th century ended and the *grand siècle* (great century) began, the role of literature, particularly poetry, in the defence of French was further strengthened by the poetic and linguistic activities of François de Malherbe (1555–1628): 'Finally Malherbe came, and was the first in France to convey the correct tone in poetry'[4] (Boileau-Despraux, 1674 *L'Art poétique*). Malherbe was official court poet to Henri IV (1589–1610), Marie de Médicis (Regent: 1610–1614) and Louis XIII (1610–1643) and, most importantly, a protégé of Cardinal Richelieu (1585–1642). This role at court and at the centre of political activity gave Malherbe an extremely influential position and sealed the alliance of language and power that had begun with François 1er. Although he had at first been influenced by the poets of the *Pléiade*, Malherbe moved away from their adherence to classical forms and insistence on creativity in the native language to insist on purity of form and strict compositional rules.

His insistence on applying rules marked the start of that highly protective and defensive attitude to the language still to be found in its modern defenders and sometimes considered by speakers of other languages to be both hyper-sensitive and typically French. Two words characterise the view of French at this time: *prestige* and *autorité*. Like Walter (1988: 96), Chaurand (1999: 231) reminds his readers that from this time on, French, rather than being viewed as a living, changing means of facilitating communication 'presents first of all the image of something with <u>prestige</u>, preserved and protected with jealous care, at the expense of its varied and free expressive possibilities.'[5] (Chaurand's underlining).

The new rule-based view of the language was at first disseminated largely by the literary *salons*, 17th century social gatherings in the homes of wealthy noblewomen, who regularly invited influential figures (mainly men) from the fields of literature, the arts and politics to discuss their ideas and read their works. Language was a frequent topic and the rules were strictly applied so that invention and creativity were eventually stifled and the typically French *chasse aux néologismes* (hunting out neologisms) became a regular pastime. In the heightened atmosphere of the *salons*, powerful political figures and literary giants met regularly.

The alliance between political power, *autorité* and language had already been evident under François 1er in the 16th century. However, as Lodge (1993: 169) explains, the sources of power and the underlying conflicts in French society were, by the 17th century, more complicated and the nature of the monarchy had changed. With the development in Paris of the new bureaucratic class, economic and therefore political power was not the exclusive preserve of the court. Various groups, the court, the legal profession and the bourgeoisie, each sought to dominate. Social tensions ran high. For the group that could establish their form of the language as the norm, there would be substantial political benefits. Thus Richelieu, as part of his move to centralise political power in the hands of the court, was determined to establish the language of highly educated court administrators as the standard. In this way, the alliance between language and power was strengthened.

According to Chaurand (1999: 232) and many other commentators: 'It is to Richelieu that we owe the first, the main and the emblematic confusion between political authority and the internal force of the language.'[6] In the terms used by Cooper (1989), this means that status planning and corpus planning were already intertwined in internal language planning. It was as a result of the 'emblematic confusion' between the two that in this period the French convinced themselves that 'our language is a fragile creature which must continually be watched over and controlled'[7] (Chaurand, 1999: 232).

It was therefore, as Cooper (1989: 3–11) and Spolsky (2004: 63–65) so clearly show, politically and socially highly significant that in 1635 Richelieu obtained from the king, Louis XIII, letters patent for an existing 'academy of music and prose'. The *Académie française* was charged with establishing and monitoring stringent rules to maintain the language in a fixed state of order and purity. This concern with the corpus was never completely separate from the more ambitious aims involved in status and acquisition planning. Fumaroli, a present-day academician (quoted on the web site, *Académie francaise, Language, Le français, langue de la nation*) says that Richelieu founded the *Académie* to 'give to the unity of the kingdom forged by political power, a language and a style which would symbolise and cement that unity.'[8]

It is important to note that achieving this political unity resulted in marginalisation of other social groups and their ways of speaking and writing, and in a concentration of power in the hands of a very small, highly educated and ambitious group of courtiers. This intimate connection between the supreme political power in France and the language has continued, although the nature of that supreme power has changed:

> Cardinal Richelieu had proclaimed himself the protector of the Academy. When he died, this protection was exercised by Chancellor Séguier, then by Louis XIV and, following him, by all the succeeding kings, emperors and heads of state of France.[9] (web site, *Académie francaise, Language, Le français, langue de la nation*)

We examine the ongoing role of the *Académie française* in Chapter 3, pp. 50–55.

The *Académie* web site also recalls that one of the stated aims of Richelieu's ambitious project was *de la [la langue française] rendre pure et compréhensible par tous* (to make it [the French language] pure and understandable by everyone). The apparently laudable aim of codifying the language so that all French people could understand one another echoes Article 110 of François 1er's 1539 *Ordonnance*: '*qu'il n'y ait, ni puisse avoir, aucune ambiguité ou incertitude*' (so that there should not be, nor could be, any ambiguity or lack of clarity). It also however begs the questions of which of the languages of France was to be the vehicle of the centralised power and who were the people capable of understanding, speaking and writing it. The mantra of comprehensibility for all was to be reiterated by the revolutionaries, but it would not be until the 20th century that the massive efforts of radically different kinds of political power would eventually achieve, for a variety of political ends, the imposition of something approaching a single national language capable of boasting that it was at last universally comprehensible.

One of the most influential figures in the history of the language in the 17th century was the *académicien* Claude Favre de Vaugelas (1585–1650). He was charged by the *Académie* with the preparation of the dictionary – one of four works it set out to produce in order to meet the terms of its statutes. In the century of its creation, the *Académie* itself published only the dictionary. It was Vaugelas who wrote a grammar of French: *Remarques sur la langue française* (Remarks on the French Language), an extremely influential work which fixed the rules of *'le bon usage'* (correct usage). Vaugelas was subsequently credited with being *'l'organe le plus accrédité du meilleur et du plus pur parler de la France'* (the most respected voice of the best and purest speech of France) (Sainte-Beuve). As later chapters show, the importance of the purity of the language, a concern of both Richelieu and Vaugelas, is still agitating the *résistants* and it is an idea also characterising attempts to defend language in other countries (Chapter 5).

The *plus pur parler de la France* was furthered strengthened by the appearance in 1660 of the influential *Grammaire générale et raisonnée de Port-Royal* (General Logical Grammar of Port-Royal) and in 1694 the long-awaited first edition of the dictionary of the *Académie* finally appeared. So, at the start of the 18th century, the French language was already allied to political power and defended, codified, controlled and protected to a degree unknown in other European countries.

Enlightenment and Revolution: The 18th Century

For the purposes of this study, the first notable linguistic event in the 18th century was the 1714 Treaty of Rastadt, which established French as the language of diplomacy throughout Europe, a status it was to maintain until the Treaty of Versailles in 1919. The consciousness of the prestige enjoyed by French during those years is still evident in the way some of its modern defenders think, speak and write about it.

This was the century of the Enlightenment, and French thinkers were at the forefront of the dramatic new intellectual developments in Europe. Fumaroli shows the extent to which the French language dominated intellectual life in Europe during this century 'where the French are at home everywhere, where Paris is the second homeland of all foreigners, and where France is the focus of interest for Europeans'[10] (2001: 9).

Numerous codifications (grammars) of the language appeared during the century of the Enlightenment, but an event still resonating in the national consciousness was the essay written by Antoine de Rivarol (1753–1801) for the competition organised by the Berlin Academy in 1783: *Discours sur l'universalité de la langue française* (Discourse on the universality of the French language) (web site, *Universität Wien*, <u>Rivarol text</u>).

The fact that the competition was organised in Berlin is striking testimony of the widespread view held at the time that French was the universal language. Thus, even in cases where the focus of attention was apparently exclusively on language (corpus), awareness of its potential for the extension of political and cultural influence and status outside France was never entirely absent. The remarks made about the mission of the *Académie* by Maurice Druon (1995), the then *Secrétaire perpétuel*, prove that this conviction has endured: 'to give reliable rules to our language, to maintain its purity, to ensure that it is always able to speak with precision about all arts and sciences, and so to protect the characteristics which make it universal'[11] (web site, *Académie française*, Statutes). This preoccupation with universality – apparently a specific feature of French – is found in the writings and pronouncements of both private and government defenders of the language today (for example Gilder, 1993).

The world was to change dramatically before the end of the century with the French Revolution and once again the close links between language and politics were to be reinforced. This time, it was not a king or his administrators who took control of the language, but the *Convention* and again it was for what were apparently the best of patriotic motives. The new Republic – *une et indivisible* – needed a language worthy of it, a language spoken and understood by all its citizens. In the country of *Liberté, Égalité, Fraternité* the continued existence of a multiplicity of languages, dialects and patois could not be tolerated. In this matter of language, *Égalité* emerged as more important than *Liberté* (Spolksy, 2004: 65). The speaking of many languages was an impediment to the universal dissemination of the new political ideas. Thus Bertrand Barère declared to the *Comité du salut public* (Committee for Public Health): 'In a democracy, to leave the citizens ignorant of the national language, unable to exercise critical judgement over [government] power, this is to betray one's country'[12] (web site, *Université Laval*, Revolution).

It was Barère who, in 1794, for clearly proclaimed political reasons, started the offensive against dialects and patois, associating them with barbarity and vulgarity: 'these barbaric corruptions and vulgar speech forms which can now only benefit the fanatics and the counter-revolutionaries'[13] (Leclerc, 2005). They had already been stigmatised by the *Encyclopédie* (1751) (web site, *L'ABC de la langue française*). Barère also foreshadowed some of the current debates in the European Union about the cost of maintaining linguistic diversity. His comments in his *Rapport sur les idiomes* (Report on Speech Forms) presented to the *Convention* on 27 January 1794: 'What huge expenses we have had providing a translation into all the languages of France of the laws of the first two national assemblies'[14] (Leclerc, 2005) can be compared with remarks in Brussels about the prohibitive cost of translation and interpretation for the increased membership of the Union (Castle, 2004).

Following Barère's comments, the *Comité de l'instruction publique*

(Committee for Public Education) set up by the *Convention* asked the *Abbé* Grégoire, an influential priest of strong republican convictions, to prepare a report. His *Rapport sur la nécessité et les moyens d'anéantir les patois et d'universaliser l'usage de la langue française* (Report on the necessity of annihilating the dialects and generalising the use of the French language), appearing in June 1794, did not pull any punches. For the *Abbé* the fact that French was spoken 'exclusively' in only 15 of the 83 *départements* was a clear denial of the republican rights of the non-French speakers. The continued use of the patois (*idiomes grossiers*) was insufferable: it would prolong '*l'enfance de la raison et la vieillesse des préjugés*' (the childhood of reason and the longevity of prejudices) (Leclerc, 2005). The resulting decree of 2 *Thermidor* (20 July 1794) instituted what has been called a reign of linguistic terror. Any document not written in French would be illegal, and any servant of the Republic who drew up a document in a language other than French could be imprisoned for six months and deprived of all his goods and rights. The decree was suspended shortly afterwards, in September 1794, but some aspects of it were re-instated by the later decree of 30 *Vendémiaire* (17 November 1794): 'In every part of the Republic, teaching is only in the French language.'[15]

Resistance to these draconian steps was strong and in the absence of sufficient schools (to replace the outlawed church schools), teachers and finance, many village schools continued to use local languages. Throughout the century, works appeared on the patois (web site, *L'ABC de la langue française*), a trend that was to grow in the following century as the study of languages developed. Nevertheless, the role of French as the national language was inevitably strengthened with the setting up of the new centralised republican political institutions where only French was spoken and where all documents were written in French. Its role as the universal international language began to weaken, as neighbouring states, now regarding republican France as an enemy, began to fight against the preponderance of French in diplomatic circles.

The attention of the revolutionaries, however, was on internal politics, rather than on the desire to obtain international power and influence. The important changes in language planning at the Revolution were:

- insistence on a coherent national language policy;
- the identification of the language as an integral part of the nation; and
- the conviction that political unity could only be achieved by linguistic unity.

These attitudes remain strong today and are frequently used to defend France's policy of internal monolingualism, for example, in discussions about regional and minority languages.

Education and the Defence of French: The 19ᵗʰ Century

The *Terreur linguistique*, instituted by the decisions of the *Convention*, continued in the 19ᵗʰ century. This was a defence of French for apparently convincing political motives, but it had enormous cultural costs and aroused strong resistance. Universal education was still not available, so the effects of the decision to impose French were limited. Nevertheless, official attitudes to regional languages, dialects and patois remained extremely judgemental. Breton aroused particular venom. A letter from the Prefect of Finistère to the Minister of Education in 1831 insists that it is essential that the state should 'by every possible means encourage the impoverishment, the corruption of Breton . . . It is absolutely necessary to destroy the Breton language'[16] (Leclerc, Breton, 2005). It was even suggested that the clergy should help by only accepting children who spoke French as first communicants. Thus a form of cultural genocide was instituted by the state.

The 19ᵗʰ century is marked by a number of important changes in education: the creation of the *lycées* by Napoleon in 1807; the institution of elementary state schooling by Louis-Philippe in 1832; the creation (following the suggestion by Talleyrand in 1794) of *une école par commune; une École normale par département* (a school in every commune; a teachers' training college in every department) by Guizot, Minister for Education in 1833. All these developments strengthened the hold of French on the education system and on French children. Anyone who wished to find employment in the public sector had to be able to write standard French, since the entrance examinations were in French.

Although the increasing availability of schooling as the century progressed led to the reinforcement of French and to the concomitant weakening of other forms of speech and writing, the Duruy report in 1863 stated that there were still 7.5 million French citizens (out of a total of 38 million) who spoke no French. It also confirmed the staying power of the *patois*, which children continued to speak at home, tending to forget most of the French they had learned as soon as they left school (Leclerc, Breton, 2005).

External influences were also increasingly important throughout the 19ᵗʰ century. The power of the press began to be felt and the creation of the *Agence Havas* (later to become AFP: *Agence France Presse*) strengthened the influence of France and the French language outside France. To enshrine the earlier codification of the language, many large and influential dictionaries of French were published in the 19ᵗʰ century. The *Académie* continued to publish successive editions of its dictionary, as obliged by its statutes, although, after four editions in the 18ᵗʰ century, there were only two in the 19ᵗʰ century: in 1833 and 1876. Among other important dictionaries were the original Larousse (1856), *Le grand Dictionnaire universel* (1876) and the first Littré (1873). It was also during this century that the word *'linguistique'* was first recorded (1833) and that the *Société linguistique de Paris* (Linguistic Society of Paris) was founded (1864). This marked the development of new attitudes to the study of language and inaugurated a new age of professional linguistic analysis. It is however notable that, even after repeated scathing criticism of its members' lack of professional linguistic qualifications (for example, Brunot, 1932), the *Académie française* has never, since its inception, given a high priority to the opinions of professional linguists.

The trend to enforce French as a single national language at the expense of regional languages was greatly strengthened by the laws passed by Jules Ferry, Minister of Education, between 1881 and 1884. Ferry's profoundly influential educational philosophy was contained in the three words *'gratuité, obligation, laïcité'* (free, compulsory, secular) (web site, France, Government of, <u>Senate</u>, Teaching). Although Ferry is apparently silent on the subject of regional languages, by making primary education in French free and obligatory until the age of 12 years, and training French-speaking *instituteurs* (primary school teachers) to deliver it, he created ideal conditions for the extinction of the despised 'lower' forms of language and their replacement by French.

A new development towards the end of the century was the interest in 'defending' French by actively propagating its use outside France. Judge (1993: 14) suggests that this may partly have been a reaction to unfavourable attitudes to France following the Franco-Prussian war. The invention of the new word *francophonie* (the act of speaking French) by a French geographer, Onésisme Reclus, in 1880 indicates that there was a growing interest in the speaking of French outside France, and this is confirmed by the creation in 1883 of the *Alliance française* whose mission was to: *'propager la langue française dans les colonies et à l'étranger'* (spread the French language in the colonies and in foreign countries) (web site, *Alliance française*, <u>Mission</u>). This involved both status and acquisition planning in other countries. The list of some of the names of those behind the setting up of the *Alliance* shows wide support from influential figures in public life – but again there are no names of linguists (Chapter 3, p. 56). Over succeeding years the *Alliance* was extended to Africa, South, then North America, the Far East and Asia. Classes for foreigners started in Paris in 1893 (Désirat & Hordé, 1976: 80). The *Alliance française* is now synonymous in many parts of the world with the idea of French language and culture. It has never though been exclusively concerned with language, nor entirely free from political involvement in its activities, as the discussion of its modern role in Chapter 3 confirms.

The publication of numerous books on patois and dialects (web site, *L'ABC de la langue française*) showed that interest in regional forms of speech had continued, in spite of the forces ranged against them. In the 19th century literature flourished, books became more widely available, the number of newspapers published grew significantly and the phonograph was invented. Each of these developments contributed to the dominance of French and tended to weaken other forms of speech and writing.

So at the end of the 19th century, the tradition of codification of the language corpus was strongly entrenched, the imposition for political purposes of French as the sole national language throughout France and the colonies was being vigorously pursued, especially through the highly centralised education system, and interest was growing in *la francophonie* (Chapter 3, pp. 67–74) and the propagation of French outside France.

Responses to the Modern World: The 20th and 21st Centuries

With the new century came further developments designed to strengthen the position of French both inside and outside the country. Thanks largely to Ferry, education was now universal and was everywhere delivered in French. Outside France, even before the outbreak of war, French was promoted by French educational establishments run by the *Mission laïque* (founded in 1902) and the *Alliance française* (1883) with financial help from the *Ministère des affaires étrangères* (Ministry for Foreign Affairs) (Désirat & Hordé, 1976: 80). The involvement of the Ministry of Foreign Affairs in language politics has steadily increased since this time. The outbreak of war in 1914 and the ensuing social upheaval brought speakers of every kind of patois and dialect together and cemented the role of French as the language of communication. In his song '*Ça fait d'excellents Français*' (They all make excellent Frenchmen), Maurice Chevalier reminds us amusingly how men of all kinds, from all parts of France, served in the army together, communicating with one another as best they could in French.

The growing number of newspapers in France took the language to every part of the country and the colonies and the beginning of radio broadcasts in the 1920s and of television in the 1950s ensured that French was the language of the increasingly powerful media. The *Union internationale des journalistes et de la presse de la langue française* (International Union of French Language Journalists and Newspapers) (since 2001 the *Union internationale de la presse francophone* – UPF (International Union of the French-speaking Press)) started in 1950. The importance of the media in the external defence and promotion of French was further marked by the political decision in 1984 to create, as part of an extension of *la Fran-cophonie*, the French language television channel TV5, now broadcasting in Europe, Canada, Latin America, Africa, Asia and the USA (web site, UPF).

The speed of technological innovation meant that inside France terminology became a problem, since the tendency was to adopt the English-language terms for new inventions, and many of these words were (and are) felt not to be suitable in French. Thus, the first official government institutions with the task of defending the language at home were concerned with terminology as an aspect of corpus planning. From the long list of legal measures related to the language in the 20th century (web site, *Légifrance*), it is immediately apparent that the majority of them concern the new vocabulary demanded by technological changes.

The *Commission de terminologie technique* (Commission for Technological Terminology), set up in 1933 was the first of several government bodies to have responsibility for creating new terms (Désirat & Hordé, 1976: 89). From this time on, it becomes difficult to keep track of all the government agencies involved with terminology and vocabulary. The *Office de la langue française* (Office for the French Language) was set up in 1937, but disappeared in 1942. The 1950s saw the creation of the *Comité consultatif de langage scientifique* (Consulting Committee on Scientific Language) (1952), the *Comité d'étude des termes techniques français* (Committee to Study French Technical Terms) (1954) and the *Office du vocabulaire français* (Office for French Vocabulary) (OVF) (1957) (Désirat & Hordé, 1976: 90–91). The *Commissions de terminologie pour l'enrichissement de la langue française* (Terminology Commissions for the Enrichment of the French Language), an initiative of Georges Pompidou, began in 1972 and *Franterm* was set up in 1980 (Offord, 1994: 76). The passing of the Loi Toubon in 1994 led to the creation in 1996 of the '*Commission générale de terminologie et néologie*' (General Commission on Terminology and Neologisms).

This plethora of institutions preoccupied with the lexical corpus is reflected in popular attitudes to language. Many users of a language equate it with its vocabulary and are prepared to go to great lengths to defend words. This is clearly exemplified in the March 2004 campaign by Bernard Pivot (*100 Mots à sauver* (100 Words to Save)) to save disappearing words (Busnel, 2004). It is important to note that the more balanced analysts of the French language have been at pains to point out that the introduction of new words, rather than signalling the imminent demise of the language, is a proof that it is alive and healthy. Inroads into the syntactic system of the language on the other hand may be a proper cause for concern.

Other institutions dealt with the defence of the language beyond the borders of France. The OVF (Bengtsson, 1968: 31–35) was the most influential of the institutions dealing with terminology, going well beyond its brief to deal internally with matters of vocabulary, and setting up the _Fédération underline_internationale_ pour la sauvegarde et l'unité de la langue française_ ✳ (_International_ Federation for the Protection and Unity of the French Language (my underlining)) in 1963. This was followed by the _Sommets de la francophonie_ (Summits of the French-speaking World) (Désirat & Hordé, 1976: 90), dealt with below and in more detail in Chapter 3. The following year, in his book _Parlez-vous franglais ?_ (Do you speak Franglais?), Étiemble (1964) sounded the alarm and made an emotional call for the French to resist the degradation of their language, symbolised by the debased mixture of French and English which, he claimed, was replacing French. Étiemble's predictions of the early disappearance of French prove to have been greatly exaggerated, but his book was a landmark. It put the question of language firmly on the popular agenda and started the wave of language protection activities by private individuals, a remarkable feature of the late 20th century. The availability of the Internet has, as the next section shows, given a new impetus to non-governmental intervention in questions of language.

Apart from the concern with the corpus of French technological terms, there are three other essential and intertwined strands in the increasingly labyrinthine history of the defence of French, both inside and outside France in recent times:

(1)   the accelerating pace of official government activity, particularly through legal measures;
(2)   the development of _la Francophonie_; and
(3)   initiatives by private individuals and groups.

(1) Legal measures relating to language are essentially internal matters. Some idea of their scope is given by the fact that, while there had been some relatively small-scale laws passed in the first 50 years of the century, three major laws related to the use and teaching of French (_Loi Deixonne_, 1951; _Loi Bas–Lauriol_, 1975; _Loi Toubon_, 1994) were passed in the second half of the century. The _Loi Toubon_ is now the main legal defensive measure for the protection of French inside the Republic. Another indication of the increasing recourse that is being had to the law is the fact that from 1973 (the date from which _Légifrance_ supplies details) and 2004, there were in France 143 laws or decrees relating to the French language. Legal measures are only a part of government defensive action. They are examined in more detail in Chapter 2, pp. 24–29.

The most obvious sign of government intervention is the creation and what might be called repeated re-creation of government agencies (in addition to the various bodies working on terminology) charged specifically with attention to linguistic matters and the defence of French. These organisations deal with Cooper's three types of planning: status, corpus and acquisition. They operate both inside and outside France and are, in Ager's terms (1996: 54–63) examples of 'constituent' policy agencies: 'institutions and organisations established by – or in some cases supported by – the state in pursuance of it aims' (Ager, 1996: 54). The French have a particular fondness for bodies of this kind and, as the numerous government reports on language matters attest, they have a tendency to feel that social and political problems can be solved only by the creation of a powerful government organisation. This has led to a series of agencies, potential overlap and diffusion of effort.

In March 1966 the *Haut comité pour la défense et l'expansion de la langue française* (High Committee for the Defence and Expansion of the French Language) was created by President de Gaulle's Prime Minister, Georges Pompidou. The inclusion of 'expansion' in the title, signalled that its role was external as well as internal. This double role has remained, sometimes combined in a single agency, sometimes performed by separate agencies. In 1973, under President Pompidou, it became the *Haut comité de la langue française* (High Committee for the French Language) which President Mitterrand replaced in 1984 with two agencies: the *Comité consultatif* (Consultative committee) (concerned with *la Francophonie*) and the *Commissariat général à la langue française* (General Commissariat for the French Language) (concerned with the language in France itself).

These were replaced in 1989 by the *Conseil supérieur de la langue française* (Higher Council for the French Language) (CSLF) and the *Délégation générale à la langue française* (General Delegation for the French Language) (DGLF). With the creation in 1993 of a *Ministère de la culture et de la francophonie* (now *Ministère de la culture et de la communication*), the DGLF was attached to the new ministry. A further separation between internal and external language matters took place in 1995 and in 1996 the position of the DGLF again changed as it became a permanent inter-ministerial group. With the growing interest in minority and regional languages (Chapter 2, pp. 29–34), the title again changed in 2001 under President Chirac to become the *Délégation générale à la langue française <u>et aux langues de France</u>* (General Delegation for the French Language <u>and the Languages of France</u>) (web site, DGLFLF gives details). Chapter 3, pp. 60–64 and Table 3.1 give more information on this powerful organisation.

(2) The development of *la Francophonie* (the capital letter is important) is the second of the three striking developments in the latter part of the 20th century (Chapter 3, pp. 67–74). France's involvement in this movement is

a reflection of its foreign policy rather than the result of language policy. In the initial stages, various groups of professionals throughout the world who had in common the use of French as their working language (Chapter 2, pp. 20–24) began to set up associations or professional groups. At the same time, from 1960 onwards, Léopold Sédar Senghor, President of Senegal, with the Presidents of Niger and Tunisia, began to work towards an association to link the various francophone countries. The *Organisation Internationale de la Francophonie* (International Organisation for Francophonia) (OIF) celebrated, in 2006, the centenary of the birth of Senghor, revered as its founder. De Gaulle was at best lukewarm on the idea of a francophone group of countries, as was Giscard d'Estaing.

It was not until 1970 that the *Agence de coopération culturelle et technique* (Agency for Cultural and Technical Cooperation) (ACCT) was set up at a conference held in Niamey. The fact that this agency had not originated in France and did not depend on Paris may help to explain its cool reception in France. Canada was less than enthusiastic but finally in 1986, during the presidency of François Mitterrand, the first meeting of the heads of the French-speaking states was held in Paris and the post of *Secrétaire d'état chargé de la francophonie* (Secretary of State in Charge of Francophonia) (attached to the office of the French Prime Minister) was created. Reflecting the increasing political importance attached to Francophonia, the post of Secretary of State became in 1988 a post of *Ministre délégué à la francophonie* (Minister with Portfolio for Francophonia), and the distinction between *la francophonie* (people whose language is French) and *la Francophonie* (official actions by and in support of those areas in the world where French is spoken) was established.

After the first *Sommet de la Francophonie* (Francophone Summit) in Paris in 1986, there has been a series of *sommets* (1987, 1989, 1991, 1993, 1995, 1997, 1999, 2002), held mainly outside France in other French-speaking countries. The tenth *sommet* was held in Ouagadougou in 2004 and the eleventh in Bucarest in September, 2006. The choice of location for these meetings resulted from a deliberate decision to emphasise the fact that *la Francophonie* was an initiative not of Paris but of the former French colonies. The decision at the sixth (1995) *sommet* that the movement would have, from 1997 on, a permanent *Secrétaire général* (Boutros Boutros-Ghali) – a spokesperson and symbol of *la Francophonie* – again shows the increasing desire to capitalise on the potential of the movement. In 1998, it took the title of *Organisation Internationale de la Francophonie* and its present (2006) General Secretary is Abdou Diouf (web site, France, Government of, OIF, Diouf).

What does the chequered history of all these government agencies reveal about government intervention in language planning and policy? The organisations seem frequently to change their names; the details of their mission change; their relationship with the government and the ministry on which they depend for funding and support, also change; their influence and effectiveness vary with the changes of government; there are tensions between them and the whole policy area becomes ever more difficult to control. Their direct relationship with the language is increasingly tenuous as it becomes a symbol and an icon of shared social and political values. The lack of continuity and the confusion caused by the re-naming and re-positioning of the government agencies cannot fail to limit their efficiency and to give an impression of successive governments involved in crisis management rather than controlled long-term planning. As far as *la Francophonie* is concerned, there is a strong feeling in some quarters in France that this immensely costly and badly organised movement is achieving little. Some feel it is scarcely more than governmental window dressing (Arnaud et al., 2002; Colin, 1997; Vinatier & Xvolt, 2002a, 2002b).

(3) The third strand in the accelerating defence of French at the end of the twentieth and the beginning of the 21ˢᵗ century is the growing number of actions by private individuals and organisations referred to in the Introduction. Some of these were described by Offord (1994: 80–81) who noted the wide range of views expressed, from moderate to extreme, and the differences in discourse between the various agencies. The stridency of some of the publications by private associations is in contrast to government publications. These on the whole, maintain a non-polemical tone and, while they may – for obvious political reasons – err on the side of optimism, they do not issue inflammatory or dramatic statements. When Offord was writing in 1993, there were at least 300 organisations of various kinds recorded in the publications of the DGLF (where the Internet was apparently not yet mentioned). Many of these organisations are ephemeral and, as Offord found (87–88), tantalisingly difficult to contact!

In 1995 five of these groups applied for, and obtained, legal status as associations of legitimate public interest. There are now only three with this status: ALF (*Avenir de la langue française*), DLF (*Défense de la langue française*), ASSELAF (*Association pour la sauvegarde et l'expansion de la langue française*) (AIF, 2003: 43). The large number of small associations like these tends to dilute their efforts but to some extent this is rectified by umbrella groups, AFAL (*Association francophone d'amitié et de liaison* (French Association of Friendship and Support)) for example. Membership lists and numbers are difficult to obtain. The financing for these groups is fragile. Those with legal status receive a limited amount of funding from the DGLFLF but otherwise, they, and those without this status, are reliant on members' subscriptions, sponsorship and donations. Those supported by the DGLFLF are charged with reporting, through the complaints of their members and other concerned citizens, contraventions of the 1994 *Loi Toubon*. They are able, as the DGLFLF itself is not, to bring cases against the offending companies or agencies. Chapter 2, p. 28 explains that few of these complaints actually get to the courts, and even fewer result in fines. The confusion and fragmentation of this sector is damaging to the public image of the defence of French and seriously limits the effectiveness of the activities undertaken.

The much abbreviated chronological table (Table 1.1, p. 18) gives some idea of the escalation in the numbers of private, semi-private and individual defensive associations and of how defensive activities have been increasing in France in recent years.

Added to these events are the growing numbers of activities (many only marginally related to language) organised by the various official agencies of *la Francophonie*: the summits, the annual Francophone Day and many others. There is also increasing activity by organisations such as the various Gaullist and republican movements and the movements for French sovereignty that consider the defence of French an essential (although not the central) part of their action. The role of some of these and their sometimes remote connection with the defence of language is examined in Chapter 4, pp. 90–98.

The dramatic growth of the Internet in the intervening years since Offord wrote is shown by the fact that virtually all of the defensive organisations now, in the 21st century, have Internet sites. The confusion and overlap reported by Offord have unfortunately only been accentuated by the new medium. Several organisations apparently have the same postal address and their memberships sometimes overlap. The same names crop up in a number of organisations so it is difficult to get a clear idea of how many different people are active members, seriously involved in fighting for French. The ALF claimed in 2003 (web site, ALF) to represent 6000 defenders of the language but it is difficult not to conclude that problems in obtaining information are an indication that numbers are in fact relatively low. Nevertheless, Table 1.1 reveals an increasing number of groups and heightened public visibility in some quarters. These groups (*alliances, associations, agences, comités, sociétés* . . .) feel very strongly that it is necessary to take up arms not only in defence of their language but increasingly of their culture, their nation, their Republic, their identity (see Chapter 6).

The number of private organisations has certainly multiplied, but any chance they might have of influencing government decisions or initiating powerful popular action has probably diminished. The emotional appeals for people to sign petitions, for government referenda, for concerted action, are unlikely to bear fruit, especially since those who are the most outspoken defenders of the language tend to belong to an older generation. They do not always find it easy to communicate with young speakers whose version of French they may scarcely recognise. Impassioned books,

Table 1.1 Non-government Defence of French

1791	*Société des amateurs de la langue française* (*Urbain Doumergue*)
1835	*Agence Havas* → (1944) *Agence France Presse*
1864	*Société linguistique de Paris*
1958	*Défense de la langue française* (DLF – closely associated with the *Académie française*)
1964	*Institut international de droit d'expression et d'inspiration françaises* (IDEF: 09.06.64)
1974	*Association francophone d'amitié et de liaison* (AFAL)
1985	Bernard Pivot – *Dictée* competition: *Dicos d'or* *Association pour la diffusion internationale francophone de livres, ouvrages et revues* (ADIFLOR)
1986	*Académie francophone* (associated with AFAL)
1990	*Association pour la sauvegarde et l'expansion de la langue française* (ASSELAF)
1992	*Alliance francophone* (06.02.92) *Avenir de la langue française* (ALF: 04.12.92)
1994	*Droit de comprendre* (29.07.94)
1998	*Conseil national souverainiste*
1999	*La Carpette anglaise* ("English Doormat" award for mis-use of French)
2001	*Porto Alegre* I (Global network of parliamentarians) (29.01.01) *Forum francophone international* (FFI – an internet umbrella group of 52 associations set up by ALF: 07.10.01) *Appel FFI de Villers-Cotterêts*
2002	Porto Alegre II – *Atelier sur la diversité linguistique* (02.02) Public meeting organised by the *Comité Valmy* (24.05.02) *Pétition pour la défense de la francophonie* (08.07.02) Appeal by the *Comité Valmy* for *Assises de la République* (22.09.02) *Journée européenne des langues* (26.09.02) Demonstration organised by the *Comité Valmy* and the FFI (14.11.02)
2003	*Assises nationales des langues de France* – Lyon (07.10.03) *Appel FFI*
2004	Bernard Pivot – *100 Mots à sauver !* (An appeal to save dying words)
2005	*Grande marche citoyenne pour la diversité culturelle* (09.10.05)

articles and petitions are, sadly, more likely to relieve the frustration of those who write them than to sway popular opinion or influence government policies. The difficulty of changing the course of linguistic development by active intervention – whether by private or constituent (government) groups – is another of the questions examined in Chapter 6.

This selective history of the defence of French from the 16th century to the present day has painted a picture of a language closely connected to the power structure and the élites who govern France. The French language, love and respect for which is transmitted to all French children by the centralised education system, can also be a political tool of great effectiveness and this potential has been recognised by successive forms of government. Difficulties arise as, in the course of time, more and more diverse bodies are created and more and more activities are undertaken in defence of the language: efforts are diluted, boundaries blurred and focus lost. The different types of language planning tend to merge, internal and external defensive actions are combined. In the growing concentration on political, social and economic aspects of language planning in France, in Europe and throughout the world, the focus on the language itself – corpus planning – is tending to disappear. For all the agencies described here, with the exception of the *Académie française* and perhaps some of the private groups, the national language is now defended as an intensely powerful symbol of the cultural, social and political values underpinning French society. Chapter 2 looks in more detail at some of the emerging themes and trends in recent phases of the defence of French: a potent and revered national and international icon.

Chapter 2

The Dynamics of the Defence of French: Some Contemporary Themes and Trends

French-speaking Professional Groups

This chapter looks at some of the ways the defence of French has adapted to a changing social and political environment. Internal and external pressures on speakers of French have led to appropriate defensive actions and to adaptations of the profile of official language policy, as defined by Cooper (1989: 89). The first organisations examined here are the groups of French-speakers whose professions have an international dimension and bring them into contact with English as a lingua franca (pp. 20–24). The importance of the legal responses in France to the perceived threat from English is another essential aspect of the dynamics of the present-day defence of French (pp. 24–29). A third recurrent and powerful theme is regional and minority languages (pp. 29–34), an area where pressure is applied on the government both from within and from outside France. This leads to a consideration of French in the European Union and reactions to decisions in Brussels (pp. 34–45). Each of these will be examined in turn, and we conclude with an analysis of the use of the Internet in defending French (pp. 45–49). Chapter 3 then looks in more detail at the powerful official agencies for the defence of French.

Those who use French as their working language have been banding together since before the Second World War, but many more organisations were formed in the second half of the 20th century. Their object is economic and political rather than specifically linguistic – an example of status planning. These organisations act as international pressure groups, actors in Cooper's terms, to influence French language policy in France and in other countries, their ends being to ensure that those who control the linguistic culture of their working environment act to ensure that it remains French. Their means are essentially persuasive and they may

Table 2.1 Professional Groups

1950	*Union internationale des journalistes et de la presse de langue française* (International Union of Journalists of the French-speaking Press) (UIJPLF → UPF)
1960	*Conférence des ministres de l'éducation nationale des pays francophones* (Conference of the National Ministers of Education of the Francophone Countries) (CONFEMEN)
1961	*Association des Universités partiellement ou entièrement de langue française* (Association of Universities Partially or Entirely [using the] French Language) (AUPELF → AUF)
1967	*Association internationale des parlementaires de langue française* (International Association of French-speaking Members of Parliament) (AIPLF → APF)
1969	*Conférence des ministres de la Jeunesse et des Sports des pays francophones* (Conference of the Ministers for Youth and Sport of the Francophone Countries) (CONFEJES)
1979	*Association internationale des maires et responsables des capitales et métropoles partiellement ou entièrement francophones* (International Association of Mayors and Civic Leaders of Capital Cities and Towns Partially or Entirely [using the] French Language) (AIMF)
1987	*Institut de l'énergie des pays ayant en commun l'usage du français* (Institute for Energy of the Countries Who Share the Use of French) (IEPF, see web site).

have little direct input into the decision-making process. They illustrate how difficult it is in a globalised world to make a clear distinction between internal and external policies.

Interest in such groupings grew at about the same time as Senghor was trying to gather support for an international group of francophone countries. As the selective list in Table 2.1 shows, those who chose to work together in this way had the potential to be very influential politically: journalists, ministers of education, universities, members of parliament and mayors of cities. The groups are designated by frequently abstruse acronyms and have, like the defensive organisations mentioned in Chapter 1, a tendency to change, and sometimes to simplify, both their name and their acronym (see Table 2.1).

The first group to be recognised internationally was the *Union internationale de la presse francophone* (UPF; see web site), created in 1950 as the *Union internationale des journalistes et de la presse de langue française* (UIJPLF) and renamed in 2001. It has now become a recognised non-governmental organisation, with representation at the UN, UNESCO and the OIF. It has more than 3000 members from the media and is active in

110 countries worldwide. Each year it holds international meetings – for example at Ouagadougou in 2004 in conjunction with the tenth *Sommet de la francophonie*. It has held several conferences in Europe, meetings for the French-language press in Arab countries and *États généraux* in 2001 and 2004. It holds training seminars, mounts exhibitions on the French-language press and publishes a bi-monthly bulletin, *La Gazette*, available on the Internet.

The *Conférence des ministres de l'éducation nationale des pays francophones* (CONFEMEN; see web site), was set up in 1960. It is now known as *La Conférence des ministres de l'éducation des pays ayant le français en partage* (Conference of the Ministers of Education of the Countries Sharing the Use of French) and claims to be the oldest of the official francophone organisations. The CONFEMEN includes 33 countries and 2 associated Canadian state governments – Quebec and New Brunswick. Its activities promote the influence of the systems of education in the defence and promotion of French. It operates at ministerial level, encourages cooperation between member states, endeavours to integrate their (French-language) education systems in the ongoing process of development, facilitates the exchange of information and seeks, through cooperation, to pursue common educational (and linguistic) aims (web site, CONFEMEN, Aims).

The CONFEMEN works at a similar governmental level with the *Conférence des ministres de la Jeunesse et des Sports des pays francophones* (Conference of the Ministers for Sport and Youth of the French-speaking Countries (CONFEJES; see web site), created in 1969. There are 36 countries and the 2 Canadian state governments in this organisation. It works to help young people to be better integrated into society through participation in sport as a recognised component of continuing, life-long education. Through sport, it aims to improve the socio-economic status of young people in participating countries. The *Jeux de la Francophonie* (Francophone Games), which it has been organised since the Quebec *Sommet de la francophonie* in 1987, are held every four years. Unlike the Olympic Games, or the Commonwealth Games (the inspiration for their creation), they include a cultural as well as a sport component. The fifth games were held in Niamey (Niger) in 2005.

The formation in 1961 of the *Association des universités partiellement ou entièrement de langue française* (AUPELF, now *Agence universitaire de la Francophonie* (Agency for Francophone Universities (AUF; see web site) was a Canadian initiative. It underlined the cultural and political potential of the defence and promotion of French in higher education. The AUF has 494 member institutions and operates 8 *Programmes d'action* (action programmes) for academics, students and educational establishments. These include programmes based on the French language and *la Francophonie*, on the environment and information technology, and student exchanges. It publishes an Internet newsletter with information on conferences, jobs, prizes and news items. It has been instrumental in setting up *pôles d'excellence* (centres of excellence) in various fields in the participating institutions.

The *Association internationale des parlementaires de langue française* (AIPLF, now *Assemblée parlementaire francophone* (Francophone Parliamentary Assembly (APF; see web site), founded in 1969, includes 73 parliaments throughout the world. It works to defend democracy, the rule of law, the International Declaration of the Rights of Man and cultural diversity. It organises conferences, training programmes and regional assemblies of members. It provides observers for elections and within it, as in many of the original francophone groups, specialist groups have tended to form, for example the *Association des secrétaires généraux des parlements franco-phones* (Association of General Secretaries of Francophone Parliaments (ASGPF; see web site) and the *Réseau des femmes parlementaires* (Network of Women Members of Parliament; see web site). The APF works very closely with the OIF and with the *Agence intergouvernementale de la franco-phonie* (Intergovernmental Agency for Francophonia (AIF)) and has direct access to heads of government at the *Sommets de la Francophonie*.

At local government level, the *Association internationale des maires et responsables des capitales et métropoles partiellement ou entièrement francoph-ones* (now the *Association internationale des maires francophones* (International Association of French-speaking Mayors (AIMF; see web site) offers an international platform to the heads of the governing bodies of franco-phone cities. It is also closely attached to the OIF and seeks to reinforce democracy at a local level, to encourage decentralisation and help local governments to carry out their task. It runs training programmes and seeks to extend best practice in municipal government. Like the other organisations mentioned here, it defends French and its use throughout the world but its agenda is never purely linguistic.

Finally, the *Institut de l'énergie des pays ayant en commun l'usage du français* created in 1987, but now, reflecting changes in the problems facing the world, the *Institut de l'énergie et de l'environnement de la francophonie* (Fran-cophone Institute for Energy and the Environment) (IEPF; see web site). This is also one of the official francophone organisations. It arranges con-ferences and exchanges of information and personnel on subjects such as energy policies, climate change, bio-diversity, sustainable development, environmental policies and compliance with treaties. It has a number of specialist groups and networks (for example, RELIEF and MÉDIATERRE) and, like all the other organisations, provides access to many publications, either web-based or in hard copy. It maintains a number of databases: *Liaison énergie francophone* (Francophone Energy Liaison); *Objectif Terre*

(Objective Earth); *PRISME* (*Programme international de soutien à la maîtrise de l'énergie* (International Programme to Support Energy Control)); and *Atlas des experts en biomasse* (Atlas of Biomass Experts) for example. The French language is the means of communication for the IEPF but none of its programmes is specifically dedicated to the defence of the language.

In addition to these groups at high level, there are many other organisations for those whose working language is French. All of them work to support their members and to exert pressure on the makers of language policy. They draw strength from their shared language, but most (unlike the *Académie française*, or professional linguists) have little concern with the specifics of its defence or with the way it is developing. One group with some specifically linguistic concerns and which, more than others, feels itself threatened by English, is the airline pilots. In 1976, following the hotly contested decision by Air France to discontinue the use of French in the operation of Concorde and Airbus, the pilots formed the *Association internationale des navigants de langue française* (International Association of French Language Airline Pilots – AINLF), now called, in memory of the revered French aviator and author Saint-Exupéry, *Courrier Sud* (see web site). In 2002 they joined with a similar organisation of air traffic controllers and in 2003 added French-speaking aeronautical engineers to their membership. Their site has a link to the DLF web site which was given as an example of an influential and serious group with a well-kept Internet site maintained by the AUF (p. 47).

As it becomes clear how many independent groups like *Courrier Sud* are active, it is possible to glimpse the extent of the economic and political importance of a shared working language and of the pressure being brought to bear on government policy-makers. The ends of these groups and those of the *résistants* are very different, and there is little if any interaction between the two sectors. Pragmatically, French is for these groups their preferred communicative tool. They do not feel obliged to take up arms in a language 'war', but they are prepared, for economic and professional reasons, to fight for their right to a French-speaking working environment.

The Legal Response

A theme emerging very strongly, particularly in the second half of the 20th century, is the recourse by the French government to legal measures of defence to regulate the language internally. The groups referred to in Chapter 1, pp. 16–18 are frequently bottom-up associations. Although they may be linked to official organisations, the impetus for their creation usually comes from their members. They respond to difficulties or embarrassments they have encountered in trying to work in their language and decide to take joint action to prevent further erosion of their linguistic rights. Further, they may find considerable professional or economic advantages in being part of an extensive international French-language network. These motivations may lead them to seek redress through the application of the law, but they are not directly instrumental in the passage of defensive laws.

The legal defence of French, on the other hand, is top-down, initiated at the highest level of government and backed by the full weight of national political power. The means used are authority and force, rather than promotion and persuasion, and the actor here is the French government, focusing on specific language behaviours that (it believes) can be regulated by legal means. Many of the laws relate, for example, to the education system and the languages taught in the schools. At the end of this section, and also in Chapter 6, the success of the language protection laws is assessed. The Internet provides many factual commentaries on the law in France as it relates to language. Some of these are on Canadian sites and, although the Canadian situation is not addressed here, they are very informative about France. The book by Grau for the Canadian Government (1981, web site) and the *Université Laval* site are particularly helpful, as are the official French government sites, for example *Legisnet*, the *Ministère de la Culture et de la Communication* (Ministry of Culture and Communication), the *Conseil constitutionnel* (Constitutional Council) and *Légifrance*.

First, to examine the main legislation since 1950. As Chapter 1, pp. 13–14 showed, there was an abundance of decrees and legal pronouncements in that period, but in the last 60 years four important laws stand out:

1951	*Loi Deixonne* (11 January 1951)
1975	*Loi Bas–Lauriol* (31 December 1975)
1992	*Loi constitutionnelle* (25 June 1992)
1994	*Loi Toubon* (4 August 1994).

Since it refers to regional and minority languages, the *Loi Deixonne* is discussed in the next section.

Given that concern with the language has for so long been a constant of French political and cultural life, it may seem strange that constitutionally the language was not protected until 1992. There were though many other references to the language in various laws and decrees, so it is paradoxical that, as recently as 29 June 2001, *Voxlatina* should issue, on behalf of one of the private associations defending the language, the *Société française des traducteurs* (French Society of Translators), a petition against the use of English in French law (web site, *Société française de traducteurs*, Petition).

This was addressed to nine highly ranked members of the government, including the President of the Republic (Jacques Chirac) and the Prime Minister (Lionel Jospin). The many measures already taken to protect the language had not been sufficient to stem the invasion of English, and the private sector therefore felt compelled to intervene as a subordinate actor to use different means on the primary actor – the government. This combination of private and official action is typical of many areas of language defence in France.

Following a number of texts imposing the use of French in specific professions, the *Haut Comité de la langue française* (Chapter 1, p. 14 (i)) indicated in 1972 that a single general law was required (web site, *Université Paris* 2). The *Loi Bas–Lauriol* (*Loi No. 75–1349 du 31 décembre 1975*) is very broad in its scope. In the France of President Giscard d'Estaing and Prime Minister Jacques Chirac, this law, named after the two people most closely involved in its formulation, sought to establish the obligatory use of French, and only French, in any and all matters to do with describing and presenting goods, in advertising them orally or in writing, and in all documentation relating to goods sold in France. Foreign goods sold in France could, if their names were well enough known, be excepted from this law but infractions would be punished in accordance with the 1905 law on the repression of fraud.

All information on the radio and the television was to be in French. Contracts for any type of work done in France were to be written in French and could contain no foreign word or expression, unless these had been officially accepted by one of the commissions of terminology or specifically covered in Decree No. 72–19 of the 7 January 1972, concerned with the enrichment of the French language. All written documents relating to the official public domain were to be in French. A breach of this article could result in the withdrawal of government finance. If necessary, for example in public transport, a translation or translations could accompany the French text.

We can measure the speed of changing conditions, and of the business environment becoming first multi-national then global, as we in the 21st century reflect on the passing of such a law, on the belief that it could prevent the use of foreign languages in commerce, in business documents and in the workplace. There were scathing comments from foreigners and a very small number of prosecutions, not all successful, and in any case, the penalties imposed were difficult to impose and not high enough to deter the multi-nationals. The law served mainly as a point of reference for those who viewed with mounting alarm the increasing use of English (not specifically mentioned in the law).

The next important legal intervention, reflecting the growing importance of the European environment, was in 1992. One of the consequences of the signing of the Maastricht treaty on 7 January 1992, was a growing conviction in France that French might cease to be an official language in the European Union. Among the various constitutional amendments to the 1958 Constitution of the Fifth Republic after Maastricht was a change to the Constitution aimed at preserving the status of French. The *Loi constitutionnelle* (Constitutional Law) No. 92–554 of the 5 June 1992 adds to the existing Article 2, which mentions the flag, the national anthem, the rallying cry of *Liberté, Égalité, Fraternité* and the principle of democratic government, a new first sentence: *La langue de la République est le français* (The language of the Republic is French). Such a statement had not been thought necessary in earlier constitutions, but its principal aims were to respond to private and political actors, and to reassure those who were concerned about the future of the language, especially in the changed political situation in Europe. There was increasing concern that the new political arrangements in Europe would mean a significant loss of sovereignty for France. As pp. 34–45 show, this anxiety has become more acute with the passage of time, as the European Union is enlarged and as it moves towards closer political union between the members.

Finally, in 1994, came the *Loi Toubon*, so named because Jacques Toubon was the *Ministre de la culture et de la francophonie* (Minister for Culture and Francophonia) in the government of Édouard Balladur at the time. The *Loi Bas–Lauriol* had not stood the test of time. New developments in the world economy and far-reaching social changes showed its inadequacies. The *Loi Toubon* was meant to be a revised version of the earlier law, providing for better protection for the language in numerous fields of public life and in advertising. It is a clear example of status planning and has generated a great deal of comment, both inside and outside France. Most foreigners, and even some French people, have regarded it with some amusement but it is taken utterly seriously by the groups defending the language. It was criticised by the *Conseil constitutionnel* because it limits freedom of expression but was eventually passed in August 1994.

The first article of the *Loi Toubon* echoes the 1992 change to the constitution, proclaiming that the French language is *'un élément fondamental de la personnalité et du patrimoine de la France'* (a fundamental element of the character and the inheritance of France). The law covers all aspects of work, education, research, public life, the media and advertising. The part of the law dealing with the media aroused the most comment in France. There was an outbreak of cartoons, ironic references to the impossibility of applying the law and puns and jokes about the name Toubon (it lends itself to humorous interpretations, for example, *tout bon* (everything's fine). Many people in France were alarmed at the totalitarian overtones of this strengthening of the government's powers in relation to the national language and there were protests both inside the *Assemblée nationale* and from members of the public.

In 1996, not long after the law was passed, the *Délégation générale à la langue française*, the actor whose task it was to defend and protect the language inside France, joined forces with the *Direction générale de la Concurrence, de la Consommation et de la Répression des Fraudes* (DGCCRF) (General Directorate for Competition, Consumer Affairs and the Repression of Fraud) (web site, France, Government of, <u>DGCCRF</u>) in a campaign to alert various branches of the legal profession to the need to act on the provisions of the law in the area of government services. The DGLFLF (whose powerful political, economic and social role in language protection is examined more closely in Chapter 3, pp. 60–67) relies on the defensive organisations it sponsors to initiate legal action against those who infringe the *Loi Toubon*. The number of prosecutions for the years from 1994 to 2001 shows that usually fewer than 20% of complaints were actually found to be infractions of the law. The 2005 figures (web site, France, Government of, <u>DGLFLF</u>, Reports, 2005) were the lowest for 10 years.

In most cases a simple reminder of the law is issued and no penalty is imposed. There were no prosecutions by the courts until 1997 (390 cases brought – 127 successful prosecutions) and the number has steadily diminished in subsequent years. In any case, the penalties it is possible to impose are not severe. They are what is described in French law as fourth class penalties. However, the €580,000 fine imposed in March 2006 on General Electric Medical Systems for not translating documents used by its technicians was a landmark, and other companies are in the firing line (*L'Express*, 2006b). This may mark a new confidence in the application of the *Loi Toubon*, as part of what *L'Express* calls a growing *patriotisme linguistique*.

Disappointing as most of the results of the law so far may be, its very existence and the penalties it provides for (the means) are reassuring to French people concerned about their language, even if the process leaves something to be desired. A. Judge (2002: 66, 71) finds in the annual reports of the *Délégation* to the parliament evidence of a shift of emphasis in the means of applying the law from the traditional Jacobin emphasis on punishment to a greater reliance on advice and encouragement. In spite of this, many of the defensive organisations referred to in Chapter 1, pp. 16–18, especially those funded by the DGLFLF, continue to regard it as a solemn duty to bring infractions of the *Loi Toubon* to the attention of the authorities. They take the legal framework of the law very seriously, not least in so far as it concerns their own status. Among the many texts relating to language to be found on *Légifrance* are those to give legitimacy to the associations, covering them for their activities in defence of French. AFAL, ALF, ASSELAF and DLF for example, among the more serious of the groups, apply regularly for confirmation of their legal status (and hence their right to DGLFLF funding) and the application must be renewed every three years (relevant texts are: NOR: MCCB9800367A, 1998; NOR: MCCG0100377A, 2001; see *Légifrance* web site).

The reality is that the increasing influence of globalisation makes the application of a law such as the *Loi Toubon* progressively more difficult. Further, as time goes on, it becomes harder to reconcile the *Loi Toubon* with European law. Like other member states, France is now bound by a growing number of laws formulated in Brussels. Because these concern free circulation of goods and services within the Union and consumer protection and health, they not infrequently contain language provisions in conflict with the requirements of the *Loi Toubon*. The section on pp. 34–45 will take this question of the growing influence of Brussels further.

The laws governing language use in France are by far the most stringent in the Union. Whether or not they can ever be seriously applied and effective remains an open question. They are a response to the political environment inside and outside France and while the actors are extremely powerful and have access to appropriate means of enforcement, the overall effect of the panoply of legal defence remains limited. The close connection between official language policy and commercial and political agendas in discussion of France's high-profile activities in favour of language diversity at UNESCO and at the World Trade Organisation is mentioined in a different context in Chapter 3, p. 80. The next section looks at the changing attitudes in France to policies concerning regional languages and dialects.

On the Fringe? Regional and Minority Languages

It might seem that this third theme, the changing ways the French have reacted to the wealth of regional languages and patois spoken within their nation and its overseas departments and territories, is not central to a consideration of how and why they have defended the national language. There are several reasons why this is not so and indeed remarkable parallels can be observed between the history of regional languages threatened with extinction by French and the defence of French against English in the 21st century. It is fascinating to observe the debates between the government and the regional language movements and to compare this with the way the groups defending French approach the European Union and the UN. Beginning in the early 1990s, there has been a notable and dramatic shift in government attitudes to regional languages. These have moved from being *'ces jargons barbares et ces idiomes grossiers'* (these barbaric corruptions and vulgar speech forms) to being accepted as a valued part of the national linguistic heritage. The question arises: Why was this change in policy – if not always in attitude – felt to be necessary?

The monolingual situation in France, the existence of a single language spoken by virtually every citizen and strongly protected and defended, has only come about by the imposition of a ruthless policy of destroying other contenders for the position. As Chapter 1 showed, it was at the time of the Revolution that the policy became explicit, specifically in the report prepared by the Abbé Grégoire. Attitudes did not soften in the post-revolutionary period, and the highly centralised education system put in place by Jules Ferry at the end of the 19th century succeeded in virtually eradicating all languages except French from schools, universities, the professions and the public service.

The success of the 18th and 19th century policies was nonetheless only partial. Throughout the 19th century there were many publications devoted to regional languages and this continued in the 20th century. Scarcely a year went by without articles, books and other activities supporting the retention of regional languages, particularly *breton* but also *occitan, corse* and *provençal* (*ABC de la langue française*, web site, <u>Chronologie</u> 7). It was as if the very high-profile campaign to impose French gave to these languages a black-market value. They continued to be prized, to be widely spoken, especially in homes and in the family. Private movements of defence were set up early in the 20th century, but from the first they found they needed allies in the political sphere. This led to increasing marginalisation of the purely linguistic issues and, in some cases, to alliances with extremist political groups.

The example of *breton* illustrates this. In 1919, after the First World War (which had further weakened the position of regional languages), the movement *Breiz Atao* (*Bretagne toujours* (Brittany Forever)) was set up. This became in turn the *Parti autonomiste breton* (Breton Autonomy Party) (1927–1931) and then (in 1931) the *Parti nationaliste breton* (Breton Nationalist Party). Similar developments occurred for *occitan, corse* and *tahitien*. Politicians and political groups, sometimes left wing and increasingly extremist, working for greater recognition of their region, for less centralisation, for independence, used the existing movements for the defence of language as a launching pad for their activities. By the end of the 20th century, linguistic and political aims had fused into single movements. Chapter 4, p. 97 describes important similarities in this respect between groups defending regional languages and those defending French.

The last section showed how, in response to changes in society and to various kinds of political pressure, government intervention by legal means accelerated in the second half of the 20th century. A similar escalation can be observed with regional languages. Against a background of increasing national and even international protest, the public government discourse continued to support the exclusive use of French and to refuse to consider that the regional languages had any rights. This went on until as late as 1980 when France, in ratifying the *Pacte international relatif aux droits civils et politiques* (International Pact on Civil and Political Rights), refused to ratify the section on linguistic minorities on the grounds that there were none in France. Indeed, even in 1992, by the inclusion in the Constitution of the sentence *La langue de la République est le français*, the government appeared to be affirming its continuing monolinguistic policy and denying rights to linguistic minorities. This is in stark contrast to the fact that, prior to the signature of the European Charter for Regional and Minority Languages, the 1999 Cerquiglini Report, commissioned by the government, identified 76 languages spoken in France and its overseas departments and territories, by far the highest number of all the member states (Cerquiglini, 2004).

In the second half of the century there had been a profusion of legislation gradually giving limited rights to some regional languages. This began slowly with the passage, as the result of continued representations by regional members of the *Assemblée nationale* (National Assembly), of the *Loi Deixonne*. Passed in 1951, but not officially applied until 1969 with further delays in the provision of the necessary resources, the *Loi Deixonne* (web site, France, Government of, MCC) states in Article 1 that its purpose is to 'seek the best means of promoting the study of languages and dialects in the regions where they are used'.[17] The text was the result of negotiation and compromise. It was substantially modified to make it acceptable to the parliament and hence can be interpreted both as a defence of some of the more outspoken of the regional languages (*occitan, basque, catalan* and *breton*) and as a defence of French (web site, *ABC de la langue française, Chronologie 7*).

This paradox is explained by the fact that the law encouraged the study of regional languages only in so far as they may help in acquiring a better knowledge of French. Primary and nursery school teachers are encouraged to use the local language 'whenever it will benefit their teaching, particularly for the study of the French language.'[18] (Article 2). The law was very limited in its application since it allowed – but did not enforce – the use of the local language, where the situation justified it and where the teacher was able to speak it. Such teaching was optional and required the agreement of the family. Some small provision was also made for the use and teaching of the specified local languages in secondary schools and teachers' training colleges (Articles 5 and 6).

From the point of view of language policy, this is a classic example of a confusion of types (acquisition, status) and of covert and overt ends (Cooper, 1989: 98, Question 4). The policy aimed simultaneously to satisfy the regional pressure groups and to reassure those in favour of mono-lingualism and a single national language. It led inevitably to a badly articulated policy whose means and process (Cooper, 1989: 98, Questions 6 and 7) were never clearly defined. The result was a law whose effect (Cooper, 1989: 98, Question 8) could never satisfactorily be measured.

Unsurprisingly, the *Loi Deixonne* failed to satisfy the supporters of regional languages. The Minister of Education therefore set up a commission to study the question. It published its findings in 1965, affirming that the *Loi Deixonne* had failed to deliver progress. It proposed a much more pro-active policy on regional languages, but teaching remained optional and in the elementary schools teachers were still to use the regional language *'pour aider et enrichir la connaissance de français'* (to help and enrich knowledge of French) (web site, Canada, Government of, CSLF, Publication D 118). This same publication affirms that any progress in this area is certainly not due to government and legal interventions and describes the activity of the French government in this area as *'très sporadique, au mieux des hypothèses, et regressif, au pire des hypothèses'* (very sporadic, hypotheses at best and at worst regressive). The report from the Ministry of Education's Commission, although accepted in its entirety, predictably did not radically change the situation.

The government continued to tinker with the regional language policy. Some concessions were made for Corsican in 1974 (*Décret* 74–33, 16 January 1974) and regional languages were mentioned in both the *Loi Haby* and the *Loi Bas–Lauriol* in 1975. A possible turning point came with the election of François Mitterrand in 1981. Already in his *110 Propositions* (policy statements before the election) he had included: '56: The promotion of regional identities will be encouraged, minority languages and cultures respected and taught'[19] (Mitterrand, 1981). He had a personal conviction that France could only gain from such a policy, as is shown in his 1983 speech to a conference at the Sorbonne. Speaking now of immigrants and their languages and cultures he said:

> In every case they [immigrants] have represented a gain, a profit, something more and not something less for her [France] . . . In every case it [the presence of immigrants] has meant something more.[20] (Mitterrand, 1983).

To some extent the policies of the Mitterrand governments did in fact produce improvements in the situation of the regional and minority languages. From the election in 1981 until the end of the century, there were at least 16 laws, decrees or circulars dealing with minority languages (Corsican, Tahitian, Polynesian languages among others), mainly concerned with their place in education (web site, France, Government of, <u>MCC</u>, *Loi Deixonne*). Savary, Minister for Education in the Mitterrand government, responded to the express wish of the President that people speaking regional and minority languages should have the right to use them. The Savary Circular (1982), extending rights to all languages, and the *Loi Savary* (26 January 1984) (web site, France, Government of, <u>*Légifrance*</u>) giving government funding for them are frequently quoted although their effectiveness is equally often queried.

Meanwhile, the international, and particularly the European, environment was changing. Activities in favour of minority cultures and languages were increasing and this encouraged action in France. It seemed that real progress was at last being made, but two research projects by the *Institut national des études démographiques* (National Institute for Demographic Studies (INED); web site) produced, in 1993 and in 2002, reports on two research projects that were far from encouraging. The first report (Héran, 1993) notes the failure of the *Loi Deixonne* and educational policies in favour of regional languages, the *écrasante domination du français* (overwhelming domination of French) and a dramatic diminution in the numbers of people speaking minority languages with each successive generation. Héran asks an important question: 'Can we really expect the education system to revitalise a heritage it helped to destroy in the past?'[21]

The second report, known as the Clanché Report (Héran *et al.*, 2002), also makes gloomy reading. Again it mentions the persistent and growing dominance of French but adds a reference to the spread of English since the time of the 1993 enquiry. This report '*confirme la domination indiscutable du français*' (confirms the undisputed domination of French) but '*révèle aussi la richesse du patrimoine linguistique*' (also reveals the richness of the linguistic heritage). Showing how far thinking has changed, it concludes with the affirmation, and many in France would not accept this, that: 'French is the crowning glory of this heritage; it is not destroying it.'[22] A similar point is made by the linguist Claude Hagège (1987: 148) and by Bernard Poignant (author of a report on regional languages for Lionel Jospin in 1998) in *Le Monde* in 2003. Poignant says that, while the future for these languages is certainly not rosy, French has no need to fear their continued existence: 'French is well established; the Republic is not threatened; national unity is not in question.'[23] Several environmental changes had occurred between the two INED research projects to account for a change of tone. Both internal and external pressures were building. There was a growing perception among policy-makers that attention should be directed to outside threats (English in particular) while strengthening what had rather suddenly become known as the cherished national linguistic heritage. Further, there had been increasing pressure from Brussels, particularly from the Council of Europe, for all countries in the European Union to protect linguistic minorities. This led to the most recent change of name of the government organisation, the DGLF (Chapter 3, pp. 60–67). This change is interpreted by some observers as purely cosmetic. While it may not indicate the change of heart the regional language groups long for, it is a clear pointer to the fact that the government now considers it expedient to publicise its acceptance of regional languages.

We can measure the far-reaching change in official government attitudes to regional and minority languages by quoting from the 2004 mission statement of the DGLFLF: '[T]he languages of France contribute to the creativity and cultural influence of our country. . . . we hold them in common, they are part of the heritage of humanity.'[24] (web site, DGLFLF). In 2005, the DGLFLF *Rapport au parlement* (web site, France, Government of, DGLFLF, Reports, 2005) is even more positive in tone: 'The multiplicity of languages is a reality which is seen increasingly positively in France, as an image of the past but also as a project for the future.'[25]

It is indeed paradoxical that those who have been responsible for imposing the all-powerful national language, the language once so proud of the ruthless elimination of all regional speech forms, should now find it appropriate, in defending itself from English, to embrace and nurture its diverse multi-lingual heritage. Could it be that this policy was adopted – at least to some extent – to give France the credibility it needs so that it can call on its allies to help it defend linguistic and cultural diversity on the world stage at the UN? Is it, in fact, another aspect of the defence of French?

France's attempts to put its house in order in regard to regional and minority languages have been enacted on the European stage, rather than in France itself, and the next section moves to the European context.

Beyond the Fringe: Europe

In the latter part of the 20th century, the political focus in Europe, and in the wider world, was on the one hand on globalisation and on the other on an increasingly narrow nationalism and on the problems and rights of minorities, particularly ethnic minorities. There was increasing agreement that the human rights of these groups included linguistic rights: continuing to enjoy the expression of their culture of origin, and the very important right to continue to speak what was for some their native language, for others the language of their parents or grandparents.

The issue of human rights as it refers to minorities and their linguistic rights is examined in detail in Grin (2003: 9–10, 81–86) and in S. Judge (2002: 73–106). Judge notes (105) that the assumption that the right to use a traditional language is a basic human right is increasingly accepted by the Council of Europe and the European Union, so posing a 'major problem for the French who will probably be forced to rethink the whole basis of their constitutional refusal to recognise minorities' (106). The increasing attention given to the rights of minorities appears to run counter to moves to create closer political links between member states. Links between regional and minority groups have become more frequent and as they support one another, they tend to espouse the federalist policies so feared by republican France. The web site of the *Organisation pour les Minorités Européennes*, for example, describes itself as: 'The website of Stateless Nations, national, cultural and linguistic minorities, native peoples, ethnic groups, areas with strong identity and federalist or separatist tendencies in Europe'.[26]

That these developments provoked very strong feelings in France is clear from two constitution-based judgments in the 1990s. In 1995, the *Conseil d'état* decided that the Constitution, which recognises only one language and does not accept the political or legal existence of minorities in the Republic, prevented France from ratifying the *Convention-cadre pour la protection des minorités nationales* of the Council of Europe (web site, *Université Laval, La politique des langues régionales et minoritaires*, section 12). Similar arguments relating to the indivisibility of the Republic and to the constitutional definition of a single national language were evoked in relation to the European Charter, so that in 1999 the *Conseil constitutionnel* decided that the terms of the constitution made it impossible for France to ratify the Charter. This decision was welcomed not only by language defenders but also by the political traditionalists who felt that there was a danger of 'diluting' and weakening the dominant culture by encouraging the continuation of a number of minority cultures, some openly opposed to traditional European ideals of democracy and tolerance.

It is against this background of exclusion that the November 2005 riots in France must be considered. The feelings of rejection nurtured by powerful centralised policies on language and culture came to a head. Such an explosion had long been predicted, but successive governments had done little to diffuse the situation. By choosing to focus on a perceived danger to the Republic and concentrating on the need for assimilation and integration, they had themselves created an explosive environment and this could now pose a greater threat than inclusive policies would have done. The challenge of managing this environment, of accepting diversity, will continue to confront French governments in the 21st century.

The minority groups have long felt that it was an infringement of their human rights (Grin, 2003: 9, 24–25) if they were prevented from enjoying their culture and language of origin. The conflict over minority languages was, and is, especially divisive in France, a country long priding itself on being a *terre d'accueil* (welcoming country), the birthplace of the *Déclaration des droits de l'Homme et du citoyen* (Declaration of the rights of man and of each citizen, 26 August 1789) on which the Republic is founded. At the same time, France places a high value on integration and the universal acceptance by all citizens of the values and culture of the Republic and on the power of the national language to ensure unity. Thus the movement to secure protection for minority and regional languages has not been universally welcomed in France.

The opposition in France to what eventually became the Council of Europe Charter on Regional and Minority Languages (text on web site) is just one, but possibly the most important of a number of issues relating to language in Europe in the 1990s. This can only be touched on here. In chronological order, these issues are: (1) the diminishing use of French as a working language in the Union; (2) the Council of Europe Charter; (3) the question of European patents (*brevets*); (4) enlargement of the Union; (5) the European Constitution. It is clear from this list that during the last decade of the 20th century it became increasingly difficult to separate questions of language policy and protection from the political context. The behaviours which government language policy in this area seeks to influence are in fact rarely linguistic. The increasingly overt ends of government actions are political and are concerned with the unity of the Republic. Seeing this, some of the protective groups, particularly the private groups, have become so involved with political associations of various shades of opinion that they appear to have lost not only their independence but also their focus on language. This development will be the subject of Chapter 4, pp. 98–106.

(1) The working languages of the European Union are the languages of the member states – 20 languages since the enlargement in May 2004. According to the 1958 Treaty of Rome, each of the institutions could decide how to interpret this official equality in its own working practices. In the Parliament, all languages are used; the European Commission works in three languages: English, French and German and the Council of Europe makes largely pragmatic decisions on how many languages and which ones will be used. The Court of Justice uses French. Although English is widely perceived as the main threat to French and other languages in the Union, the entry of Great Britain in 1973 did not at first disturb the linguistic equilibrium (Leparmentier, 2004: 1), and the first movement for wider use of English came not from the UK but from Sweden, Finland and Austria, admitted in 1995, countries with a marked preference for working in English rather than French.

The weakening of French in the Union is symbolised by the call from Romano Prodi, then President of the European Commission, suggesting in 2001 that English should be the single working language of the enlarged Union from 2004. This earned him opprobrium in France and also the 2002 *Carpette anglaise* (English Doormat) (see web site), a 'prize' awarded by the association *Droit de comprendre* (Right to Understand, see web site) to notable French and foreign personalities who mistreat French and promote the cause of English. There continues to be widespread concern in France about the lessening use of French in all the institutions of the European Union, concern that is deepened by the problems of enlargement.

In 2003, the *Assemblée nationale* received a report, commissioned from Michel Herbillon, on linguistic diversity in the European Union (Herbillon web site). Table 3.7 puts the report in context. The motivation for this report was the forthcoming enlargement of the Union on 1 May, 2004 and the report will be referred to again under that heading. The report quantified the decline in the use of French: in 1986, 58% of the documents of the European Commission were in French; that proportion had fallen to 30% in 2001 and the decline was even more noticeable in the Council of Europe. The Herbillon Report was accepted in its entirety and led to a resolution adopted by the *Assemblée nationale* on 6 January 2004: *Résolution sur la diversité linguistique dans l'Union européenne* (Resolution on Linguistic Diversity in the European Union) (web site, France, Government of, *Assemblée nationale*).

Perhaps the most interesting aspects of the Report and the resulting Resolution are the constant references to the coupling of language and culture, to linguistic and cultural diversity, to pluralism and to multilingualism. This is a clear sign that these have now, in the 21st century, become essential features of French government foreign policy (Chapter 3, pp. 74–81). It reveals a considerable widening of the behaviours the government is attempting to influence and targets a far broader range of people than hitherto. It essentially envisages a globalised language/cultural policy, with France as the leading actor in Europe and at the UN.

Within Europe, it is recommended that all French officials and civil servants in the Union use French exclusively and reference is made to Prime Minister Raffarin's Circular of 14 February 2003 (NOR: PRMX0306461C – *Journal Officiel* du 21.03.2003, pp. 5034–5035) (web site, France, Government of, MCC, Raffarin Circular). The circular insists on the importance of strict adherence to the terms of the *Loi Toubon*. The Report and the Resolution further endorse first, the learning by all school pupils in the Union of two foreign languages and second, the requirement accepted in May 2003 that all civil servants recruited by the enlarged Union should henceforth also have two foreign languages before they could be promoted.

Both government agencies and private defensive groups share the conviction that the future of French is closely tied up with the European Union and that if the battle for French is lost in the Union, it cannot be won elsewhere. Speaking in an interview for *L'Express* about the 2004 *Semaine de la francophonie*, the Minister (*Coopération et Francophonie* (Cooperation and Francophonia)) Pierre-André Wiltzer (2004) affirmed: 'We are well aware that the main battle front for the future of French is the European front.'[27] He refers to yet another government inquiry into the language, commissioned in 2004 by Jean-Jacques Aillagon, Minister for Culture and Communication, in charge of the CSLF, which draws similar conclusions (Table 3.7).

There is therefore a strong political will to maintain and defend French in the European Union. In spite of a panoply of measures taken by the government to strengthen French in European institutions and to cope with enlargement, it seems increasingly doubtful that the move to use English, initiated by speakers of English as a second language, can be halted (Phillipson, 2003).

(2) A second struggle on the European front is concerned with regional and minority languages. As Chapter 2, pp. 29–34 showed, there is a long and involved history of the diverse languages of France and this took a dramatic new turn in the 1990s. The European Charter for Regional and Minority Languages, adopted by the Council of Europe in June 1992, and open for signature in November that year, introduced a new phase. France was very unwilling to sign the Charter and did not finally do so until 1999, when it agreed to only 39 of the 95 clauses. Two weeks later came the decision of the *Conseil constitutionnel* that the Charter was contrary to the Constitution: France has still not ratified the Charter and arguments continue to rage over whether or not it should do so.

The hesitation of France was mainly due to the conviction expressed by many political figures that the Republic would be weakened if languages other than French were given rights in the legal and administrative sectors. The typical French response to a problem of this kind is to commission a government report (Table 3.7). The government of Prime Minister Lionel Jospin commissioned no fewer than four reports (web site, France, Government of, <u>MCC</u>, Jospin Reports). Following an initial report on how the *Charte* was to be interpreted in the light of the 1994 *Loi Toubon* (web site, France, Government of, <u>MCC</u>, Jospin Reports, Report 1998(a)), there was another in July 1998 by Bernard Poignant on regional linguistic and cultural matters (*Langues et cultures régionales* (Regional languages and cultures) (web site, France, Government of, <u>MCC</u>, Poignant Report; see also p. 33); a third study, presented to the Prime Minister in October 1998, was commissioned from Guy Carcassonne (web site, France, Government of, <u>MCC</u>, Carcassonne Study) on the legal and constitutional implications of the Charter. Finally a further report (*Les Langues de la France* (The Languages of France) (web site, France, Government of, <u>MCC</u>, Cerguiglini Report) was prepared in April 1999 by Bernard Cerquiglini, head of the DGLFLF and also Director of the *Institut national de la langue française* (National Institute for the French Language – INLF).

Each of these concluded, for different reasons, that it would be possible for France to sign and ratify the Charter without causing unwelcome political damage at home. The arguments over legal and constitutional aspects, and the interpretation of some sections and terms of the Charter are very technical. From the beginning, it was clear that purely linguistic matters were not the focus. These have been overshadowed by the political dimension. The movements for the defence of regional and minority languages were vocal in their insistence that France should ratify the Charter, while opponents claimed that the Charter was the first step in creating a federal Europe, a Europe of regions rather than a Europe of nations, a melting pot where the sovereign rights of participating nations would be lost. It was pointed out that the Council of Europe (which had prepared the Charter) was not an elected body, that there was even a danger that France might lose Alsace and Lorraine. The ASSELAF, for example, entitled its contribution to the debate (web site, ASSELAF): '*La Charte européenne des langues régionales ou minoritaires : un danger pour la République*' (The European Charter for Regional and Minority Languages: A Danger for the Republic). Some groups opposing the Charter argued that there were already many laws covering the use of these languages in France and to suggest that more protection was required was ludicrous (for example web site, *VIGILE*).

Against all the heated rhetoric and the impassioned pleas to save the Republic and the nation, can be set the equally extravagant views being expressed by the minority language groups. We have already seen that the opponents of the Charter moved seamlessly from the defence of French to the defence of the Republic. The defendants of the Charter, among whom are many members of the government and the general public, as well as the minority language groups, feel there is greater political advantage in France aligning herself with other European Union members and in strong links between the regions. They were therefore equally speedy in espousing the federalist cause. It appears from successive IFOP opinion polls that numerically the defendants were (and are) more numerous than the opponents. In 1994 77%, and in 2000 82% of those polled were in favour of a change to the Constitution to enable the Charter to be ratified (web site, ASSELAF). The opponents however are more voluble.

Support for the Charter is dismissed by the opponents as a betrayal of the French people by the ruling élite. This is a particularly bitter internecine conflict, as Lecherbonnier (2005) argues in his analysis of the motives of influential sections of French society:

> Why do they want to kill French? Civil servants to advance their careers, businessmen to make money, researchers to hide their nationality, politicians in submission to so-called market forces.[28]

This example may explain the failure so far of the Charter's defendants to convince the government that ratification is in France's interest: the power and the vociferous nature of republican opposition point up deep divisions in France's internal politics – divisions the government is understandably loath to confront.

The Charter had never been purely a linguistic question. For some, opposition to minority languages had become indissolubly linked with republican values, with nationhood and with sovereignty. For others, it was inextricably entwined with human and minority rights and with multi-culturalism. The confrontation over the Charter has radically changed the nature of language defence in France, pointing out the fundamental conflicts characteristic of French political life and highlighting the opposition between Jacobin republicanism and Girondin inclusiveness. (Chapter 4, pp. 90–97 will look again at the political implications for France of ratification of the Charter.)

The ongoing debate over the Charter is therefore crucial. Not only has it crystallised and polarised opinions in France, it has also created new and sometimes surprising alliances between the defenders of French and other mainly political groups with vested interests of various kinds. It has become increasingly difficult for the *résistants* to speak of the defence of French in isolation from the narrow views on sovereignty that political expediency dictates should henceforth be associated with it.

(3) After the upheavals caused by the Charter in 1992 and its eventual signature by France in 1999, the next major event to cause alarm and despondency was an agreement reached in London in June 2001. This was the Convention on the Delivery of European Patents, generally referred to as the *Protocole de Londres* (London Protocol) (web site, France, Government of, Senate, London Protocol). The association of the name London with this agreement is significant, since the Protocol is widely believed to be specifically concerned with the strengthening of English at the expense of other European languages, notably French and German. Again, France has signed, but not ratified this agreement.

The London Protocol provides for a simplification, and thus for a reduction in the cost of the process of obtaining a patent in Europe. By removing the necessity for costly translations at various stages of the process, the Protocol makes it easier and cheaper for foreign companies and investors to obtain a *brevet* (patent) and therefore to sell their goods and services in the European Union. The furious reaction of some of the protectors of French to the new system is based on the conviction that it is directly inspired by malign forces in the United States whose aim is to destroy French (and other languages) and so to gain world dominance. Arguments continue to rage about the effect of the London Protocol, but its opponents are convinced that it weakens French inventiveness and creativity, destroys the livelihood of translators and contributes (with the connivance of the French government!) to the destruction of the language. The vocal protests of translators in France led directly to an increase in private defensive measures.

Feeling betrayed by the government, they turned to popular protest. One of the results of this was the formation in 2001 of the FFI (web site, *Voxlatina*), an umbrella group of 52 defensive associations. The historical, republican and emotional resonance of the title FFI is deliberately emphasised by the use of words like *résistance*. The FFI then issued, on the 7 October 2001, on the *Voxlatina* web site, its Villers-Cotterêts Appeal: *L'Appel de Villers-Cotterêts*. This direct evocation of the 1539 *Ordonnance de Villers-Cotterêts* is another instance of the attempt to enlist national pride for the cause of defending the language. The fact that, in May 2004, the *Appel* had been signed by fewer than 400 people is perhaps a reflection of the limited popular appeal of defensive rhetoric.

On the other hand, the *Rapport Grignon* (Grignon Report) prepared for the Senate in June 2001 (web site, France, Government of, Senate, Grignon Report), argued that there were very considerable advantages for France in ratifying the Protocol, but the association of translators, *Association des professionnels de la traduction des brevets d'invention* (Association of Professional Translators of Patents – APROBI) was scathing in its criticisms of the new patent arrangements. It goes so far as to claim that: 'The London Protocol would kill off, once and for all, the cultural and linguistic diversity which is the wealth of Europe'[29] (web site, APROBI (b)). In March 2006 another proposal to ratify the Protocol was withdrawn – a withdrawal hailed as a victory for the APROBI and the FFI (web site, *Voxlatina*).

From our point of view, the Protocol and the arguments about patents are less important than the reactions they provoke about language and the attitudes expressed by those who oppose them. The contrast between government statements and the outpourings of non-government agencies is acute and points to a sharpening focus and a heightened tone in private defensive movements. Although the weight of numbers is on the side of the government, it finds itself, as so often in matters pertaining to the language, trying to reconcile a number of opposing realities: internal pressure to protect and maintain the status of French, economic expectations as expressed by French business, and the weight of external (European) assumptions. In this balancing act, it is unlikely that anyone will be completely satisfied.

(4) The fourth aspect of the defence of French in Europe is concerned with the enlargement of the Union in May 2004. The French government had long been aware of the problems the increase in the number of languages from 11 to 20 might create and this was one of the reasons for the 2003 Herbillon Report (Table 3.7) and the resulting Resolution by the *Assemblée nationale* (web site, France, Government of, *Assemblé nationale*, Herbillon Resolution). The recommendations of the Resolution dealt with problems of translation and interpretation and sought to maintain the place of French as one of the main languages within the Union. It recommended keeping the current status of French, refusing any attempt to increase the number of meetings where no interpretation was provided and seeking a compromise between linguistic pluralism and economic reality. One of the ways to arrive at such a compromise would be to have what is known as an asymmetrical interpretation regime, so that each person could speak in their own language, but there would not be simultaneous interpretation for each of the pairs of languages. (These would increase from 110 to 420 possible combinations).

The most concrete action taken by the French was to institute a training programme for civil servants in the new member countries so that they could learn French before May 2004. In 2003, 3200 people attended the language courses set up by the French government in their country of origin and special sessions were held in Avignon for ambassadors and other high level diplomatic staff (Leparmentier, 2004: 2). The circular issued by the Prime Minister in February 2003 (web site, France, Government of, MCC, Raffarin Circular) also emphasised the importance of pro-active measures to maintain the role of French in the enlarged Union and recommended a strong defence of plurilingualism both in Europe and in France. Frequent questions in the *Assemblée* were answered with a strong reiteration of the government view, always with a reference to the need to balance costs and a desirable outcome for the French language (for example, web site, DLF, Voisin text).

It is as yet too early to judge the outcome of the enlargement, but the fact that many of the new member countries use English as a lingua franca causes gloomy predictions of a speedy move to a monolingual Union, promoting 'with the constant help of the civil servants of Blairite England, the removal, not only of French, but of all the other languages of Europe'[30] (web site, Daguet, *Voxlatina*,). Academic interest in the question is signalled by the hosting at the Sorbonne in April 2004 of a high-level conference entitled: *L'élargissement de l'Union européenne et les langues* (The enlargement of the European Union and Languages).

(5) As the disquiet about enlargement and its effect on French grew, so did concern about the work of the European Convention and the eventual move to a European Constitution. This concern reached its height in the preparations for the referendum on the Constitution in May 2005. The Constitution is the fifth and last of the European aspects of language defence considered briefly here. France was certainly not the only country in Europe where there was a real fear that the Constitution would radically weaken national sovereignty, but it is possibly the only one where movements whose primary purpose was once to defend the language are now so closely allied with political movements in defence of sovereignty. These two topics – language and sovereignty – find common cause in France where they are more hotly debated than elsewhere in the Union.

Following the Declaration of Laeken in December 2001, a European Convention was set up under the presidency of the former French President, Giscard d'Estaing. In the run up to enlargement, it was given three years to produce a Constitution to bring the institutions of the Union closer to the citizens of all the member countries and provide a political modus operandi for the enlarged Union. The Convention was to report to the Inter-governmental Conference (IGC) in Brussels in December 2003. Prior to this meeting, there was a great deal of political activity in all member states. The 2003 IGC in Brussels failed to come to an agreement. France was one of many member states that refused to agree with the proposed text. Many of the arguments and fears aroused by the Charter for Regional and Minority Languages were revisited in Brussels in 2003 and again in 2004 when the Constitution was finally signed in Rome. After signature, the ratification process continued in 2005. Another article on *Voxlatina*, this one warning against the power mania of the Germans and the advantages they hope to get from a Constitution, makes it clear that the battle was being waged on more than one front: '*Espoirs . . . mais ne baissons pas la garde*' (Hopes . . . but we mustn't let our guard down) (web site, *Voxlatina*, Bollmann).

The demands for a referendum in France were met and on 29 May 2005 the French, to the surprise of many, voted strongly against the Constitution. The 'No' Vote in France, with the similar vote in the Netherlands on 1 June 2005, has effectively halted, or at least stalled, the move towards greater political union in the European Union, the date for ratification having been delayed for 'a period of reflection, explanation and discussion' before further examination of the situation (web site, *EUROPA*).

The motivation for the French rejection of the European Constitution has been interpreted in various ways, some at least of which have little to do with the Constitution itself and none of them directly concerns the language. The sovereigntists rejoiced at what they interpreted as a massive endorsement of their republican agenda. *Libération*, in an article entitled *Chef-d'oeuvre masochiste* (see web site), was not alone in claiming that France had seen in the referendum the chance to express concern about a number of issues not primarily concerned with the Constitution. It was, Serge July said, a referendum on the performance of the governing élites (in the government, in Brussels, in the media – all those in favour of a France governed from on high); on liberalism (for or against competition; for or against globalisation); on France (its role and power in Europe); on social problems. Ager (1999) has shown how attitudes to language in France relate to the substantial insecurities in French society revealed by this analysis in *Libération*, and how they lead to problems of identity and image.

An example of how the language defence groups in France fit into the opposition to the Constitution is provided by the activities of the FFI. The week before the 2003 Brussels meeting, the FFI launched a demand for a referendum at a demonstration in Paris. Convinced that the Constitution would enshrine *l'anglo-américain* as the common and finally the only working language of the Union, they had been very active in the years since Laeken, producing texts on the status of languages for inclusion in the putative new Constitution (web site, FFI, Constitution), but they had met with little response from the French government. Their call to attend the demonstration states that it is '*Pour l'indépendance, pour la souveraineté de la France*' (For French independence and French sovereignty) (web site, *Voxlatina* Demonstration).

A strong call for a referendum, and for a 'No' vote, also came in early 2004 from the *Rassemblement pour l'Indépendance et la Souveraineté de la France* (Assembly for French Independence and French Sovereignty – RIF) (web site, RIF; web site, *Voxlatina* Dossier du Non). In April 2004, the RIF publicly endorsed a motion in favour of French and Francophonia proposed by the President of the FFI and of ALF (web site, *Voxlatina* ALF). This, and subsequent coverage on *Voxlatina*, shows how some associations for the defence of French have found common cause with political groups working to stem the tide of increasing European political unity. These alliances are further analysed in Chapter 4, pp. 98–106. Even acting in concert, the influence of such groups appears to be limited.

The European theatre of operations presents a difficult and constantly evolving challenge for action in defence of the language. Clearly any fight for the future of French in the 21st century, in Europe or elsewhere, will not be confined to linguistic objectives. The examination of some of the problems faced by France in the European arena has shown conflicting environmental pressures and mutually incompatible demands on the government, not all of which can be satisfied. Here as in other areas of the defence of French by government action, policy weaknesses may partly be attributed to the failure to set precise goals. Exceptionally, the measures put in place prior to the enlargement of the Union, well planned and with limited but clear goals, supported by appropriate means and with in-built measures of effect, may be considered a successful example of diffusion, acquisition and status policies.

The private defensive organisations, confronted with evidence of the continuing decline in the use of French, and despairing of government efforts, have realised that they must band together and find political allies if they are to make their voices heard and successfully influence policy. The Internet gives them new weapons for the modern battlefield.

Technology and the Defence of French: The Internet

In the last decade of the twentieth and the first decade of the 21st century, a striking development in the defence of French has been the enormous growth in the use of the Internet, both by top-down official government organisations, by bottom-up private groups and by individuals. The balance of power is clearly, here as elsewhere, on the side of the government, but there are features of the Internet that make it the ideal instrument for the weak and politically vulnerable. In particular, the financial cost of setting up a site is rarely a deterrent, although the continuous cost in time and effort of maintaining a site is sometimes not taken into account.

From the point of view of all those concerned with defending French, particularly private individuals and associations, the Internet was a boon. It allowed them, for minimal cost, to air their views to a wider audience, to recruit like-minded individuals to their associations, to get 'signatures' on petitions, to advertise publications, meetings and demonstrations and to appeal for funds. The Internet, through easily established electronic links, is also an excellent way to provide connections with allied organisations. The use of the Internet is also a case where to some extent the medium is the message. Albert Salon (Co-founder and President of the FFI) says in an interview (2004a) that the Internet is proving to be an *'allié de grand poids'* (a heavyweight ally) in the defence of French. Promoting French language sites on the Internet, whatever their content, can be seen as one way of combatting the overwhelming (but diminishing) dominance of (American) English in this new medium.

Nevertheless, the specific features of the Internet appear tailor-made to accentuate the problems of fragmentation and dispersal identified in the last section of Chapter 1. While it is reasonably easy for a motivated individual to set up a web page, its maintenance requires regular and constant oversight by a qualified person. It is the absence of this costly continuity and discipline that in part explains all the pages that fail to load, the sites with misleading and undated or out-of-date information needing to be removed, the links that do not work. There is also the more serious problem that some sites and files can corrupt computers – a powerful disincentive to further research. In organisations where membership changes frequently it is virtually impossible to guarantee adequate maintenance of web sites. It is unfortunately also the case that the Internet allows the publication of views and information not subject to any kind of editorial oversight. Anyone can say anything – but how can the truth of these statements be assessed? How many people are paying attention? Are the same people setting up a number of sites?

Excellent sites disappear without explanation (dicosdor.fr for example). There is a mass of similar and confusing acronyms (ALF, AFAL, AFRAV, ASSELAF, as shown in Chapter 1). As you navigate around the various language sites, the real meaning of the 'web' becomes apparent. Many sites find it easier to post long lists of *liens* (links) than to give clear and detailed information. Thus once you are connected to one of the associations for the defence of the language you can rapidly be linked to a multitude of other organisations. It is unfortunately impossible to tell how many of these sites may have been set up by the same small group of people and most of them do not reveal the number of hits the site has had.

Provided the links are still active, something that can certainly not be guaranteed, this is a heady experience at first. It can save costly time navigating the web and having the URLs of a host of other related organisations can be a considerable advantage. It gives a quick overview of the field and its ramifications and can help with further research. On the other hand potential sympathisers with the language cause may be disillusioned when they are connected to some strange organisations with whose aims they disagree, possibly quite violently. There is a morass of inter-linking and self-referential sites.

A distinction must be made between sites presenting information about the defence of French, often in the context of the history of the language, and the sites of associations actively engaged in defending the language. On the whole, because of their purpose, the historical and informative research sites are more objective and use calmer language than the sites of the active defenders. Many of the research sites are created by linguists, universities or government agencies, are subject to editorial control and are regularly updated. The sites of universities are generally reliable, and many supply full details of teaching materials and edited references. The excellent *Université Laval* site is a case in point but there are many other useful and reliable sources. The government sites are carefully maintained by qualified technologists and are generally easy to navigate. Their facts are reliable and they are an excellent source of primary documents, but it must be remembered that they are obliged to follow the government's political agenda and that it may be unwise to take some of their statements at face value.

This caveat applies even more to the content of the activist sites. They may also be subject to some editorial control, but this will usually be by a dedicated individual or group in sympathy with the views of the site's creators and therefore not unbiased. Many of them seem to be the work of enthusiastic and committed individuals whose seriousness and real purpose it is difficult to assess. The effectiveness and durability of these sites is often dependent on the energy of one or two individuals. Continuity cannot be assured if these highly motivated people for some reason cease to be active. Some of the more ephemeral sites present unsubstantiated, and possibly misleading personal views in the guise of attested historical fact. Others are more serious. The site *L'ABC de la langue française*, to take just one example, is the work of a single committed author who makes every effort to be frank, disinterested and objective. He supplies a great deal of relevant and constantly updated information – most of which can be verified elsewhere, responds to queries about his site and posts a list of links to primary source documents. This is particularly useful as it includes a personal assessment of each link by the web master.

Essential for those interested in the defence of French are the two very different sites of the DLF and *Voxlatina*. The President of the DLF is Jean Dutourd of the *Académie française* and it enjoys the support of the DGLFLF, so ensuring that it has a special status. Its web site is well maintained by the *Agence universitaire de la francophonie* (AUF) and it has multiple links to official agencies, covers legal and historical aspects of the defence of French and gives information on its activities. It is an elegant and authoritative – but scarcely independent – site, apparently balanced in its approach, easy to navigate and agreeable to use. It promotes the French language in various ways. Its aims are to: '*Découvrir les richesses de notre langue, l'enrichir et la faire rayonner, en défendre l'emploi*' (Discover the richness of our language, enrich it and promote it, defend its use).

Very different is *Voxlatina*, which urges those who visit it to: '*Défendez votre culture. Soutenez la Francophonie et la Latinité*' (Defend your culture. Support Francophonia and Latin languages). This is the site of FFI-France. It performs a very useful task in scanning the press, in keeping track of political and legal developments relating to the French language and *la Francophonie* and in promoting the active involvement of its members through petitions and demonstrations. It describes itself as '*Le premier journal du monde latin et de la Francophonie*' (The leading news source for the Latin world and Francophonia) and covers Belgium, Canada and other francophone countries. As its name suggests, it is pragmatic enough to support linguistic diversity and publicises defensive activities not only on behalf of French, but also (occasionally) other Latin languages. It lists 130 so-called defensive organisations (many with no apparent focus on language) to which it provides links, but is also closely connected to other sites with strong political affiliations and whose main purpose is not the defence of language (see Chapter 2, pp. 45–49 and Chapter 4, pp. 98–106).

Apart from the government sites and those of the universities, the number of sites involved, however loosely, in actively defending French is difficult to establish. There is a disconcerting tendency for sites whose sole purpose is apparently to 'defend the language' to blur gradually into those where the defence of language is part of a much wider and sometimes more doubtful political agenda. Neither these, nor the government sites, feel the need to define what is meant by defence, nor do they explain what they mean by language. There is a deliberate attempt to harness emotional responses to perceived language threats rather than to present a reasoned case. From the language sites of defensive associations there are pointers, either by Internet links or by giving contact details, to a multitude of other organisations:

- Gaullist groups such as *Rassemblement gaulliste* (others are *Jeune France* and the Charles de Gaulle site);
- associations whose purpose is to defend France's sovereignty in the face of perceived threats from Brussels (the financial/political site *Europe, Une, Libre, Grande* and right wing political sites such as *France politique*);
- religious organisations: *Catholiques pour les Libertés économiques*;
- right-wing political bodies: *Action française*;
- green groups: *Confédération des Écologistes indépendants*;
- those of all political shades wanting to defend the Republic: *Avenir France République* (this group lost its government approval in 2002), *SOS République*. (See various web sites)

A tangled web, and one which again, like French attitudes to the European Constitution, reveals, as Ager (1999) notes, multiple insecurities in French society, problems with identity and with France's image. These insecurities are a concern for both the right and left in politics and both value France's language policies, ever more loosely defined and emotionally charged, as a guarantor of values they hold dear. 'For the Left, [the defence of the national language is] Republican, Revolutionary in origin and supportive of human rights. For the Right [it is] French, pure and solidly based in defending the identity and true nature of France' (Ager, 1999: 222).

The motivation of those involved in language defence is therefore frequently contradictory. Rather than linguistic issues, political concerns and various other covert agendas, evident in France since the time of François Ier, now dominate. Chapter 3 considers some of the motivations of the major government agencies and looks more closely at their activities.

Chapter 3

Official Agencies: The Language of Power

L'Académie française: The Grandmother of Them All

This chapter examines the roles of the four great official agencies for the protection and promotion of French. It takes the four agencies in approximate chronological order, beginning with the *Académie française* (1635). The second section deals with the *Alliance française* (1883) and the third and fourth sections cover the *Délégation générale à la langue française et aux langues de France* (DGLFLF, originally created as the *Haut Comité pour la défense et l'expansion de la langue française* in 1966) and the *Organisation international de la Francophonie* (OIF) for which the rather arbitrary date of 1986, the first Francophone Summit in Paris, is chosen. Although there had been considerable activity well before that time, this date may be said to mark the first fully official participation by France in the movement. The chapter then concludes with a fifth section on government policy in the area of language, as implemented by the various agencies of the Ministry of Foreign Affairs (*Ministère des Affaires Étangères* (MAE), and an assessment of its effectiveness.

In the framework of this book presented in the Introduction, these five actors fit into different categories. The *Académie*, as we saw, stands virtually alone as an official organisation that continues to focus almost exclusively on language inside France and therefore on corpus planning – although it is also concerned with status planning and maintaining the prestige of the language. The *Alliances* have widened their focus as the need for government support has become more obvious and more controversial and are now active inside as well as outside France in a broad spectrum of cultural activities. The DGLFLF is a political arm of the government concerned mostly with language planning inside France and its focus is mainly on the political realities and processes characterising corpus planning. It is also involved in areas of acquisition, status and diffusion planning. These three types of planning are also the concern of the OIF and the MAE. They

50

promote the external image, influence and power of France and for them the language is one – perhaps the most important – of the status symbols allowing the politicians to defend and extend that power.

The *Académie française*, with its long history of concentration on the language itself, has emblematic status not only in France but in other European countries who may either envy the French their tradition of language protection, or find that the *Académie* makes a great deal of fuss to little effect. It is one of the oldest of French institutions and this alone gives it a unique position among the various academies in Europe (Table 5.1) and in the world. In France it is a national icon, a proud symbol of a long tradition, of the love and respect the French have for their language. In the centuries since it was set up in 1635, its purposes have varied little and its strongly anchored traditions confer on it an aura accorded only to the most revered and enduring symbols of the national culture.

The history of the *Académie*, as presented in the one-page list of dates on its web site (*Académie française*, <u>Dates</u>), is understated in the extreme: the 'creation' by Richelieu, the various letters patent and statutes governing its activities, its memorable green uniform, the admission of the first woman in 1980 and the election of the first female Perpetual Secretary in 1999 and, spread over more than three and a half centuries, the publication of nine editions of its dictionary. This summary gives little idea of the hubris surrounding its activities or of the extreme seriousness with which its 40 members – *les Immortels* (the Immortals) – and the French public regard *la Compagnie* (the Company).

The institution continues to be of considerable interest to scholars of language planning. The history of its founding and of the social conditions making it possible to create such an institution are analysed by Cooper (1989: 3–11) as an early example of language planning. For him 'the founding of the *Académie française* is unintelligible without reference to its social context' (11). Spolsky (2004) describes the *Académie* as 'one tool of language management, an organisation with state authority to protect the French language' (66). Before its foundation in 1635, a group or *compagnie* of educated and influential individuals, interested in literature, language and the life of the mind, had been meeting in one another's homes. Richelieu, in Louis XIV's centralised France, saw the political possibilities of stabilising the language and regulating its use so that it became a way of consolidating royal power. Colbert saw similar possibilities in creating centralised institutions for literature (*L'Académie des inscriptions et belles-lettres* (1663)), for science (*L'Académie des sciences* (1666)) and for the visual arts (*L'Académie des beaux-arts* (1648; 1803)). The fifth academy, for moral and political sciences, was created in 1795. The first three, and subsequently the other two, were amalgamated into the *Institut de France*.

Since its foundation in the 17th century, the *Académie* has continued to meet almost without interruption. The royal academies were disbanded by the *Convention* in 1793, but re-organised under Napoleon in 1803. Apart from those ten years, the academicians have met regularly, and since 1805, they have met under the cupola in the *Collège des Quatre-Nations*, now the *Palais de l'Institut*. When one of the 40 members dies, existing members elect a replacement for the vacant *fauteuil* (armchair) and there is an intricate process of voting and speech-making by a proposer and by the new member. Every aspect of this is governed by tradition. The members of the *Académie* wear, like other members of the Institute, a special green uniform, designed in 1803.

The roles of the *Académie* are also largely unchanged with the passing of time, although at the end of the 20th century some important new activities were added. The web site now affirms that the *Académie* has two roles: to keep watch over the French language and to administer financial support programmes. These two activities are scarcely equal. The *Académie* devotes by far the larger part of its time and effort to the first of these, the one normally associated with it in the public mind: 'to work with all possible care and diligence to provide reliable rules for our language and to make it pure, eloquent and able to deal with arts and sciences'[31] (Article 24 of the Statutes) (web site, *Académie française*, <u>Statutes</u>). It is also the role given greatest prominence by the immediate past *Secrétaire perpétuel* (Perpetual Secretary), Maurice Druon, who takes a very traditional view of language and of the work of the *Académie*, a view he frequently expresses with great force. As Chapter 1 showed, all the heads of state since Louis XIV have had a policy of protecting the *Académie* and promoting its work thus giving it a very powerful position in French culture.

The original statutes stated that the *Académie* was charged with producing a dictionary (Article 26 of the Statutes), a grammar, a manual of rhetoric and a treatise of poetics (web site, *Académie française*, <u>Statutes</u>). In the event, only the dictionary was produced by the *Académie* itself. In the years following its creation, other scholars produced authoritative works in the other three areas. The dictionary, as the public face of the work of the *Académie*, has attracted most attention. The extraordinary slowness with which it is produced (the first edition in 1694, the ninth currently appearing in sections) is legendary and the subject of much disparaging criticism: 'The complaints and jokes provoked by the slowness of the Dictionary are almost as ancient as the Academy itself'[32] (web site, *Académie française*, <u>Preface, 9th edition</u>) . It is nevertheless true, as Maurice Druon further comments in his preface to the ninth edition, that such a task cannot be hurried and that the successive editions of the Dictionary are a national monument, an enviable record of the mutations of the language over the centuries.

The year 1996 was important for the defence of French and brought new responsibilities for the *Académie*. This was the year of the creation of the *Secrétariat général de la Francophonie* (General Secretariat for Francophonia). It was also, following the introduction of the *Loi Toubon* in 1994, the year of the passing of the *Décret No. 96–602 du 9 juillet relatif à l'enrichissement de la langue française* (Decree No. 96–602 of the 9th July relating to the enrichment of the French language) (web site, *Adminet* Decree 96–602) signalling a further important but cumbersome addition to the traditional role of the *Académie*. The decree relates to terminology and replaces an earlier Commission by a new *Commission générale de terminologie et néologie* (General Commission on Terminology and Neologisms) and subordinate specialist commissions attached to the Prime Minister.

This legal intervention indicates a growing concern with the flood of new terms coming in to French at the end of the century, and gathers together the major government defensive agencies (notably the DGLFLF and the *Académie française*) with high-ranking representatives of business and industry in an attempt to help the language to keep pace with technological and industrial developments and create French terms in place of foreign (mainly English) ones. The role of the *Académie française* in the deliberations and activities of the Commission is decisive. It is to be involved in all the discussions and is to have the final say. No new term can be approved until the *Académie* has pronounced that it is a suitable addition to the language: 'No revision can be published without the agreement of the *Académie française*.'[33] (Article 13 of Decree 96–602).

The second role of the *Académie*, distribution of funds, was not foreseen at its creation, but became possible as generous benefactors donated or left money to the institution for the purposes of furthering its basic aims. Sixty prizes associated with the promotion of French are awarded by the *Académie* and in 1986 it began to award the *Grand Prix de la francophonie* (Grand Francophone Prize) as a symbol of its interest in the promotion of French outside France. This is a significant addition to the list of prizes, since the activities of the *Académie* had hitherto been concerned with metropolitan France. It bears witness to the increasing importance of *la Francophonie* and to the creation in 1984 by the government of the two agencies: the *Comité consultatif* (concerned with *la Francophonie*) and the *Commissariat général à la langue française* (concerned with the language in France itself) (Chapter 1, p. 14).

The protected status of the *Académie* as a supremely reliable national institution is confirmed by the fact that among the minor tasks it has acquired over the years is the distribution, on behalf of various small literary and learned associations, of funds for closely defined purposes in no way related to its principal role: limited financial assistance for small numbers of *familles nombreuses* (large families) or for widows, and scholarships.

The election of Hélène Carrère d'Encausse as the first female head of the *Académie*, *Madame le Secrétaire perpétuel*, in 1999 has marked a slight, but perceptible shift in the public pronouncements of the *Académie*. The web site now refers not only to the work of regulating the language in France but also, in a reference to the importance of *la Francophonie*, it mentions *tous ceux qui pratiquent notre langue* (all those who speak our language) and goes on to say that the *Académie* 'takes action to preserve the qualities of the language and follows those changes which are necessary.'[34] Part of the web site (*Questions courantes* (Topical questions)) is devoted to problems of language and to answering questions about the language from its users.

Many of these problems are grammatical, a surprising fact perhaps considering how much of the *Académie*'s time is taken up with the preparation of the dictionary, commissions of terminology, spelling reforms, hunting foreign words and neologisms, and other matters to do with vocabulary. From the start, the *Académie*'s involvement in aspects of the structure of the language has been peripheral. Its grammar, when it did finally produce it, was widely criticised by linguists (for example, Bengtsson, 1968; Brunot, 1932) and by the public. The Preface to the ninth edition of the dictionary illustrates the imbalance between lexis and syntax, asserting that the simple and sometimes apparently banal examples given in the dictionary are there to illustrate the correct grammar of the language. Linguists agree that, while changes in vocabulary are rarely harmful and indeed essential in a living language, changes in syntax are a much more worrying sign of the influence of another language and of possible decline. This perception does not appear to underlie the work of the *Académie*.

The section of the site dealing with *Défense de la langue française* (Defence of the French language) (web site, *Académie française*, <u>Defence</u>) continues to define the role of the *Académie* at the start of the new century in terms that reveal that the reactionary and traditional views, which have done so much to arouse mistrust and even hostility, still prevail. It sees the language as threatened by the growth of English, or 'more precisely, American [English], which is tending to invade minds, the written word, the audio-visual media.'[35] So, at the start of the 21st century, the vital continuing role for the *Académie* is to defend the vocabulary of French against invasion from English words. It continues its *oeuvre régulatrice* (work of regulation), giving shape to such changes as may be necessary, but has not forgotten that it has a centuries-old duty to police correct usage of French.

Words have attributed to them an essential role in defining and maintaining the national cultural status quo. The attitudes of members of the Dictionary Commission are very revealing. They are quoted as saying, for example, 'an institution which preserves words is at the same time the guardian of the values they express'[36]; 'to defend words is also to save the ideas they express.'[37] In a claim that will astonish both linguists and ethnologists, the dictionary affirms that '[t]he [French] language has reached the peak of its capacities which have made it, for two centuries, the language of the élites of the whole world'[38] (web site, *Académie française*, Preface, 9th edition).

The Preface contains re-affirmations of the universality of French and of its unique qualities of clarity and precision that Rivarol would easily recognise: 'the French language, which is analytic and has unmatched syntactic richness, deserves to remain the language of reference for everything, beginning with international treaties, which requires an over-riding precision of thought.'[39] Similarly, in the section of the web site dealing with the beginning of the century (*A l'aube du XXI*[e] *siècle*): 'We are here to define and recall what is permanent, and thus to be the main servants of the supreme values of our civilisation'[40] (web site, *Académie française*, History). Inflated claims of this kind can only diminish the rightful respect due to this august and remarkable institution. They do not give added prestige or seriousness to the *Académie*, to its work or to the French language.

L'Alliance française: The Friendly Face of French

In chronological order, the *Alliance française*, founded in 1883, is the second oldest of the big official institutions working to promote French. It has never had the power and *éclat* of the *Académie*, nor has it sought them. While virtually everyone in France has at least heard of the *Académie*, many are unaware of the activities of the *Alliance*. Blaise (2001) calls it the *grande dame du secteur associatif* (great lady of the voluntary sector). Its unique status is difficult to define, since it is both a private (non-profit) and a government-funded association, both French and foreign. The far-sighted patriots responsible for setting it up were men of great influence, many of whom had had experience of living outside France and had been closely involved in government and in education. The aims and the structures they gave to the new institution ensured that it operated quietly and effectively, with a minimum of fuss and public attention.

It also differs from the *Académie* in the views it holds on language, culture and the place of French in the world. The end of the last section showed how some members of the *Académie* see these matters. The contrast between the views of Maurice Druon quoted there and those of Maurice Bruézière (1983) writing at the time of the centenary of the *Alliance* could hardly be greater. Since the views of Druon are shared by many of those defending French today, it is worth quoting Bruézière at some length, although allowances must be made for possible exaggeration in painting the ceremonial portrait of a 100-year-old lady. He writes (1983: 6):

> Languages, cultures and civilisation are what they are and they occupy the space in the world that History has given them. It has never stopped reducing or enlarging that space as it wills. Should one language seem one day to be more useful than others, or even more suited to express certain aspects of civilisation, what does that matter to us? Tomorrow, things will have changed and only the mind may possibly be eternal.[41]

Kessler (1999: 375) interprets the activities of the *Alliance* in a far less idealistic light. She quotes the bulletin of the *Alliance*:

> The French language engenders French habits; French habits lead to the purchase of French products. A person who speaks French becomes a client of France.[42]

This, she says, is a philosophy arising from two political motivations: foreign policy and colonial policy. For her, the creation of the *Alliance* was an early example of a politically expedient alliance between the government and private defenders and promoters of French (1999: 375). Thus the humility and inclusiveness of Bruèzière's statement does not give the whole picture. Nevertheless, he reaffirms his conviction of the openness of the *Alliance* elsewhere in his book (1983: 239): 'The *Alliance* is in favour of respecting civilisation. No, not just French civilisation, which is only one form of it, but various civilisations. Thus its purpose is to engage in cultural dialogue.'[43] As we shall see, the innovative and imaginative internal structures put in place when the *Alliance* was founded are precisely suited to achieve the kind of dialogue and reciprocity Bruézière speaks of.

The group of men who decided to create what became known as the *Alliance française*, although remarkable for its breadth, did not contain linguists. It included Ferdinand de Lesseps (its President from 1887–1889), Louis Pasteur, Ernest Renan, Jules Verne and Paul Cambon (web site, *Alliance française*). After the Franco-Prussian war, there was a feeling that France and the French language and culture may have been losing some of its prestige in the world. The founders felt that one way to combat this would be to create an association to support the language and culture throughout the world. Rather than imposing French, as had been done in the colonies, they thought it would be possible to use existing groups of French speakers and francophiles throughout the world to set up partnerships in various countries. From the beginning, the focus was on other countries, on sharing and participation – ideas the rest of the world appears to have discovered at the end of the 20th century. As a Power-Point presentation prepared by the *Alliance* puts it: 'The association called the *Alliance française* is charged with teaching the French language in the world, organising cultural events and bringing together the friends of France in foreign countries'[44] (web site, *Alliance française* <u>PowerPoint</u>).

From its beginnings in 1883, the *Alliance* had considerable government support (Kessler, 1999: 374). It spread quickly to other countries and in 2003 it was active in 130 countries, with 1072 local associations throughout the world. Although it has been through difficult periods, it has always been able to modernise – as is shown by the introduction of new statutes in 2000 and the current debate on new structures and statutes. It has continued to fulfil the founders' wishes, devoting itself, in partnership with local francophiles, to the teaching of French language and later, to a lesser extent, French culture. Its presidents have been outstanding men: Poincaré and Doumer were Presidents of the Republic, de Lesseps, Duruy, Poincaré, Bédier, Duhamel and Henriot were members of the *Académie*. Throughout its existence, it has had the full support of the heads of government, notably in recent times of de Gaulle, Mitterrand and Chirac.

A steady expansion continued in the first half of the 20th century, with the creation of *Alliances* throughout the world and the development of the *Alliance française* in Paris, which had oversight of all the others. The opening of the school of French at the Paris *Alliance* in 1919 was an important step forward. This school teaches students from all round the world and has continued to modernise, for example with the creation of a multi-media centre in 2002. The 1930s were years of crisis, but the situation gradually improved. The Second World War was a particularly difficult time for the *Alliance*, unable to function under German occupation. In a moving declaration sent to all member associations on 20 April 1942 (Blaise, 2001), it explained the reasons for the temporary closure and transfer to London. The speech by General de Gaulle in Algeria on the 60th anniversary in 1943 therefore had special psychological (and political) importance:

> [E]levated values will not be preserved through an outrageous intellectual nationalism. . . . it is through free spiritual and moral relationships, established between ourselves and others, that our cultural influence can be extended to the advantage of all and that, in return, our worth can be developed.[45] (web site, *Alliance française* <u>De Gaulle</u>)

The post-war period saw continuing expansion in foreign countries and huge growth in the school and student numbers in Paris. The *Alliance* began to go far beyond its original brief, developing a close involvement with *la Francophonie*, creating new teaching programmes and establishing teacher training courses, working with institutions teaching French language and culture both at home and abroad. It now organises competitions and examinations and works closely with the *Direction des Relations Internationales* (Office of International Relations) of the Ministry of Education. With the *Association pour l'enseignement du français à l'étranger* (Association for Teaching French Abroad) and other government cultural and educational centres such as the *Instituts français* (French Institutes) it is part of a strong worldwide network presenting the public face of the French language, language teaching methods, French culture and education. Each *Alliance* works with the French embassy and cultural services in its home country in the promotion of the cultural policy of the government. The *Alliances* also now cooperate with similar agencies of other governments – the British Council, the Goethe Institute, the Dante Alighieri Society.

The management structures of the *Alliance* are unique. Each *Alliance*, wherever it is located, is an independent organisation set up according to the laws in the country where it operates. While the directors of the *Alliances* are part of the official French government *Services culturels* (Cultural Services) and are appointed by Paris, all other personnel are recruited locally, sometimes locally trained and have local contracts. The buildings are usually owned by the local *Alliance* Committee, composed of volunteers and benefactors, and responsible for the financial health of their *Alliance*. The whole enterprise is founded on the idea of partnership and response to local needs. Thus each *Alliance* is different from the others. At times in its history, this has seemed quaintly old-fashioned. At the start of the new century, it appears as an outstanding 'new' idea.

Some of the founders certainly had high ambitions and thought that the *Alliances* were the ideal way of restoring French *grandeur* and re-establishing the superiority of French. Cambon, for example, *'prône le maintien et l'extension de l'influence de la France par la propagation de sa langue'* (advocates maintaining and extending the influence of France by the promotion of its language) (web site, *Alliance française*, PowerPoint). These aims have given way, as the quotation from Bruézière showed, to a far more tolerant and tempered approach. Changes in the environment in which the *Alliances* operate have meant that the emphasis now is on the teaching of French by native speakers and on the promotion of French culture. The *Alliances* now aim to offer a credible alternative, in cultural terms, to the dominant English-speaking American model. This does not involve vituperative attacks on *les Anglo-saxons*, but an insistence on the right to be different, on the need for sharing and openness. This means that the original focus on the French language articulated in the founding documents is now far less clear.

The new approach could of course be seen as simply a new form of political correctness and it is certainly true that, although local needs and cultures are respected, the *Alliances* do not operate in a politics free zone but are ever more closely tied to the cultural policies of France. They are now increasingly dependent on the Ministry of Culture for some of their funding and on the French *Attaché culturel* in their country for approval of their actions. Jacques Chirac, in his message on 27 January 2004 for the 120th anniversary of the *Alliance*, insists on the one hand on France's late 20th century motto: *la diversité culturelle et linguistique et le dialogue des civilisations* (cultural and linguistic diversity and the dialogue of civilisations) while on the other he re-states an unshakeable belief in the superiority of French and its inherent suitability for expressing in an international context French values of tolerance and democracy, French culture and learning, French politics and economics (web site, *Alliance française*, <u>Chirac</u>).

In his statement released for the same anniversary Jacques Viot, President of the *Alliance*, devotes a section to 'cultural' politics but confines himself essentially to questions of finance. He concludes by side-stepping the cultural issue, saying: 'because of its status as a private association and because it is integrated into the host countries, it [the *Alliance française*] is particularly well placed to encourage cultural dialogue and to develop the values of exchange, sharing and friendship,'[46] (web site, *Alliance française*, <u>Viot</u>). The PowerPoint presentation claims: 'It [the *Alliance française*] is entirely removed from political or religious considerations.'[47] There is nevertheless constant reference to and acceptance of French government cultural policies (if not politics) so it would be naive to take statements such as this at face value.

The *Alliance*, as it has moved away from its traditional emphasis on language, has already accepted a considerable degree of government direction. The government decision to keep it under the oversight of the MAE, although the DGLFLF was moved to the Ministry of Culture, certainly kept it within a more powerful ministry but in fulfilling its broader cultural role, it has accepted as its partner organisations not only the Ministry of Education (*Ministère de l'Éducation nationale* – MEN) but also influential sections of the MAE: the Directorate General for International Cooperation and Development (*Direction générale de la coopération internationale et du développement* – DGCID), within which is the Directorate for Cultural Cooperation and French (*Direction de la coopération culturelle et du français* – DCCF) (Table 3.6).

The *Association française d'action artistique* (French Association for Artistic Action – AFAA), a close partner of the *Alliance*, is jointly funded by the MAE and the Ministry of Culture, and was, from its foundation in 1922 until 2006, the principal official exporter of French culture. For Kessler (1999: 382) the AFAA is a good illustration of how government cultural diplomacy works: sponsors are encouraged, private organisations are welcome but control remains the prerogative of the state. Because the state assumes the right to choose which cultural activities to sponsor and the selection criteria are not revealed, government cultural policy (both internal and external) frequently arouses criticism. By promoting activities chosen by the state, the *Alliance* loses a degree of its cherished independence.

The *Alliance française* is now at a turning point in its history. Since the 1990s, various government reports on French cultural services abroad (Table 3.7, pp. 78–79) have revealed a growing disquiet – among both members of parliament and the general public. In particular the 2001 Daugé Report (web site, *Académie française*, <u>Daugé</u>) found many weaknesses in the system and it was crucial for the *Alliance*. The annual reports of the *Alliance* itself reveal a mounting concern with financial problems, and those for 2004 and 2005 show that, for the *Alliance* to continue, it must be prepared to accept increasing levels of government aid. There is a price to be paid for this and it involves acceptance of a greater degree of government involvement than many think is reasonable. The new management structure will separate the language school in Paris from the international division which, in return for government help, will be expected to act as an agent of government cultural policy. That the polemic surrounding this change has sometimes been bitter should not surprise us. In spite of the continued involvement of local management and finance in *Alliances* throughout the world, the organisation is perilously close to losing its valued independence and becoming another instrument of government status planning.

The next chapter returns to the connections between language policy and politics in a wider sense. The growing reality of a political agenda for the *Alliance* constitutes yet another move away from the predominance of language in cultural planning and an example of government manipulation. In the international arena the stakes are high and the government clearly appreciates symbolic value of language.

La Délégation générale à la langue française et aux langues de France: Official Action

Chapter 1 (p. 14) gave some idea of the complications involved in trying to trace the various stages of the <u>DGLFLF</u> and other government agencies. The successive changes of name (Table 3.1) make it particularly difficult to follow the development of this, the first purely governmental agency and the political institution most explicitly dedicated to the defence of the French language, as distinct from other cultural concerns.

It was created in 1966 (two years after Étiemble's book made *le franglais*

Table 3.1 History of the DGLFLF

Date	President	Title
1966	De Gaulle	*Haut-Comité pour la défense et l'expansion de la langue française*
1973	Pompidou	*Haut-Comité de la langue française*
1984	Mitterrand	*Comité consultatif à la langue française; Commissariat général à la langue française*
1989	Mitterrand	*Conseil supérieur de la langue française; Délégation générale à la langue française*
2001	Chirac	*Délégation générale à la langue française et aux langues de France*

Table 3.2 Ministry of Culture and Communication – Structure 2006

Ministry of Culture and Communication
Minister for Culture and Communication
Direction: General administration
Direction: Architecture; Heritage
Direction: Archives
Direction: Development of the media
Direction: Books and reading
Direction: Music, dance, theatre, performance
Direction: Museums
Delegation: Visual arts
Delegation: Development and international affairs
Delegation : Délégation Générale à la Langue Française et aux Langues de France
National centre for cinema
Regional directorates for cultural affairs
Departmental services – Architecture and heritage
Inter-ministerial office for the quality of public buildings
Public establishment dependent on the Ministry

Source: MCC web site

a topic of lively popular debate), an initiative of de Gaulle's Prime Minister Georges Pompidou, who felt that an official response to widespread concern about the state of the French language was required. From 1966 until 1996 it reported to the Prime Minister. Since May 1986, when the position of a supporting minister for Francophonia was created, it has also reported to the minister with responsibility for Francophonia. Its various changes of title are shown in Table 3.1.

Within the MAE (Structure, Table 3.6), a separate Ministry for *la culture et la Francophonie* was created in 1993 (now the *Ministre délégué à la Coopération, au Développement et à la Francophonie*) and from 1996 the DGLF has been attached to the Ministry for Culture and Communication (MCC). It is now, as the tables in this chapter show, an administrative sub-section of the civil service in the Ministry of Culture, headed by a full-time professional administrator, the *délégué général*. It is thus involved in policy-making at the highest level and its presidents, vice-presidents, *rapporteurs* (reporters [a role specific to the French system of government]) and commissioners have been men of distinction (web site, DGLFLF History). It is currently (2006) headed by the linguist Bernard Cerquiglini (see Table 3.2).

Table 3.3 shows the internal structure and principal areas of activity of the DGLFLF.

Originally, the mission of the *Haut-Comité* in 1966 was to:

> examine appropriate measures to ensure the defence and expansion of French, to establish the necessary links with competent private organisations, especially in the areas of cultural and technical cooperation and to instigate or encourage any and all initiatives related to the defence and the expansion of the French language.[48] (web site, *Haut-Comité pour la défense et l'expansion de la langue française*)

The name of the institution changed as environmental factors (Cooper, 1989) exerted different kinds of pressures: in response to historical developments and to changes in society, the role it was expected to fulfil was altered. It is possible to measure the extent of the changes in the organisation by comparing the 1966 founding statement above with the 2002 statement by Bernard Cerquiglini (van Dixhoorn, 2002). In response to a question about the changed mission of the DGLFLF, the *Délégué général* gives three main purposes for the institution he directs:

- 'a policy which is favourable to the development and the spread of the French language . . . to help it to progress'[49];
- 'the use of French in France and outside . . . respect for French as a language of international organisations . . . prepare for the enlargement of Europe . . . promote French in the essential context of European and worldwide multi-lingualism'[50]
- '[work for] pluri-lingualism within the national borders'.[51]

The first of these corresponds to all intents and purposes to the 1966 mission and involves principally corpus planning. It covers: the ongoing work in the various Commissions of Terminology, ensuring that French

Table 3.3 Structure of the DGLFLF (Ministry of Culture)

Délégation générale à la langue française et aux langues de France
Délégué général   *Délégué général adjoint*
Missions:

• Use and spread of the French language
   – Legal; Annual report to parliament
   – Plurilingualism; French in the world; Francophonie
   – Use of French by the scientific community

• Competence in French; fight against illiteracy
   – Competence in French and education
   – Fight against illiteracy; national action

• Development and modernisation of the French language
   – Publicity
   – Terminology commissions

• Languages of France   – Observatory for language use

• Communication and public awareness
   – Publications, trade fairs, seminars
   – Internet site
   – Press office; Protocol

Source: MCC web site

is able to function in developing areas of science and technology without having to resort to the use of foreign terms; the attempt to introduce spelling reforms; the feminisation of job titles; and (since 1994) monitoring compliance with the *Loi Toubon*.

The other two show dramatic and recent shifts in government thinking and policy. The second concerns diffusion planning, with a particular emphasis on protecting the status of French. It reflects a shift beyond internal concerns and adopts the terms that have become government buzz words (*plurilinguisme*, for example). The third, again as an element of status planning and the advancement of the national language, acknowledges the existence of other languages in France and the new political power they have acquired. In using the term 'pluri-lingualism' it declares an acceptance of the fact that people may speak more than one language. It does not commit itself to the defence of the regional and minority languages.

The 2001 change of title, adding 'and the languages [plural] of France' reflects the new government stance. The DGLFLF web site describes the additional functions in the following way: 'The DGLFLF contributes to the preservation and promotion of the languages of France, that is, languages other than French which are spoken in territorial France and are part of the national cultural heritage.'[52]

The labyrinthine nature of the various developments leading to the present-day DGLFLF makes it very difficult to describe its functions clearly. Because of the overtly political nature of the organisation, many of the changes have resulted from the intricacies of political intrigue and this is probably impossible to unravel. There have also been a number of constant tensions contributing to the apparent lack of direction that has character-ised the DGLFLF and its predecessors and these have been highlighted each time the government or its cultural and linguistic policies have changed.

To select just three:

- First, an apparently exclusive concern with questions of vocabulary and terminology led to confusion with other agencies, wrangles and slow progress.
- Second, financial tensions caused by changing government priorities meant that there was sometimes (particularly since the transfer of the *Délégation* from the MAE to the Ministry of Culture) not enough money to carry out the tasks prescribed for both the DGLF (and its predeces-sors) and the various agencies concerned with *la Francophonie*.
- Third, the problem of reforming the spelling system (Introduction) again reared its head and absorbed time and money that could have been spent on other activities: 'the sacred fire [of protecting and defending the language] was extinguished, smothered by the question of the reform of the spelling system'[53] (Hadoux, 1997).

Additionally, the personalities involved changed continually. Meanwhile, in the eyes of some of its defenders, including members of the *Académie française*, French was losing ground to English and government intervention was inadequate and failing to defend it.

This points to yet another tension marking the recent history of the DGLFLF – the tension with the *Académie*. There are various indications of this uncomfortable situation. The statutes of the *Académie* (and, indeed the terms of the 1996 *décret relatif à l'enrichissement de la langue française* (web site, France, Government of, <u>MCC</u>, *Enrichissement*)) give it the final say in all matters to do with the use of the language, including, notably terminology. It is not always clear where the line is drawn. For example, when the DGLF published its suggestions for spelling changes in 1990, the *Académie* at first appeared to support them, but later was more guarded; the publication in 1991 by the DGLF of its *Dictionnaire des termes officiels* (Dictionary of Official Terms) was felt to be trespassing on the *Académie*'s prerogatives.

The list of appointments to key positions in the DGLF shows frequent changes in those positions as changes occur in governments and in policy. Some names however recur, for example that of Bernard Cerquiglini, the current *Délégué général*. He was *Délégué général à la langue française* from 1989–1993, and again from 2001 when the words *et aux langues de France* were added. A professor of the history of the French language in the *Université Denis Diderot* (Paris) he is a civil servant and is seconded to work at the DGLFLF.

During his first period as *Délégué général* Cerquiglini advocated far-reaching spelling reforms and more recently was in the forefront of the movement to create feminine forms of the titles for various jobs and professions, for example: *Madame la Ministre* instead of *Madame le Ministre*. (Becquer *et al.*, 1999). Both of these topics polarise speakers of French and notably accentuate the rift between, on the one hand, the *Académie* and private defenders of the language and, on the other, the DGLFLF and some professional linguists. Bernard Cerquiglini is described by one of his interviewers as '*du côté des évolutionnistes plutôt que des normatifs*' (on the side of the [linguistic] evolutionists rather than of those who [seek to] impose norms) (van Dixhoorn, 2002).

As far as the defence of the language is concerned, this outline of the evolution of the DGLF shows clearly how a national history of several centuries, and a DGLF history of nearly 40 years, of defending monolingualism and imposing French appears to have given way within a surprisingly short time to the promotion of linguistic and cultural diversity. Certainly, there had been some years of discussion and preparation, particularly since the proposal for a European Charter for Regional and Minority Languages, adopted by the Council of Europe in June 1992, but the new direction took many people by surprise and provoked some sharp criticism. Bernard Cerquiglini's plain-speaking interview (Cerquiglini, 2002) after taking office as the *Délégué général* of the newly re-christened organisation in October 2001, marks a determinedly new stage in the long history examined here. He returned to the topic the following year (Cerquiglini, 2003) and, particularly since his work as *rapporteur* on the European Charter in 1999, has strongly championed the cause of the regional and minority languages of France.

He is well aware of the potentially confusing volte-face in government policy on this issue but his attempt to reconcile apparent contradictions in the role of the DGLFLF is not entirely convincing:

> [W]hat has changed today is that for the first time since the State interested itself in language, an organisation [the DGLFLF] is trying to follow simultaneously a policy in favour of the national language

and in favour of the other languages. Until now, for regrettable historical reasons, . . . the two activities have been seen as distinct, if
not opposed to one another. . . . Today, we have to envisage the two
approaches at one and the same time.[54] (Cerquiglini, 2002: 1)

This attempt to keep both balls in the air has been reflected in the two
inquiries carried out for the DGLF by the INSEE (*Institut national de la statistique et études économiques* (National Institute for Statistics and Economic
Studies) see web site) and the INED (*Institut national des études démographiques*
(National Institute for Demographic Studies) see web site). Chapter 2, p.
33; referred to these (Héran, 1993; Héran *et al.*, 2002). The surveys provide
the first results of the *Observatoire des pratiques linguistiques* (Observatory for
language use – Table 3.3 above) set up by the DGLF in 1998 at the request
of the then Minister for Culture. No study of similar scope had been carried
out since the time of the Abbé Grégoire (Chapter 1, p. 8).

Another recent activity of the DGLFLF is the *Assises nationales des langues
de France* (National Assises [meeting] for the Languages of France) called
by the new (and short-lived) Minister for Culture in the Raffarin government in October 2003. This unprecedented meeting reflected the growing
influence of decentralisation in French political thought and brought
together representatives of a wide variety of organisations, political tendencies, local, regional and national government and language activists
(web site, DGLFLF, *Assises*). Its purpose was to try to create a new tool for
making and implementing language policy and to create a Statute for the
Languages of France. It was marked by 'a very spirited debate, at the heart
of which is the will to give to the languages of France a credible status and
legal protection'.[55]

Four conclusions were drawn from the meeting:

(1)   There is no positive law in favour of the languages of France.
(2)   The teaching of languages in France needs to be re-thought in line
      with government policy on decentralisation.
(3)   The media should be encouraged to take positive action in favour of
      the languages of France.
(4)   It is necessary to ensure that the languages of France are modern
      and creative.

These suggestions have produced little change. Recent (2005) action by
the *Conseil supérieur de l'audiovisuel* (CSA) (see web site; Chapter 6, p. 151)
shows that the media are still being 'encouraged' to take a responsible
attitude to language, but many observers continue to be very dissatisfied
with the limited results the CSA produces.

The final decision was to revive the *Conseil national des langues et cultures régionales* (National Council for Regional Languages and Cultures), set up in 1985 under the Mitterrand government: *Décret 85–1006 du 23 septembre 1985* (web site, *Adminet*, <u>Decree 85–1006</u>). This later changed its name to *le Haut Conseil des Langues et Cultures de France* before disappearing. *Plus ça change . . .*

The likelihood of there being any speedy outcome from the *Assises* is small. With changes in the composition of the government, activities such as these tend to be postponed. Thus the DGLFLF, ignoring apparent contradictions in its role, is taking a high-profile line on the question of the languages of France and its influence could be decisive. Nevertheless, and in spite of the government policy of increasing decentralisation, the conviction that only a central, government body can oversee language use and development and that this must be supported by appropriate national laws remains a typically French approach to the problem. It is re-iterated by the many government reports on language policy (Table 3.7). The changing policies of the DGLFLF represent an attempt to reconcile conflicting environmental pressures within France, in Europe and in the wider world and to implement appropriate language strategies.

One of the challenges facing the DGLFLF is to convince the French that it is possible to operate diffusion policies to protect and promote the national language and at the same time defend the minority languages. Unsurprisingly given the long history of state intervention and control, it is apparently not possible to re-think the overriding role of the highly centralised government in the area of language. This is again exemplified, albeit in a different mode, in the following section on *La Francophonie*.

La Francophonie: Commonwealth and Common Wealth?

The fourth of the big official agencies in this chapter is the OIF (see web site). This is the most extensive and far-reaching of the agencies acting in the defence of French. Because of the extensive use of the words *francophonie* and *francophone*, it is very difficult to define these terms when they are used in the name of an official organisation. Chapter 1 (p. 15) showed that there is a difference implied between *la francophonie* and *la Francophonie*. Neither is concerned exclusively, nor even principally, with the defence of the French language. *La francophonie* is used to refer to all the people in the world who use French partly or entirely as a language of communication in their everyday lives. When it is spelt with a capital letter, *la Francophonie* refers to the group of governments or countries using French as a working language, those accepted by the OIF as full members, associate members, observers or special guests. Certainly, *la francophonie* is a subject of consid-

Table 3.4 *La Francophonie* – Administrative Structure

(1) French government agencies:· • Assistant Minister for Cooperation, Development and French – MAE • Service for Francophone Affairs – MAE (administration of the five direct operators: OIF, AUF, AIMF, *Université Senghor, TV5*) • Directorate General for International Cooperation and Development – MAE • Minister for National Education, Higher Education and Research – MEN • Higher Council for the French Language – Prime Minister; DGLFLF – MCC • General Commission for Terminology – Prime Minister; DGLFLF – MCC
(2) OIF (central organisation of the member states): Five Direct operators: • *Agence universitaire de la francophonie* (AUF) • *Agence de la Francophonie* • *TV5* • *Université Senghor d'Alexandrie* • *Association Internationale des Maires et Responsables des Capitales et Métropoles partiellement ou entièrement francophones* (AIMF)
Other partner institutions: • *Association internationale des Parlementaires de langue française* • *Forum francophone des affaires* • *Comité international des Jeux de la Francophonie*
Additional partners: • *Association francophone d'amitié et de liaison* (AFAL) and other associations and private organisations involved in francophone culture; *Fédération internationale des professeurs de français* (FIPF) • Audio-visual media: RFI, RFO *TV5*

Source: http://www.diplomatie.gouv.fr/fr/actions-france_830/francophonie-langue-francaise_1040/index.html (20.02.2006)

erable interest, but this book is more concerned with official government involvement in *la Francophonie*.

Kessler (1999: 436–437) takes a resolutely critical stance on Francophonia, defining it as an *idéologie institutionnalisée* (institutionalised ideology) or a *nationalisme multinational* (multinational nationalism). She sees as the basis of the movement a shared emotional conviction of the superiority of the French language, French literature and art, French philosophy and law as illustrated in the history of France. After a shaky start in France, it is now, she argues, an official ideology supported by political and administrative élites, literary, artistic and media milieux all of whom feel themselves threatened by the domination of English. This is only one side of the coin. As with colonialism, the picture is not completely bleak. Francophonia has many positive aspects although, as we shall see, it has now grown into a multi-headed creature the French government struggles to control.

The official agency, the OIF, is, as Table 3.4 shows, an intricately struc-

Table 3.5 Francophone Summits

Sommet	Date	Place	Themes
1	1986	Paris	Solidarity
2	1987	Quebec	Setting priorities (see above)
3	1989	Dakar	Education and training; Creation of the *Université Senghor* in Alexandria
4	1991	Paris	New structures for *la Francophonie*; Role of the ACCT
5	1993	Mauritius	The name of the *Sommet* changes to the *Conférence des chefs d'état et de gouvernement ayant le français en partage* (Conference of the Heads of State and Government which share the use of French); Economic cooperation
6	1995	Cotonou	Political cooperation; ACCT becomes the *Agence de la Francophonie*; creation of the revised *Charte de la Francophonie* (web site, UPF, *Francophonie*)
7	1997	Hanoi	Prevention of war in member countries; Human rights
8	1999	Moncton	Strengthening of democracy; Organisation in 2000 of a meeting in Bamako to assess progress; Cultural diversity
	2000	Bamako	Democracy; Good governance; Human rights
9	2002	Beirut	Responses to terrorism; Cultural dialogue; Information technology in third world countries; Re-drafting of criteria for membership; Announcement of the opening, in 2006, of a *Maison de la Francophonie*; Plans for a festival of the cultures of the francophone world in Paris in 2006
10	2004	Ouagadougou	Solidarity; Sustainable development

tured and wide-ranging organisation. It now includes over 50 participating countries. It is neither a specifically French nor a specifically language-focused institution. France is one of the members: perhaps the most powerful, but not necessarily always the most important member. While many of the activities of the OIF are administered from France, France is not the head of the group in the way that the Queen is the head of the Commonwealth. As Chapter 1 (pp. 14–16) showed, the organisation owes its existence not to France but to some of its former African colonies and this is an essential feature of the OIF and the way it functions.

The ramifications of the organisation are therefore extensive. Although now based in the MAE, it also has connections with the Prime Minister, with the MCC (through the DGLFLF – Table 3.6) and with the Ministry of Education. Its numerous partner agencies include both government and private organisations in France and abroad so that its governance becomes ever more problematic.

Table 3.5, showing the various *Sommets de la Francophonie* since 1986, further emphasises the broad sweep of environmental factors that have impacted on language policy. The wide variety of OIF activities and the changes in focus reflect a direct response to changing world conditions and a tendency to move away from strictly linguistic questions.

Since the first *Sommet*, the OIF has moved to embrace linguistic and cultural diversity, and participation in the francophone group of nations and states has become an essential arm of French government policy.

The protection and promotion of the French language does not therefore appear to be the OIF's major concern and linguistic questions are absorbed into the wider notions of cultural diversity and dialogue. It lists (in the following order) its main activities and interests:

- '*Paix, démocratie et droits de l'homme*' (Peace, democracy and the rights of man);
- '*Diversité culturelle et dialogue des cultures*' (Cultural diversity and dialogue);
- '*Développement durable*' (Sustainable development);
- '*Accès à la formation et à l'information*' (Access to training and information). (web site, OIF)

As with many statements of political objectives, these are typically vague (Kessler, 1999: 383). It will be obvious from the list that only the second heading directly concerns the French language. The widening of the activities of the AIF to include the languages spoken in member countries (Dakar Declaration, 1989) shows:

> first, the very strong influence of the former African colonies in shaping the policies of the OIF; second, a strong desire by France not to be thought of as neo-colonialist or imperialist; third, the extent to which linguistic and cultural diversity are now central planks in French linguistic policy.

Similarly, France and the francophone countries have, like the *Alliance* and the DGLFLF, moved away from a focus uniquely on French to collaborate with other language groups and the countries where their languages are spoken. There are strong links between the OIF and similar organisations for Spanish, Portuguese and Arabic as part of a wider concern with worldwide linguistic and cultural diversity. Calvet (2002a: 192–202) analyses these alliances and suggests some possible scenarios for the future.

The language mission of the OIF, subsumed under 'Cultural diversity and dialogue', is mainly implemented by its executive arm, the Paris-based *Agence intergouvernementale de la Francophonie* (Intergovernment Agency for Francophonia – AIF) (see web site AIF). The AIF develops cooperative programmes in the fields of education, culture, the media, the economy and good governance in the 50 countries and states that are members of the OIF. It is not easy to find details in the language domain, since the AIF is involved in very many other fields and relies on a variety of outside operators to deliver its programmes. Another complication is that the AIF network of actions in favour of the language, particularly in France, is spread over many other partner agencieswhich share a loosely defined remit to protect and promote the language. Information about the linguistic priorities of the *Agence* is given on the web site (AIF, <u>French language</u>).

Even within the language mission, there are many activities not directly concerned with the French language:

- *Enseignement et apprentissage du français <u>et des langues partenaires</u>* (Teaching and learning French <u>and partner languages</u>) (acquisition planning)
- *Le français dans la vie internationale* (French in international life) (status and acquisition planning)
- *Appui aux politiques linguistiques <u>et aux langues partenaires</u>* (Support for language policies <u>and for partner languages</u>). (My underlining)

(These three main areas of language interest are supported by grants also available through the *Agence*.)

What is perhaps surprising about this list is the inclusion of support for national languages in the partner states, although this has been an ongoing trend in the *Alliance* and the DGLFLF as they followed changing government policies. A movement originally based on the shared use of French, and sharply criticised for strengthening French at the expense of local languages (for example, Petnkeu Nzepa, 2003), has now so far shifted its language policy that support for local cultures and therefore local languages is seen as appropriate, indeed essential.

The AIF web site states that the first activity – Teaching and learning French and partner languages – is justified as a means of providing access to learning, to development and to democracy. The strategies in place in different countries reflect the differing needs of those countries. In Africa, the

AIF works in literacy programmes in local languages to ensure that they are strengthened and can interface with French. The second activity – French in international life – is directed towards international institutions and against the spread of '[le] *monolinguisme anglophone qui progresse*' (increasing English monolingualism). The institutions most concerned are those of the UN and the European Union. (There is a special AIF web site (European Union) for countries about to join, or having just joined the EU.) The use of French as a working language in these international agencies will allow the Franco-phone countries to '*défendre et faire entendre*' (defend and give voice to) the ideas and political positions of the francophone group. Finally, the third activity – Support for language policies and partner languages – recognises the fact that in many countries, particularly in Africa, support for national and cross-national languages is essential. This is part of the policy of cultural and linguistic diversity of the OIF and of France. Help is provided, for example, in publishing books in these languages.

This third aspect of OIF language policy is supported by four very wide-ranging networks:

- *Le Réseau international du français dans le monde* (International Network of French in the World) (RIFRAM);
- *Le Réseau international francophone d'aménagement linguistique* (International Francophone Network for Language Development) (RIFAL) (web sites, France, Government of, *MCC*, OIF, RIFAL);
- *Le Réseau international des langues africaines et créole* (International Network of African Languages and Creole) (RILAC);
- *Le Réseau international des littératures francophones* (RILIF).

It is not possible to give details of all the activities of the networks, but the fact that they exist is testimony to the astounding extent of the OIF activities related loosely to language. Through the OIF, funding is available for:

- training various specialists from member countries so that they can take part in international projects;
- translation and interpreting in international meetings and conferences;
- publication of books in African languages and creole.

An example of the complexity of the organisation is provided by the award, through French radio and television, of prizes (*Trophées de la langue française*) for people who '*contribuent à vivifier la langue française et à en faire un vecteur international de communication, d'éducation, de création et de culture*' (contribute to the health of the French language and make it an interna-tional tool of communication, education, creativity and culture). There are 12 partner organisations involved in the arrangements for this relatively small event alone: *TV5, France 3* (television), *Réseau France Outremer* (French Overseas Network – a radio, television and Internet organisation), the MCC, the MAE, the OIF, the AIF, the DGLFLF, the *Mission laïque*, the *Alliances françaises*, the *Communauté des Télévisions Francophones* and *Radio France*.

Although most of the full meetings of the francophone countries have been held outside France, many of the agencies of the OIF now have their headquarters in France. The growing involvement of France in *la Francophonie* has not been universally welcomed, particularly by the private organisations for the defence of French. Questions have been raised by private defenders about the efficacy of the movement (Arnaud *et al.*, 2002; Vinatier & Xvolt, 2002a and b) and there have been perennial financial problems, with the defenders of the language demanding that more money be spent on protecting the language inside France. There is also, as Kessler points out (1999: 437–438), a tendency for an anti-Francophonia movement to develop, mocking the insistence of the francophone countries on protectionism and the need for diversity. This was very apparent after the UN vote in October 2005 (see next section).

The opening up of *la Francophonie* to countries not principally, or even marginally, francophone has also provoked criticism. The movement strongly and outspokenly embraces democracy and human rights, seen as essential shared values bequeathed to the former French colonies. It has though bowed to external pressure to admit to membership Haiti, Congo, Côte d'Ivoire (a former colony), countries where, although French is an official language, these values have been openly flouted. The admission of Albania, Bulgaria and Macedonia, among others, again raises the question of admission criteria and what part the shared use of the language can possibly play in countries such as these. Their acceptance is a clear indication of the wish to gain political influence in countries in the eastern bloc hoping to join the European Union. It is interesting to reflect that, although the motivation for their admission was certainly not linguistic, some of the direct outcomes may be. Acquisition and status planning here go hand in hand – French will be taught in schools and universities in these countries and will offer a high status alternative to the invasion of English.

Many people in France believe that the loosening of the criteria for membership of *la Francophonie* has been counter-productive and that the credibility of the movement has been seriously weakened by its willingness to tolerate totalitarian governments and to accept countries where French is scarcely spoken at all, or spoken badly. This is the point of view of those who concern themselves primarily with the language. It is however entirely possible to envisage other valid political reasons for considering language as a symbol of a much wider political agenda, and including countries that do not meet strictly linguistic criteria. There might for example be historical, educational, scientific, economic, political or ideological reasons for admitting a country where the use of French is not highly developed.

Although it is not always possible to always equate French policy and OIF policies, successive French governments have been very much involved in all aspects of *la Francophonie*, and have supported its activities both financially and politically. This means that there is, both inside and outside France, a confusing collection of official agencies and activities involved in implementing 'Francophone' language policy. And there are, as the next section shows, yet further ramifications! The intricacies of the operation of the OIF and the fact that much of its activity is concentrated in countries outside France may account for the apparent lack of interest and comprehension of its function inside France. At the time of the Ouagadougou Summit, the *Express* published its international edition with the title: *Mais à quoi sert la Francophonie ?* (But what's the use of Francophonia?) (*Express*, 2004b). The wide variety of activities described and opinions expressed explains to some extent why many people in France are confused about the role of the OIF. Abdou Diouf (2006), in his New Year Greetings, makes it clear that the organisation is aware of this confusion. He describes new structures for the OIF – a new Charter and a new Strategic Framework – to be implemented in coming years. Whether these will in fact, as the *Secrétaire général* so clearly hopes, streamline and simplify the administration and enhance the effectiveness of the OIF remains to be seen.

We conclude this chapter by looking at the work of the MAE in protecting and promoting French and then assess the effectiveness of government policy and planning.

Foreign Affairs: The French Government and Language

The MAE (see web site) has an over-arching role in matters to do with the French language outside France. The importance attached to the defence and promotion of the French language and culture outside France is reflected in the high level at which the government is closely involved and in the fact that the funding for the DGCID, according to the Duvernois Report in 2000 (see Table 3.7), can still be as much as half the budget of the Ministry (Wardhaugh, 1987: 152). Table 3.6 shows the position of *la Francophonie* in the structure of the MAE.

As Table 3.6 shows, the Assistant Minister for Co-operation and Francophonia is under the direct authority of the powerful Minister of Foreign Affairs. She has wide responsibilities that include all Francophone activi-

Table 3.6 Ministry of Foreign Affairs – Structure 2006 (position of *La Francophonie*)

Minister of Foreign Affairs
Assistant Minister for Cooperation, Development and French (1 of 2 Assistant Ministers in the MAE)
Service for Francophone Affairs   *Directorate General for International Cooperation and Development*   (DGCID – 1 of 15 sections in the MAE)

Sections of the DGCID:
 • Department of Strategy
 • Department for Geographic Coordination
 • Directorate for Development and Technical Cooperation
 • **Directorate for Cultural Cooperation and <u>French</u>**
     Section for Cultural Cooperation and <u>French</u>
     Section for <u>French</u>
 • Directorate for Scientific, University and Research Cooperation
 • Directorate for External Audio-visual Services and Techniques of Communication
 • Mission for Non-governmental Cooperation

ties and co-operation with the international organisms and partner associations involved in the Francophone group. She has full access to all the resources of the MAE and relies, in particular, on two groups within the Ministry: the *Service des Affaires Francophones* (Service for Francophone Affairs) and the DGCID. Looking for language-specific activities in the DGCID is reminiscent of a game of Hunt the Thimble. The Directorate general is composed of seven sections, including the Directorate for Cultural Cooperation and Francophonia, within which is a section for cultural cooperation and French. It is here that a sub-section concerned with French is found.

The Service of Francophone Affairs has two main spheres of activity. Neither of these is primarily concerned with the language. The first concerns decisions taken at the *Sommets de la Francophonie*, at ministerial conferences of the francophone states and at the Permanent Council for Francophonia. The Service oversees the implementation in France of decisions taken by these bodies. Second, it has responsibility for cooperation with and financial oversight of the five partner agencies carrying out multi-lateral programmes for the OIF: AIF; AIMF; the international French-speaking university – *Université Senghor d'Alexandrie*; and the television channel TV5 (Table 3.4). The emphasis in these programmes is to a large extent on education and training.

The DGCID was created, as its web site states, as part of a ministerial re-organisation in 1998 when the former Ministry of Cooperation, formerly responsible for *la Francophonie*, was brought into Foreign Affairs to create a new Directorate with a wide brief in international cooperation. It suggests to the government the direction France should take in international cooperation and oversees two programmes:

- the developmental aid programme;
- the action programme for external cultural and scientific activities.

Its seven sections (Table 3.6 above) help the Assistant Minister in carrying out her role (under the control of the Minister for Foreign Affairs) as head of French government aid for development and oversee (for the Minister) all the agencies involved in French international cooperation. French policy in this area now has three main priorities :

- French aid for developing countries;
- Cultural diversity and human rights;
- France as a centre for students and researchers. (web site, France, Government of, MAE, DGCID)

The second of these is the domain of the DCCF (see Table 3.6) (one of the 7 sections within the DCGID), responsible for various sectors including the French language. On the MAE web site three main areas of activity are outlined:

- promoting multi-lingualism – which implies maintaining the importance of French in international (especially European) organisations;
- reinforcing the use of French as an aid to development in countries France is committed to helping;
- promoting French in developing countries so as to encourage new groups of people to use the language.

This is clearly a political rather than a linguistic programme, the result of status and, to a lesser extent, acquisition policies. It echoes what was found in other official agencies (apart from the *Académie*): concern for political and economic advantages for France and trendy preoccupations with cultural diversity.

The MAE works for 'linguistic and cultural diversity', through the DGCID and its DCCF. On the ground, its activities in these areas are the responsibility of a worldwide network of 151 cultural centres and institutes (the *Instituts français* in various European cities, for example) and 283 *Alliances françaises* (Chapter 3, pp. 55–60). In addition, the DCCF pays the salaries of about 800 French citizens who work throughout the world in various capacities. The MAE's linguistic diffusion policy for the teaching of French throughout the world is another essential area of activity, since the majority of people who learn French outside France do so at school or at university. Acquisition of the language is widely believed to confer on the learners a status their mother tongue does not have. In support of its vast teaching network, the MAE oversees the award of internationally recognised certificates of proficiency in French for various purposes and at various levels.

The attractive web site of the MAE makes a direct appeal to those who visit it, using colour, photographs, quotations and varied typefaces. It encourages people to speak French, shows how and why it promotes linguistic diversity and explains the importance of maintaining French as an international language. It shows how the francophone countries can help one another and also addresses the issue of spreading the use of French to countries, such as China, where it has previously rarely been taught or spoken. The psychological aspect is not neglected. There is a section on giving people a taste for French, and a user-friendly questionnaire (*La langue française et vous* (French and you)) invites visitors to the web site to answer some light-hearted questions to find out which of three types of learner of French they might be: a militant defender of the language, a waverer or a pragmatist. Positive and engaging activities like these are far more likely to have an impact on attitudes to the French language than criticism and doom-laden predictions.

Nevertheless, the defence of the language and culture and the long-standing government diffusion policies operated by the MAE are frequently criticised in France (Kessler, 1999: 380). One indicator of the difficulties faced by the MAE is the large number of government reports on French cultural and language policy commissioned by various official agencies in recent years (Table 3.7).

The list of selected reports in Table 3.7 clearly reveals a deep-seated malaise in the area of French cultural diplomacy. The successive reports have attempted to diagnose the reasons for this and their response is usually to recommend yet more government action, the creation of another government body with more clearly defined powers. By analysing the policies using Cooper's (1989) questions, it is possible to arrive at another diagnosis. As Kessler (1999: 370) reminds us, external cultural diplomacy in France is one of the oldest of government policies and France had something that might be called an external cultural policy – for example François 1er and *Soliman le Magnifique* and the treaty they signed in 1536 – before it had an internal policy in this area.

The acceptance of government intervention in cultural affairs is so old that it is almost impossible to re-think it and go back to first principles. Over the centuries the agencies and activities involved have become so

Table 3.7 Selected Reports – Cultural and Language Policy 2000–2005

Author	Title	Commissioning body	Date
Duvernois, Louis	*L'enjeu de la Francophonie au 21e siècle. Que veut la France ?* Source: http://www.expatries.senat.fr/francophonie.pdf	*Conseil Supérieur des Français à l'Étranger – Commission de l'enseignement, de la culture et de l'information*	4-9.09.2000
Tavernier, Yves *Député*	*Les moyens et les structures de diffusion de la Francophonie* Source: http://www.assemblee-nationale.fr/rap-info/i2592.asp	*Assemblée nationale – Commission des finances*	21.09.2000
Daugé, Yves *Député*	*Rapport d'information sur les centres culturels français à l'étranger* Source: http://www.assembleenationale.fr/rap-info/i2924.asp	*Assemblée nationale – Commission des affaires étrangères*	07.02.2001
Trupin, Odette *Députée*	*La politique éducative extérieure de la France* Source: http://www.assemblee-nationale.fr/rap-info/i3204.asp	*Assemblée nationale – Commission des affaires étrangères*	27.06.2001
Herbillon, Michel *Député* – Val-de-Marne	*La diversité linguistique dans l'Union européenne* Source: http://www.assemblee-nationale.fr/12/europe/rap-info/i0902.asp	*Assemblée nationale – Commission des affaires culturelles*	10.07.2003
Brunhes, Jacques *et al.* *Députés*	*Proposition: La création d'une commission d'enquête visant, à partir du bilan des politiques publiques destinées à promouvoir la langue française au plan national, européen et international, à proposer des mesures pour leur amélioration et le cas échéant, leur réorientation* Source: http://www.assembleenationale.fr/12/propositions/pion1101.asp	*Assemblée nationale – Commission des affaires culturelles*	02.10.2003

Table 3.7 (*cont.*) Selected Reports – Cultural and Language Policy 2000–2005

Legendre, Jacques *Sénateur*	*L'enseignement des langues étrangères en France* Source: http://www.senat.fr/rap/r03-063/r03-063.html	*Sénat – Commission des affaires culturelles*	12.11.2003
Legendre, Jacques *Sénateur*	*Avis – Projet de loi de finances pour 2004 : Francophonie* Source: http://www.senat.fr/rap/a03-074-14/a03-074-14.html	*Sénat – Commission des affaires culturelles*	20.11.2003
Boisseau, Yves *Député*	*Rapport (rejet) : La création d'une commission d'enquête visant, à partir du bilan des politiques publiques destinées à promouvoir la langue française au plan national, européen et international, à proposer des mesures pour leur amélioration et le cas échéant, leur réorientation* Source: http://www.assemblee-nationale.fr/12/rapports/r1277.asp	*Assemblée nationale – Commission des affaires culturelles*	09.12 2003
Legendre, Jacques *Sénateur*	*Avis – Projet de loi de finances 2005 : Francophonie* Source: http://www.senat.fr/rap/a04-075-12/a04-075-120.html	*Sénat – Commmission des affaires culturelles*	25.11.2004
Duvernois, Louis *Sénateur*	*Pour une nouvelle stratégie de l'action culturelle extérieure de la France : de l'exception à l'influence* Source: http://www.senat.fr/rap/r04-091/r04-091.html	*Sénat*	01.12.2004
Astier, Hubert	*Rapport d'évaluation de la politique en faveur du français* Source: http://www.culture.gouv.fr/culture/dglf/rapport/Astier_rapport.pdf	*Ministère de la culture et de la communication*	06.2005

numerous and, in some cases, so time-hallowed and so emotionally loaded, that objectivity is impossible. Salon (in Kessler, 1999: 387) comments that, in cultural and linguistic diplomacy:

> We [the French] have only found a virtual strategy, a juxtaposition of actions and policies, but neither a real strategy nor a comprehensive policy . . . [56]

This series of juxtapositions, this multiplicity and autonomy of decision-making structures (Kessler, 1999) means that overall goals (Cooper, 1989, VII A) have remained vague. They have not been progressively or precisely re-defined and the means (Cooper, VII B) to attain them are decided in an ad hoc way. There is therefore no established process for assessing the effect (Cooper, VIII) of the policies and, as the various reports show, impressionistic conclusions abound. External cultural diplomacy is now a huge organic growth, virtually beyond government control (Table 7.1).

Nevertheless, where goals are precisely defined, as with the enlarge-ment of the European Union, considerable and measurable successes are achieved. An outstanding recent instance of this is the adoption at UNESCO on 20 October 2005 of the Convention on the Promotion and Diversity of Cultural Expression. The OIF had begun action in this area in 2000, and following discussions with other language groups – Arabic, Portuguese, Spanish – and the Francophonia Summit in Cotonou in 2001, the UNESCO Declaration on Cultural Diversity had been adopted unani-mously the same year. There followed a prolonged period of intensive lobbying and negotiation by France (and other countries) as it became clear that the USA would strongly oppose the Convention. Only four nations did not support the Convention, resulting in a resounding victory for the French and fury in the USA which responded with threats of retali-atory financial sanctions against UNESCO. The outcomes of the 2005 decision will show whether it was a victory in principle only. Economic realities may yet limit its effectiveness, but it could be the beginning of an important new phase of cultural and linguistic diversity.

This chapter has given an overview of the impressively extensive and convoluted network of official action to defend French in the 21st century. It paints a picture of multi-faceted policies both inside and outside France within which activities related to the language itself constitute a small and diminishing part of an increasingly ambitious and diversified political programme. Within these policies, the language functions as a powerful symbol rather than as a means of communication or a linguistic artefact. The chapter also shows the way government language and cultural policies can be implemented through an ancient, venerable and venerated institu-tion such as the *Académie*, or can infiltrate the *Alliances*, whose founders showed such amazing foresight in setting up its once proud independent structures.

The work done by the MAE, and by the two 20th century government agencies, the DGLFLF and the OIF, in the short time since their creation, has increasingly reflected changing political policies and priorities and constant adaptation to environmental pressures from changing European and world situations. Government policies are based on uncertain processes. The problems they address are vaguely formulated and their goals are nebulous and imprecise. Implementation is progressively more difficult to manage and results, in most cases, are impossible to assess. Against this bleak picture, can be set successes in those situations where a well-defined planning process has been followed.

Chapter 4 looks at other aspects of language in the political landscape, first from an historical perspective and then from the point of view of some of the groups involved in language defence who seek in various ways to increase their political influence on the formation of official language policies.

Chapter 4

Language and Politics – Inseparable Partners

Rois, Révolution, Républiques

The first three chapters of this book have commented on the political implications of language policies and agencies in France. This chapter considers three of the areas where politics and language, these two important and interdependent forces in French life, interact. Historical decisions and policies on language have had far-reaching political consequences. Repercussions from those decisions are still being felt today. But the relationship between language and politics, always close no matter what type of government is ruling France, has changed in the 20th and 21st centuries. Language activists are now able to exert influence on government policy in areas outside language, particularly in relation to European affairs.

This section is not a history of the interaction between national politics and language, but gives snapshots of three different historical periods when the relationship between the two was crucial: (1) Kings and language: the 16th century and 17th centuries – from François Ier and his famous *Ordonnance* to Louis XIII, Richelieu and the *Académie française*; (2) Revolution and language: the 18th century – Revolution, the Convention and the official language; (3) Republic, empire and *la Francophonie*: the foreign and colonial policy of France, taking French to the wider world. The second and third sections of this chapter take the story up to the present time, with an analysis of the areas where the reaction between politics and language is most likely to erupt in France today. The second section considers (1) the rise of the political language movements in Alsace, Brittany, Corsica, Occitania and Savoy; and (2) the example of Alsace – the activities of the separatist parties in Alsace. The third section looks at the political implications of some of the Internet organisations defending French.

(1) Kings and language: Chapter 1 started with François Ier and the 1539 *Ordonnance de Villers-Cotterêts*. There is general agreement that cultural

diplomacy involving language is a long-established tradition in France (for example, Kessler, 1999: 369; Ostler, 2005: 403). Long before the *Ordonnance* there had been a European tradition of language serving political ends and indeed rulers have probably always used language as one of the ways of subjugating conquered peoples (for example Cerquiglini, 2000:113). Henriette Walter (1994: 286–289) is convinced that government intervention in language policy in what is now France goes back at least to Charlemagne. What she calls the 'relatinisation' of French took place at the end of the 8th century when Charlemagne, whose native language was Germanic but who had set himself to correct and 'purify' Latin throughout his empire, brought an English monk, Alcuin, to teach a purer form of Latin in France.

This was the Carolingian renaissance and it had a profound effect on the French language. For Walter 'this seizure of the language by government forces was just the first of a series of interventions which would continue to the present day'[57] (Walter, 1994: 287–289). The implication that the effect of these interventions has not always been beneficial is clear: 'Thus the State has constantly brought its weight to bear on the evolution of the French language since the late Middle Ages'[58] (Walter, 1994: 289).

Judge (1993: 9) points out that the decision by François Ier to insist on French in legal texts was a logical outcome of moves begun long before, and that Charles VIII had already in 1490 introduced language legislation. Rather than nobly defending the native language, François Ier was therefore simply following earlier developments when he decided, for essentially political reasons, to insist that all legal documents were henceforth to be written in French. (This at least is the interpretation of most commentators, but in the best French tradition, there are conflicting interpretations of the text.) Ostensibly the king was simply making sure that there were no misunderstandings and ensuring that all citizens were equal before the law: '*Afin qu'il n'y ait cause de douter sur l'intelligence desdits arrêts*' (so that there may be no cause to doubt the meaning of such documents) (web site, University of Pennsylvania). This is a seductive argument and, for differing political reasons, it has appealed to successive regimes – the *Convention* in 1793, the *Académie française* and the *Délégation à la langue française et aux langues de France* today.

By insisting on what he called the *langage maternel français*, the king was in fact excluding the vast majority of his subjects, who could neither read nor write. French was certainly not their native tongue, and thus they were to be prevented from understanding the processes and decisions of the law. By choosing to legislate pragmatically for the dominance of the language of a chosen, mediating few who were already in positions of power, he ensured that they and their language retained a superior status.

Judge (1993: 10) quotes a contemporary source approving of the king's decision: 'it was appropriate that the most important men should have in language, as they do in status, some pre-eminence over their inferiors'.[59] This is a difficult political problem and not as simple as Barère (p. 85) claimed. Perhaps one should not criticise too sharply the king who was open-minded enough to found in 1530 what would become the *Collège de France* because he disapproved of the stuffy conservatism of the Sorbonne. There was no move under François Ier to prevent the use of the other languages of France in domains other than the law and under his rule these languages continued to flourish.

The superior status accorded to those who spoke, and more importantly read and wrote, the *langue d'oïl* intensified what was at this time a potential political divide between speakers of the official language and those who spoke the *langue d'oc*. As the second section of this chapter shows, this divide developed in succeeding years and continues even today to mark linguistic and political patterns in France. The power–language axis, which was greatly strengthened by François Ier is evident in the subsequent development of French. The influence of Malherbe as an arbiter of the *langage maternel français* (Chapter 1, p. 3) was also considerably enhanced by the political power he held due to his position at court (Cerquiglini, 2000: 121). In the *salons*, other members of the court and their wives gathered with the literary figures of the age and linguistic and political alliances were formed. Richelieu, in the service of his king, Louis XIII, took advantage of these in establishing the *Académie*, consecrating simultaneously the supremacy of the language and the political power of the court.

Commentators (for example, Chaurand, 1999: 232) are clear that there was a strong political motive in the creation, or at least the royal recognition of the *Académie*. Walter (1988: 108) refers to the language at this time as '*un instrument de la centralisation politique*' (a means of centralising political power) and '*une affaire d'État*' (a concern of the state). Using language as a political tool to establish increasing power in the hands of Louis XIII and the court, as under François Ier, resulted in the continuing exclusion of many other groups from power and positions of influence. This divisive potential was reinforced by the emerging insistence by grammarians such as Vaugelas on the essential distinction between *le bon usage* (good usage) and all other ways of using the language – a distinction at least as much social and political as linguistic. Language thus became in 16th and 17th century France a way of protecting the status quo and of creating an excluded majority. The exclusion enshrined by state language policy from François Ier to Richelieu has not been forgotten by present-day language agitators.

(2) Revolution and language: By the 18th century, the political standing of France in the wider world was mirrored by the respect and admiration accorded to its language, not only in intellectual circles but also in its establishment as the prevailing diplomatic language, shown by its use for the 1714 Treaty of Rastadt. It was on to a political stage in Europe where the supremacy of French was unquestioned that the Revolution burst in 1789. By the time of the Convention in 1793 it was clear that the political face of France and indeed of the world had changed and the revolutionary government was faced with a stupefying problem of communication. If the Revolution was to be more than a passing phase in a country where the vast majority of the population had continued to speak regional languages and dialects, all citizens would now have to understand at least some of the intricate political and social arguments for which so many people had suffered and died. For the population, now released from the bondage of the *ancien régime*, language would be the key to *Liberté, Égalité, Fraternité*.

This role for the national language was foreshadowed by Talleyrand in his 1791 plea for a school in every commune in order to 'put an end to this strange inequality: the language of the Constitution and the laws will be taught there [in the schools] to everyone; and this mass of corrupted dialects, the last vestige of the feudal system, will be forced to disappear'[60] (Walter, 1988: 116). No sooner had the king been killed on 21 January 1793 than Carnot reported to the Convention on 29 January that better communications were the key to overcoming the 'indifference to the general affairs of the nation' (Kohn, 1967: 88) and that a single official language was the way to achieve this end. Rather than combatting indifference, most of those who wrote and spoke about language at this time mention two political ideals: *Égalité*, the equality of all citizens of the new Republic and the all-important concept of the single, indivisible Republic (*la République une et indivisible*). Connecting democracy, freedom and the republic, Bertrand Barère had argued in the Convention:

> The monarchy had reasons for appearing like the Tower of Babel; . . .
> Where the people are free, the language should be one and the same
> for all.[61] (web site, *Université Laval*, Revolution)

A little later, the Abbé Grégoire stated that: '*L'unité de la République commande l'unité des idiomes*' (The unity of the Republic requires unity of language).

These ideas are still important in France and are used routinely by those who, for example, oppose minority languages or the new European Constitution. Chapter 6 of this book returns to the questions of freedom and equality and the problems they continue to pose in reconciling main-tenance of the one official language with the protection of the linguistic heritage and the defence of pluri-lingualism in Europe. The state-backed establishment of French as the only official language was at the expense of linguistic diversity and richness, the very policies the French government now feels itself obliged to defend so vigorously in the European Union and elsewhere.

By the following year Barère (Chapter 1, p. 7), for the *Comité du salut publique* (Committee of Public Safety), submitted to the Convention his report: *Sur les idiomes étrangers et l'enseignement de la langue française* (On Foreign Tongues and the Teaching of the French Language) (Full text at web site, *ABC de la langue française*, <u>Barère</u>). In one of the most dramatically political statements about language ever made in France he proclaimed: 'Federalism and superstition speak low Breton, emigration and hatred of the Republic speak German; the counter-revolution speaks Italian and fanaticism speaks Basque. Let us break these causes of damage and error.'[62] Teachers of French were to be sent immediately to the benighted areas where these seditious and debased forms of speech were in use (web site, *Linternaute*). Barère's report is notable not only for its explicit linking of language and politics, but also because it marks the beginning of the attack on regional languages and dialects that was to be pursued with such determination throughout the 19th century. The results of this policy are discussed in the section starting on p. 87.

Just a few months later, in June 1794, there was a second influential survey and report on language and language policy from the Abbé Grégoire (Chapter 1, p. 8; text of the report at web site, *L'ABC de la langue française* <u>Grégoire</u>). The *Rapport sur la nécessité et les moyens d'anéantir les patois et d'universaliser l'usage de la langue française* (Report on the Necessity and the Methods of Annihilating the Patois and Universalising the Use of the French Language) reinforces the policy of imposing the use of French at the expense of what is now known as the linguistic heritage (*le patrimoine linguistique*) of France. A particularly interesting aspect of the responses received by the Abbé Grégoire is that some of his respondents in the provinces insist on the absolute necessity of eradicating the local forms of speech (Walter, 1988: 115).

Rather than being an unwelcome policy imposed from above, the insistence on French as the ubiquitous and only official language clearly found considerable support at least from those who were asked to reply to the Abbé's questions. The fact that these reports on the linguistic situation were carried out in the revolutionary era shows the strength of the new concern for *Égalité*, the equality of all citizens, and the subsequent trans-lation into linguistic policy of this ideal is perhaps not surprising. A side effect of this exclusive concentration on French was the introduction of attitudes of moral superiority towards other languages spoken in France, attitudes sanctioned by the subsequent actions of the revolutionaries and persisting to the present day.

Yet another problem with present-day resonances emerges from reading the report of the Abbé Grégoire: he was apparently convinced that the political state of the world made it impossible, as was desirable, for everyone to speak one language. No other country had yet managed, even within its own boundaries, to 'render the language of one great nation uniform' (Kohn, 1967: 92). This was an enterprise worthy of the French who, after their dramatic *Révolution*, were now the most politically advanced nation in the world. In post-revolutionary France, imposing a single official language was just one aspect of centralising all branches of social organisation. The Abbé's extravagant, if seductive, 'esperantist' argument, insisting on the political advantages of everyone speaking the same language, is close to revolutionary ideas. Applied to the 'imposition' of the English language by the American 'empire' in the 21st century, it is also an idea that arouses derision and opposition in France. Chapter 6 looks again at this apparent contradiction and at other paradoxes.

As a result of the Abbé Grégoire's report, the short-lived decree of 2 *Thermidor* (20 July 1794) passed draconian legislation excluding any language other than French from official documentation. A later decree, on 17 November 1794, insisted that all teaching throughout the Republic must henceforth be in French. This was when the intimate political connection, still visible today, between education and the official language was consecrated. Although it was not until the third Republic (1880–1914) that the Ferry reforms (Chapter 1, p. 10) made it possible to have a French-speaking teacher in every school (Citron, 1991: 271), the aim of using the language to centralise and control education, and thus access to the public service and most positions of power, was widely accepted.

(3) Republic, empire and *la Francophonie*: The increasing centralisation of education, the spread of free state schools later in the century (Citron, 1991: 273), wars, conscription, the growing road and communications network (Caput, 1975: 51) and a centralised civil service meant, inevitably, that French was more widely used as the 19th century progressed. A national identity was constructed around the idea of shared values and a shared language (Citron, 1991: 273). Other political decisions at this time, related to France's foreign and colonial policy, also had an impact on the promotion of the national language. From the time of the voyages of Cabot (1497) and Cartier (1534), and particularly after the foundation of Quebec by Champlain in 1608, the use of French had begun to spread throughout the world. Although it is not possible to cover adequately the

French language outside Europe, specifically the situation in Quebec, the extension of empire must be mentioned briefly. It brings into sharp focus the impact of politics on present-day language policy. French colonial policy strongly influenced the development of _La Francophonie_ (Chapter 3, pp. 67–74) and created the intertwining of linguistic and political threads that today characterise this grouping of francophone states.

The history of the French colonies gives an idea of the areas of the world where the French language spread and of the long history of Franco-British confrontation marking the colonial period (Citron, 1991: 267–268; Wardhaugh, 1987: 143–145). The first French colonial empire began in the 17th century with the foundation of a colony in what would become Canada in 1605. France laid claim to large areas of North America and extended its empire to various islands, including Haiti. The French also established trading posts in Africa and in India and in the 18th century founded island colonies in the Indian Ocean.

Subsequent conflict with the British lead to the loss of much of the French land in North America and of some of their possessions in the West Indies but a French flavour frequently persists in these former possessions. A second colonial empire was started in the 19th century with the French taking territory in North Africa and Indochina. French territories were also extended in northern, western and central Africa and in the 20th century, between the World Wars, France gained mandates over what are now Syria and Lebanon. The French language was taken to all of these areas and the list of member countries of _La Francophonie_ shows traces of French colonial policy and the influence of the language.

Chapter 1 (p. 15) showed that there was considerable resistance by successive French presidents to the suggestion in the early 1960s by the heads of some former colonies that what is now called a 'geo-political grouping based on their shared language' could be to the advantage both of the former colonies and of France itself. The motivation for what has become _la Francophonie_ came essentially from the newly independent African countries and they have continued to have a determining role in the francophone movement. The reticence of French presidents is widely attributed to their unwillingness to be seen to be playing neo-colonial politics and many felt that they were showing undue sensitivity when enthusiasm for the new group of nations would have demonstrated confidence in the governments of the former colonies.

Once President Mitterrand had grasped the nettle, France espoused the cause of _la Francophonie_ and another mammoth political organisation based on language was created. Although the propagation of French is a very minor part of the work of the OIF (Chapter 3, p. 71), the political ramifications of its language-related activities are extremely extensive. In the years since the first summit in Paris in 1986 the tentacles of the OIF have spread far and, some would argue, too wide. This is reflected in the questions asked in the press at the time of the tenth francophone summit in Ouagadougou in November 2004: for example the dossier in *L'Express* (2004b) and the article by an African journalist (*Nouvelle-Expression*, Cameroun, 30.11.2004) asking wryly *Dis, Papa, c'est quoi la francophonie ?* (Daddy, what's francophonia?) (web site, *L'ABC de la langue française, Aigreurs francophoniques* (Francophone bitterness)).

Apart from confusion both in France and in other countries about what the francophone movement actually is, this aspect of the language-related policy of the French government is now under attack from two directions: predictably, some citizens of the former colonies point to the use by France of the international organisation as a neo-colonial agency, dedicated to destroying traditional languages and using the language of the colonial usurper to strengthen French control over lucrative commercial deals. This is the view of some disaffected and disappointed African writers, for example of Petnkeu Nzepa (2003) and others writing in *Présence francophone*.

On the Internet the writing is even more critical with the creation of sites such as *Survie* and *Stop-françafrique* using a highly imaginative vocabulary to accuse France of systematically pillaging the African nations and shamelessly manipulating political regimes for commercial advantage. In the run up to the tenth francophone summit in Ouagadougou in November 2004, for example, *Survie France* declared on its web site:

> Since the sixties France has knowingly chosen to use its linguistic influence as a means of domination which allows it to maintain its economic and political influence.[63]

On the other hand, supporters of *la Francophonie* inside France, seeing the enticing possibility of a powerful geo-political group to rival the British Commonwealth and, more importantly, the large and influential informal group of countries under the sway of the United States, are also bitterly critical of the way France's francophone policy has developed. Chief among the critics are the private and semi-private organisations for the defence of French, for example Vinatier and Xvolt (2002a and b) and Arnaud and his fellow authors Guillou and Salon (2002). There are several causes for their attacks. The recent decision to reorganise the funding for the OIF and the DGLFLF is seen by these observers as a deliberate intention to lessen the involvement of France in *la Francophonie* and thus to limit severely the power of the movement to be a credible counterpoise to the Anglo-Saxon hegemony they so distrust. Another cause for disquiet is the way membership of *la Francophonie* has been extended (Chapter 3, p. 73).

There are two worries about this: first, countries where French is an official or important language, including some of the former colonies, do not always meet the political criteria for admission. Many people in France are embarrassed by the inclusion of these countries in *la Francophonie* and feel that in the eyes of the world the whole organisation has lost credibility. In addition, a number of countries where French is scarcely spoken have been admitted for openly political and commercial reasons rather than because of a shared ideology. This too discredits the movement and, they feel, greatly weakens attempts to defend the language. Again, many of the members of the francophone group feel very strongly that France has not, as the British have done, set up arrangements for preferential status for citizens of the francophone countries, particularly as far as immigration and working and educational visas are concerned. African graduates are turning towards America and this is a bitter pill for France to swallow: '*Découragés par les règles d'immigration, 80% de nos diplômés [des pays franco-phones d'Afrique] se tournent vers l'Amérique*' (Discouraged by the rules for immigration, 80% of our [of the African francophone countries] graduates are looking towards America) (*L'Express*, 2004b: 20).

French governments are clearly never going to please all those who feel they have a stake in *la Francophonie*. At best they can only juggle with the opposing interests of the conflicting groups and this in itself must weaken the very organisation which for many people held out the best hope of creating in the modern world a universally accepted role for the French language. The next section considers another way that political decisions, taken for what no doubt seemed the best of motives, have disappointed those who placed such high hopes on the values France has traditionally stood for: the separatists who now seek their *Liberté, Égalité* and *Fraternité* outside the *patrie*, the mother country.

Dependence or Independence? The Separatist Parties

The next two sections of this chapter give an overview of the situation of separatist parties in France founded on language claims: first a brief history of the rise of some of these movements and second – just one of many possible examples – the situation in Alsace.

The rise of the political language movements: Following the political decision by the *Convention* to try to impose a single official language, the regional languages of France were subjected to persistent and deter-mined attacks by the state (Chapter 2, p. 30). The severity of these attacks reflects the strength of feeling in the revolutionary and post-revolutionary periods, the absolute conviction that the unity of the Republic was essential and that a single language was both a proof of that unity and a vital means of achieving it. The offensive against regional languages doubly excluded speakers of other languages since it became necessary for all citizens, if they wished to prosper in the new political climate, not only to speak French, but to read and write it well. The linguist Brigitte Schlieben-Lange (2000), writing in 2000, gives a penetrating analysis of some of the outcomes of the language policy of the Revolution:

> The legacy of revolutionary linguistic thought is double. On the one hand it imposed the identification of political unity and linguistic unity, an identification which no language policy has been able to avoid up until the present day. On the other hand, it created the model of a well made language, built on the principles of analogy [and] which would replace the whimsical historic languages by eradicating all the seeds of possible diversification.[64] (Quoted in notes from the web site, University of Toronto, Schlieben-Lange)

The aim of instituting a single language was not easily achieved. The Abbé Grégoire had shown how widespread the ignorance of the national language was and therefore conversely how entrenched were the traditional languages. Early in the 19th century the lengthy, but ultimately unfinished, linguistic survey carried out by Coquebert de Montbret and his son (web site, *L'ABC de la langue française*, Montbret) revealed that the languages spoken along the borders of France (German, Italian and Flemish) and the regional languages in Brittany and the French Basque Country were still very much in use, although the numbers of speakers of these languages were declining. The decline of the regional languages was a source of satisfaction in some quarters and, even among those for whom it was a cause for regret, the ultimate triumph of French and the disappearance of other languages was considered inevitable.

As the 19th century progressed there was an increasing desire to document and defend the regional languages, not only on their linguistic merits but because it was becoming clear that much more than language was being destroyed. Thus in parallel with the numerous grammars and dictionaries of the French language now appearing, publishers were producing books on the patois (Chapter 2, p. 30). The titles of the books on regional languages published during the 19th and 20th centuries (for example, web site, *L'ABC de la langue française*, Publications) are very revealing. They are evidence of a strong desire to defend the linguistic heritage but they also show a concern for 'purity', and with it a demand that the French language be delivered from interference from these linguistically inferior forms. This highly judgemental attitude is a legacy from the revolutionary period. It is apparent in the recurrence in the titles of these books of derogatory terms referring to the patois as, for example, *expressions impropres* (unsuitable expressions), *les patois ou idiomes vulgaires* (dialects or vulgar speech forms), *expressions vicieuses* (perverted expressions), *fautes (de langage)* (errors in language), *langage vicieux* (depraved language), *provençalismes corrigés* (Provençal speech forms corrected) (my underlining).

Books with titles such as these nurtured the resentment fostered by official government attitudes and ultimately created a breeding ground for increasingly determined regional activities dedicated to preserving local languages. It was a small step from here to the explicitly political and increasingly strident and violent regional separatist movements that characterised the end of the 20th century.

Chapter 5 shows that the tendency in the 20th and 21st centuries for language activists to be increasingly involved in overtly political action is not confined to France, but is evident to varying degrees throughout Europe. Each country's unique historical, political and social background has produced a characteristic pattern of action. Whereas in Germany, Italy and Spain the repression of regional and minority languages is associated with relatively short-lived fascist regimes, in France this repression has been enshrined in government policy since the Revolution. Although there appears to have been a fairly broad consensus among people in positions of power that the regional languages must be destroyed if the goals and ideals of the Revolution were to be achieved, at the grass-roots there was resistance and resentment of the government's insensitive policy. Some linguists interested in the history of language and in the new field of dialectology attempted to document the 'disappearing' patois and others tried to help the process by writing books about how to remove all traces of non-standard speech.

There were other publications and associations (especially after the eventual appearance in 1831 of Montbret's book on *les langues, dialectes et patois*) devoted to the preservation of the traditional speech forms. These increasingly reflected a positive attitude to non-official languages and linguistic diversity. By 1852 the ground-breaking association *Félibrige* had been founded in Provence by the poet Mistral and some of his literary friends. Its object was *la promotion de la culture méditéranéenne* (the promotion of Mediterranean culture), especially language. There were disagreements about language even within the *Félibrige* but it is important as one of the first and most influential of the organisations defending regional languages and cultures. The *langue d'oc*, Basque, Provençal, Corsican and other languages all had their defensive groups and these became increasingly politicised as the overwhelming difficulty of fighting against centralised government language policy became ever clearer.

On the government side, anxiety about the success of the single language policy was reflected in the Duruy Report in 1863–1864 which showed that many children were still speaking the traditional languages. As repression increased, societies for the protection of the various regional languages, usually with regular publications and meetings, were created. It was groups such as these that gradually moved from mutual support to political action. As the 19th and 20th centuries advanced, the battle for the preservation of these languages was gradually extended in scope to include a struggle against the highly centralised education system and numerous attempts were made to have regional languages included in school curricula. The history of the legal status of the various languages of France, particularly in the 20th century, provides clear evidence of this (Chapter 2, pp. 24–29).

With this background it is perhaps unsurprising that a tradition has grown up in France of politicised language movements, rebelling in ever more violent ways against the power of Paris. The espousal, particularly after 1945, of separatist agendas by a number of them has to some extent been encouraged by subsequent developments in the European Union, and they have sought allies not only inside but also outside national boundaries. By their nature small movements such as these are frequently fragmented, ephemeral and difficult to track down. The various lists on the Internet of separatist parties in Europe give some indication of the extent of language-based separatist political activity. These lists are usually on the sites of European groups or 'parties', alliances of smaller affiliated parties, all hoping to increase their power to influence government policy by belonging to a bigger group. In such lists the number of language-based parties given for France is consistently higher than for any other country in the Union.

In France itself the site of *Alsace d'abord* lists 34 official political parties in France; 15 or 16 of them have language-based and/or separatist agendas, and it is reasonable to assume that there is also an extensive unofficial fringe. The site of the Democratic Party of the People of Europe – Free European Alliance (*Parti démocratique des Peuples d'Europe – Alliance libre européenne* (PDPE–ALE) for example lists the names of its adherents as the *Ligue savoisienne*, the *Mouvement Région Savoie*, the *Parti Occitan, Unitat Catalana*, the *Union du Peuple Alsacien* and the *Unione di u Populo Corsu/ Scelta Nova*. Each of these parties is based, with greater or less seriousness, on the need to defend a regional language.

The names of the parties in other lists show several dedicated to each of the regional languages but the same party name rarely occurs twice. This is telling evidence of the fragmented and shifting nature (and perhaps the financial insecurity) of this part of the political landscape and of the difficulty faced by separatist groups in gaining access to real political influence and power. For Alsace for example there are, in addition to the *Union du Peuple Alsacien* on the PDPE–ALE site, *Alsace d'abord, Le Front National de Libération d'Alsace FLNA* and the *Mouvement Régionaliste Alsacien*. Brittany has produced, as well as the *Union Démocratique Bretonne*, the *Droite Nationaliste Bretonne ADSAV*, the *Mouvement Régionaliste de Bretagne*, the *Parti Breton* and the *Parti pour l'Organisation d'une Bretagne Libre* (web sites, *Alsace d'abord; Organisation pour les Minorités Européennes*) and there are several more given by *An Arvorig* (see web site).

All that can safely be said is that these appear to be the current names of some of the parties apparently in existence at the time of writing this chapter (April 2006). The situation can change very rapidly. Web sites come and go. In typically French fashion, parties split, disappear, change names, frequently choosing convoluted and cumbersome titles, clearly the result of group decisions. These are very difficult to include in zippy and memorable publicity materials. All of these features militate against the effectiveness of these groups that have chosen political action as the best means of defending their precious regional languages. In an attempt to give an idea of the political ramifications of action in favour of regional languages in France, this section concludes with an overview of two of the most accessible, moderate and apparently reliable web sites dedicated to the defence of the regional language in Alsace. It is perhaps invidious to select so small a sample, but similar conclusions could probably be drawn from an analysis of almost any of the other regional language separatist associations and parties.

The example of Alsace: Alsace, the political football of Western Europe in the last 150 years, has its own very individual language history. Nevertheless political events there could be said to mirror, certainly in a more acute form, those in other French provinces where battle is joined between the official and the regional language. In the attempt to understand the situation in Alsace, this section looks first at the site of *Verdammi*, not a political party but an activist group whose site gives an idea of the very involved situation in this frequently disputed part of France. Finally this section turns briefly to *Alsace d'abord*, one of the separatist political parties.

Verdammi points out that the political situation of language in Alsace after the Revolution was made more complicated by the fact that the Alsatian dialect was closely related to German, the language of the enemy in the wars at the end of the 19th century. There were therefore concerted efforts to impose French in the province. These were particularly successful in the towns and with the upper bourgeoisie so that, by 1871 when Alsace became German, French was embedded in the cultural heritage, and the linguistic tug-of-war between the two sides of the Alsatian heritage was echoed in social and political differences between town and country, rich and poor. After the First World War Alsace was returned to France and opposition to the draconian and insensitive French language policies of the new administration eventually gave birth in 1924 to the first of the Alsatian movements for autonomy. The policy of Germanisation, imposed during the Second World War when Alsace again became German, was similar to Nazi language policies in Germany (Chapter 5, pp. 112–118) and succeeded where the French government's policies had failed in turning many Alsatians against Germany and its language.

After the war, the return to France, the re-imposition of French and the accompanying measures against the dialect were therefore accepted without massive protests and it was not until 1968 and the *événements* that rocked the French government at that time that simmering resentment finally resulted in the creation of protest movements aimed at saving the Alsatian dialect. The action was confined largely to demands for the teaching of the dialect and of German in the schools and by 1972 there had been some success (legal measures to permit changes in the education system, see chapter 2, p. 31). The real politicisation of the language issue came in the 1980s as even the main political parties in France realised that there was a need to consider the possibility of lessening the tightly centralised control characteristic of French governments since the Revolution.

As the *Verdammi* web site puts it *'Le vent a tourné'* (The [political] wind changed) and finally many Alsatians realised that their dialect, and with it their cultural and historical heritage, was threatened. As the statistics pointed to ever decreasing numbers of young people speaking the dialect, it seemed possible that political action might be able to achieve what hand-wringing had not. It was at this same time that speakers of regional and minority languages in other European countries came to similar conclusions (Chapter 2, p. 30) leading eventually to the opening for signature of the European Charter on Regional and Minority Languages in November 1992. In the years that followed, before France finally signed in 1999, the minority language movements, realising the potential of the Charter, became very active. This spurt of activity provoked concern and counteraction from those who were convinced that the unity of the Republic was in danger.

Meanwhile, as defensive associations and language-based parties, filled with new hope, stepped up their interventions, the Alsatian dialect continued to decline. The INED reports (Héran 2003; Héran *et al.*, 2002; see also Chapter 2, p. 33) confirm the views of many commentators, including *Verdammi*, that in the period from 1962 all the regional languages have been in a decline that many do not hesitate to call terminal. While the situation for Alsatian may be less dire than for some of the other languages, it is nevertheless desperate. In Alsace, with its double French and German heritage, the disappearance of the dialect seems to herald not only the loss of a distinctive language and culture, but also *'le basculement définitif et exclusif . . . dans la sphère culturelle française'* (overbalancing definitively and exclusively into the French cultural sphere) (web site, *Verdammmi*). This immediately puts the emphasis on the political rather than the purely linguistic elements of the situation. As the regional languages weaken throughout Europe and the likelihood of saving them diminishes, there is an almost parallel increase in political activity, often of an unreasoning and extreme kind. *Alsace d'abord* constitutes one example of a language-based political party.

The title *Alsace d'abord* (Alsace first) announces what its political objectives are and where its loyalties lie. Its web site proclaims that it is *'le mouvement politique qui rassemble les forces régionalistes européennes et identitaires de la région Alsace'* (the political movement which gathers the forces for European regions and identities of the Alsace region). The words *politique*, *régionalistes* (*région*), *européennes*, *identitaires* all convey a sub-text and this, for many defenders of the national language, is insidious in its implications, proclaiming support for a Europe of the regions and so threatening the unity of the Republic. The symbolic poster of *Alsace d'abord* shows an Alsatian girl in traditional regional costume, gagged – and so prevented from speaking – with the slogan *'Rendons la parole à l'Alsace'* (Give Alsace back the power of speech).

Language is not the predominant preoccupation of the organisation. The 'hot topics' (*dossiers chauds*) on the web site give a quick picture of its aims and guiding principles: Yes to Europe, No to Turkey, the Alsatian economy, the TGVs (*trains grande vitesse*), Decentralisation, Immigration, Bilingualism. The story this tells of strong political support for Europe but total opposition to the entry of Turkey to the Union reflects the sometimes conflicting political positions many of the essentially right-wing separatist parties find themselves in: they supported the European Constitution because of its respect for regional languages and cultures but, in line with the *Front National* and other extreme parties, they are opposed to the entry of Turkey on the grounds that it is not 'European' and will be an Islamic 'Trojan Horse' in the European Union.

Alsace d'abord states that it welcomes Alsatians whether born in Alsace or newly arrived (but there are conditions as later sections make clear). It proclaims its attachment to the three identities of the region: first Alsatian, second French and third European. It supports a 'double culture', French and Germanic, and remains faithful to its history, its Greco-Latin and Judeo-Christian heritage. Its apparent openness is mirrored neither in its opposition to Turkey nor in the stand it takes against non-European immigration in its Charter.

The Charter re-affirms that the identity of the region's inhabitants is limited to three strands. The first section *'Donnons sa vraie place à l'Alsace'* (Give Alsace her rightful place), addresses the balance of power between Europe, the French state and the region. It proclaims the need for the financing of a more independent and representative regional government. The second section deals with identity. This must not be weakened by greater recognition of Islam or by 'non-European' immigration. Turkey must not be admitted to the European Union. There must be regional control of education which should be bi-lingual from the nursery school onwards. The third and final section confronts economic, social and environmental problems and law and order. Here there are repeated references to the failure of 'Paris' to understand and appreciate local realities in the areas of law, employment and agriculture.

The picture emerging here is of a political organisation seeking to attract support by espousing popular concerns and exploiting xenophobic tendencies. In spite of the message of its poster, language is not the major concern for *Alsace d'abord*. There is no mention on the web site of other languages spoken in the region or of support for a wider multi-lingual or pluri-lingual policy. Its language policy is restricted to bi-lingualism. Even then, the call for a bi-lingual education policy is the final sentence in the last section of the Charter – on identity. *Alsace d'abord*'s inclusiveness is strictly limited to the three strands of its proclaimed Alsatian identity: Alsace, France, Europe. Its separatist aims are also limited: greater decentralisation and devolution of specific powers to the region. It is therefore far more modest in its political ambitions than some of the other separatist parties, but its political and linguistic exclusiveness is extreme.

While it claims rights for Alsatian, the main regional language, and for the other regional languages in Europe, it completely ignores the language rights of other groups in the Alsace region. In this it is similar to the more recently formed (1994) *Office pour la langue et la culture d'Alsace* (Office for the Language and Culture of Alsace: see web site). The policy of *Alsace d'abord* therefore echoes the official national language policy which works for multi-lingualism and multi-culturalism outside France, but has so far failed to give recognition to the many minority languages within its borders by ratifying the European Charter on Regional and Minority Languages.

The sites linked with *Alsace d'abord* are an indication of the positions it has adopted and also of its unwillingness to exclude potential support for its political aims. Its list of 257 European political parties (15.03.2006) covers all political persuasions and is evidence of a broad European base. The *Alsace d'abord* site also gives links to various local and regional government sites in Alsace, perhaps in an effort to demonstrate its seriousness. The situation in Alsace is parallel to what is happening in the other regions of France where similar policies attract considerable support: the pursuit of separatist language- and culture-based policies sometimes meaning that moderate voters find themselves with unusual allies. For such voters presumably the compromise is acceptable if it holds out hope of ultimately achieving their aims.

The necessity for such uncomfortable compromises is nowhere more apparent than in the various private and semi-private language defence groups in France. The next section attempts, by following links from the web site of *Voxlatina*, to map the interlocking political relationships of the FFI (Chapter 2, p. 41) and the *Entente souverainiste*.

A Slippery Slope

As the defenders of French become increasingly convinced that French is threatened, the various private and semi-private defensive groups seek to improve their chances of success by forming alliances with other associations some of whose objects are similar. The associations in this section, (1) the FFI; and the (2) *Entente souverainiste*, have both been formed by amalgamating numbers of smaller groups to form a larger, but not necessarily stronger or more cohesive movement. Some of the alliances are shaky; virtually all of the member groups are small. The urgent need to find partners can sometimes ((3) below) lead to surprising collaborations.

(1) <u>The FFI</u>: The FFI, its founding group ALF and its web site *Voxlatina* were mentioned earlier, notably in the section on the Internet in Chapter 2. The aim of this section is to show how intricate and meandering are the connections between their defence of language and politics. To do this, it is useful to try to disentangle just one strand of the political alliances the FFI has formed in its commitment to the defence of French – its connection to the multi-faceted sovereignty movement in France. The role of *Voxlatina* has been crucial in establishing these alliances. Already at its creation it felt it was necessary to seek help outside the francophone world, particularly in the 'Latin' world, and it has continued to give some space on its pages to what it sees as its natural allies in what it is now politically correct to call the fight for linguistic diversity.

The Introduction mentioned that the FFI made deliberate use of initials intended to recall the legendary bravery of another FFI, the *Forces françaises de l'Intérieur*, in the defence and liberation of France in the Second World War. This new alliance of various defensive groups seeks to mobilise French-speakers worldwide in what it claims is a battle of similar importance for the future of the language and the nation. The history of its formation (web site, FFI, <u>History</u>) illustrates the search for support and the many meetings and discussions necessary for its creation. Its call for support when it was created on 3 July 2001 (web site, FFI, <u>Creation</u>) described the FFI as '*UN APPEL AUX PARTISANS FRANCOPHONES*' (A call to French-speaking partisans), a movement '*pour le redressement de la Francosphère*' (to put the Francosphere on its feet), language which, for the French, is immediately evocative of the fraught days of the 1940 defeat and the years of suffering that followed.

The intention of taking advantage of the emotional impact of the language and expressions used in the 1940s is quite explicit in the *APPEL*:

> . . . France is once again in danger . . .
> The time has come for a partisan uprising . . .
> Thus, the FFI will base itself on a New resistance, no longer only French, but of the whole of Francophonia. A resistance worthy of the great moments of the past, but embodying a vision for the future.[65]

The FFI, says the *APPEL*, will be 'open to alliances with all Mediterranean, Latin and other movements which, inspired by humanist principles, fight against the US hegemony and for a multipolar and multicultural world'. It will 'engage in frontal combat against the WASP empire and its vassals'. Starting with such aims and such language, it is perhaps unsurprising that the FFI's allies include some groups with extreme views having little or nothing to do with language. Many of these groups are, like the FFI, members of the *Entente souverainiste* (a right-wing sovereignty movement) founded just three months after the FFI in November 2001.

(2) The *Entente souverainiste*: The FFI launched the *Appel de Villers-Cotterêts* on 7 October 2001 (web site, FFI, <u>Villers-Cotterêts Appeal</u>), calling for a wide range of expressions of support for its actions in defence of French. When the *L'Entente souverainiste* was created, it appeared that it was a natural ally for the newly-formed FFI and it was given prominent billing on *Voxlatina*. Shortly afterwards, in April 2002, the *Entente souverainiste* launched its Charter (web site, *Voxlatina* <u>Entente souverainiste</u>). Declaring that: 'France is threatened with extinction and its voice in the world is being extinguished',[66] the *Entente* opened hostilities on a number of fronts of which the French language was certainly not the most important. The weakening of the language was seen as one of several factors in the destruction of national sovereignty, essentially by the United States:

> This collapse of national and popular sovereignty is part of the larger movement of globalisation, another name for Americanisation. The decline of French in the world in favour of English, the attacks on the

content of our language, the advance of cultural colonisation are the logical outcomes of this.[67]

The *Entente* – now renamed the *Alliance souverainiste* – describes itself as a collection or network of independent organisations and individuals over which it has no power. It aims to 'coordinate activities in favour of national independence and the sovereignty of France – one indivisible, inalienable, unable to be legally removed'. Its states that its sole aim is 'the defence and the reinforcement of the sovereignty of France'. It is organised into a National Sovereignty Council (whose name, it says, deliberately recalls the National Council of the Resistance). The Council is 'the political and strategic arm of the *Alliance*, leading the members and public opinion on matters of French sovereignty, the organisation of Europe and the right of peoples to govern themselves'. With this broad, even vague description of its purpose, the *Alliance* can expect to attract numerous groups who have generally similar platforms, but in the absence of detail there is scope for widely different ideologies and encouragement for various political oddities. The strongly nationalistic agenda of the *Entente* is a reminder of the similarities between the Jacobine and the sovereignty platforms (A. Judge, 2002: 55).

The formation of this umbrella group was far from simple: *entente* was difficult to achieve and internal disputes persisted. In November 2002 its founder was still talking about '*divisions endémiques*' (endemic divisions) which he cautiously described as '*délétères*' (disadvantageous) (web site, Polemia). In August 2003, a Gaullist member group worried about sovereignty was still clamouring for a *redressement de la France* and action in the *Assemblée nationale*. It issued a new appeal (web site, *Voxlatina*, *Appel au redressement*) ('the last before the ship-wreck') to all advocates of French sovereignty including the *Entente/Alliance pour la Souveraineté de la France*, setting out again the main points of its political agenda. Of the ten points listed, the defence of French (*La Francophonie, composante de la souveraineté* (Francophonia, an element of sovereignty)) does not appear until near the end, at number nine:

> 9) Saving the French language is another area, no less important, in which the challenge of independence is met. Actually, the language is not just a means of communication. It is a crucible in which, over the centuries, national unity has been forged, not only at the level of a cultural identity, but also on the political level.[68]

This is at best a muted appeal for what is seen as a symbolic and contributory rather than an essential factor in the struggle to retain or regain national sovereignty. Consciousness of the relatively low status given to language explains the inclusion of the following paragraph:

This element of our sovereignty and our identity [language] seems of no interest to many people because is it an established habit which it seems will never change. Nevertheless its importance should be emphasised in the face of the danger posed by the invasion of Anglo-American words, with the accompanying decline of our language at the international level. [These are] all results of the economic, even political domination achieved by the United States.[69]

The repeated references to the threats from American globalisation and from the English language reveal a deep-seated fear of otherness. This has not led the sovereigntists to adopt, as the government has done, more inclusive policies of linguistic and cultural diversity (Phillipson, 2003). Rather it has strengthened their narrow nationalist perspective and their determinedly exclusive stance.

These lengthy quotations from the sovereignty agenda show how easy it is, if one seeks strength through alliances, to be forced to accept a changed emphasis and to compromise on one's major concerns. Thus, as partners in the *Alliance pour la Souveraineté de la France*, the FFI and *Voxlatina* have found themselves obliged to play down the role of language and emphasise their anti-American sentiments.

(3) Allies of the sovereignty cause: The list from its web site of the movements forming the *Alliance* (web site, *Alliance pour Souveraineté de la France*, Movements) gives an idea of the groups, some of them distinctly on the fringe, with which the ALF, the FFI and *Voxlatina* now find themselves allied. These movements oppose the Amsterdam and Maastricht treaties and the Constitution but have other areas of activity which the *Alliance* does not necessarily endorse. Of the 25 members listed (see Table 4.1), none is principally a language defence group and the word language does not appear in any of the titles. Nor, by virtue of their overriding concern with sovereignty, are they associated with any of the separatist parties. One group is based in Franche-Comté and there is one in Corsica but the aims of this latter organisation are closer ties with the Republic. Not all of these parties have their own web sites, so it has not always been possible to access their manifestos or to obtain information about them. From the list a picture emerges of a strongly, even dangerously, right-wing tendency common to most of them.

The fact that many of these associations cannot be contacted on the Internet shows perhaps that they are very small. Nevertheless, the information available on the sites that do exist reveals a degree of consensus and shows an *Alliance* on the far right of the political spectrum. Each of the sites has its own further sets of links to groups seeming to become ever more extreme.

Table 4.1 Movements allied to the *Alliance souverainiste*

Party	Description
Action française (CRAF) http://www.actionfrancaise.net/	Royalist, sovereignty, nationalist
Association pour la Défense des droits de la Corse dans la République (ADCR)	Republican, nationalist
Catholiques pour les Libertés Économiques (CLE)	Christian, nationalist
Club des Jacobins 2000	N/A
Confédération Avenir-France-République (AFR)	N/A
Confédération des Écologistes Indépendants, Mouvement Souverainiste et Régionaliste (CEI-MSR)	Green, sovereignty, regionalist
Conférences Daniel Halévy	N/A
Debout la France	N/A
France Bonapartiste http://francebonapartiste.free.fr/	Bonapartist, democratic, sovereignty
Franche-Comté Renouveau	N/A
Hexagone	N/A
Identité France-Forez	N/A
Jeune France	Gaullist, republican, nationalist
La Voix des Français – Renaissance 95 http://www.vdfr95.com/index.htm	Anti-immigration, anti-Turkey, nationalist
Mouvement Démocrate Français	N/A
Mouvement des Chrétiens et des Indépendants	N/A
Mouvement Innovation Progrès Social Indépendance	N/A
Mouvement Retraité InterGénérations	N/A
Nouvelle Union Démocratique du Travail (Nouvelle UDT)	N/A
Prométhée	Gaullist, republican, nationalist
Rassemblement Gaulliste http://www.gaulliste.com/	Gaullist, sovereignty, republican, nationalist
Réflexion Citoyenne pour la France (RCPF)	N/A
Solidarité Française	N/A
SOS République http://notre.republique.free.fr/amissosrep.htm	N/A
Union pour une Politique Nouvelle	N/A

A closer look at the aims and ideologies of five of these groups (asterisked in Table 4.1) for which it is possible to obtain information on the Internet is revealing: (a) *Action française*; (b) *France bonapartiste*; (c) *La voix des Français*; (d) *Rassemblement gaulliste*; (e) *SOS République*.

(a) *Action française* is the 'leading defender of royalism in France'. Its fundamental principles are listed as:

- the restoration of the monarchy – unity, continuity, independence (of the influence of elections and public opinion), responsibility, legitimacy;
- the defence of the national interest – defence of the royalist heritage; limitation of the damaging effects of republicanism; internal and external defence of France and its territories; authority, freedom, representation of the 'real' country.

(b) *France bonapartiste* is founded on principles of democracy, citizenship, sovereignty, order and social progress. Rejecting the system of political parties, it is opposed to progressive loss of sovereignty through the European treaties and supports a Europe of nation states, not a federal Europe. It bases its action on Article 3 of the Declaration of the Rights of Man: 'The basis of all sovereignty resides essentially in the Nation. No body, no individual may exercise authority which does not explicitly come from it [the Nation].'

(c) *La Voix des Français – Renaissance 95* (founded in 1993) is also wary of political parties. It claims to be totally independent of them. It condemns the immigration policies of the last 25 years, finding them economically, socially and culturally damaging for France, for the countries of origin of the immigrants and for the immigrants themselves. Most immigrants are 'unassimilable' in France. The aims of *La Voix* are to study these problems, organise conferences, meetings and demonstrations, publish books and articles and give interviews. In this way they aim to defend the interests of the French community and bring together all those French people who wish to defend '*l'entité française*'.

(d) The *Rassemblement gaulliste* (founded in 1999) acts to promote:

- man in society; and
- the nation in the world.

The first involves promoting human dignity for both men and women, and the human mind and will. The second defines the nation as a community of men and women where reciprocal rights and duties must be respected. The community forms itself into a nation whose sovereignty is essential. Thus France must affirm its identity, its independence, its sovereignty and its willingness to defend itself. By so doing it will show the world how morality and solidarity should prevail among nations.

The *Rassemblement,* while not mentioning Charles de Gaulle or the French language in its aims, clearly feels it is continuing Gaullist principles and has strong, if somewhat vaguely expressed, views on sovereignty.

(e) The web site of *SOS République* (founded in 1999) states that it came into being to bring together sovereigntists and republicans on the left and associated with the *Rassemblement pour la République* party. It refuses to accept that the decline of France is inevitable and supports the nation in the struggles it is engaged in on economic, social, political, diplomatic and cultural fronts. It reaffirms the founding principles of the Republic so that France can emerge from its torpor and recover its power to shine in the world. 'Refusing to be duped by false republicans of the extreme left or the centre, it supports those movements, vital forces and men who are authentic sovereigntists [*sic*]' (web site, *SOS République*). Here there are equally strong views on sovereignty deriving from republican values and a rejection of some political parties.

These five movements associated with the *Alliance souverainiste* are clearly very different from one another: royalist, Bonapartist, anti-immigration, Gaullist, republican, they represent a sweep of French history and political affiliations and do not appear to be natural allies. Their support for 'French sovereignty' is unswerving, but their other motivations cover a broad spectrum. It is easy to understand that there were problems in creating the *Entente/Alliance* when such diverse organisations were involved. None of the five mentions language although there may be an underlying assumption that, in defending sovereignty, they are also defending the language as the outward manifestation of national unity. The picture emerging here is of an 'alliance' riven by internal dissension and unable to act as a strong lobby group. This is not an organisation that can be counted on to fight strongly for the language.

Beyond the groups actually in the *Alliance,* the web site also gives a longer list. This includes the 25 members listed in Table 4.1 and other movements with a less formal attachment to the main organisation. These are described as *Les Mouvements Souverainistes* and there are 46 of them. There are two language defence associations included: the *Association Francophone Avenir* (AFRAV) and ALF – a return to the start of our political peregrination. In this second list some of the tendencies in Table 4.1 become even clearer, particularly the strongly republican and potentially xenophobic views, the opposition to immigration, to Brussels and to federalism (the *Cercle Anti-Maastricht* for example). *Europe des Nations,* a group of Euro-MPs opposed to a federal Europe, is also included showing that, while the emphasis is usually on what is strictly Franco-French, there are some exceptions. The Gaullist and conservative Catholic traditions are strongly represented in the second list as are parties of the far right – *Rassemblement pour la France et l'Indépendance de l'Europe* (RPFie) (Charles Pasqua), the *Mouvement pour la France* (Philippe de Villiers) and the *Front National* (Jean-Marie Le Pen). On the other hand also mentioned, strange bedfellows indeed for the *Alliance,* are *Coordination Communiste pour la Continuité Révolutionnaire et la Renaissance Léniniste du P.C.F.* and *Gauche Révolutionnaire.*

This tracing of one strand of the political associations of the FFI has given some idea of how involved the relationships between language and politics are in France today. All three sections of this chapter have shown that government decisions to implement language policies may have very long-lasting and indeed double-edged effects. This was apparent during and after the riots that broke out in France in November 2005. For many years there had been awareness of growing violence and simmering unrest and predictions that *la banlieue* would explode. Among the many possible causes for the 2005 riots was the policy of assimilation and integration of immigrants and the imposition if a single national language and identity on all citizens.

By imposing French as the sole national language and assuming that it would be learned through the school system, the French state had, it was argued (both in France and in the foreign press), effectively gagged generations of immigrants, making it impossible for them to succeed at school or to obtain jobs. Their exclusion from mainstream French society was reinforced by inflexible policies on education and language. The political arguments for this centralisation had not changed since the Revolution, and now France, once proud to call itself the *terre d'accueil* (country of welcome), found itself accused of a deliberate refusal to take the problems of immigration seriously. Unsurprisingly this provoked a strong backlash from the right wing, whose supporters could see nothing wrong in insistence on the traditional model of a single shared national identity and language.

A. Judge (2002: 70–72) feels that, in response notably to 'cracks . . . in the system as the very foundations of the state are questioned', there has been a gradual change of language policy and a move to greater acceptance of the possibility of a pluri- and multi-lingual France. If she is right, November 2005 shows that the pace of change has been too slow. The experience of exclusion resented by so many immigrants is now giving rise to violence that demands an immediate, drastic and wide-ranging response from the government and the nation.

Again there is evidence of the contrast between internal and external policies, the outspoken espousal of multi-lingualism in Europe and at the UN, and the hesitancy over accepting pluri-lingualism and according recognition to regional and minority languages at home. As a result of the close intertwining of politics and language and increasing internal and external political pressures, the French government finds itself in a logically untenable position. It is impossible not to conclude that the contradictions between internal and external language policies arise largely from planning which is too closely dependent on political expediency.

The decision to impose a single official language within the country, for what seem to be the best of motives, can set up reactions that are still being felt centuries after the original policy was created. In France, a long period of insistence on a single language and a single identity has led to mistrust of otherness and cultural and linguistic xenophobia. The passage of time has blurred the issues so that the arguments produced at the time of the Revolution for the introduction of a language policy, highly persuasive and apparently morally and politically beyond reproach though they seemed, may to later generations seem tainted. As France is now realising, even many years later the reactions to these policies can be politically threatening for a highly centralised state. Opposition to such policies can develop in unexpected ways, can impact on mainstream politics or inspire new political movements and alliances. The 2005 riots show that, because of their intimate connection with questions of image, identity and security (Ager, 1999), aspects of such opposition can exert an influence going far beyond questions of language.

The next chapter addresses the question of whether or not these convictions are shared by France's nearest European neighbours, before Chapter 6 looks more closely at some of the puzzles and paradoxes observed in present-day language resistance in France.

Chapter 5

Languages in Other Countries: How Does France Compare?

An Overview

So far, French language policy has been examined entirely from the point of view of France and this picture now needs to be put into a wider perspective. It is easy to feel that the highly developed structures and strategies for the defence of French are unique and exist in isolation from language policies in the rest of Europe. In such a small geographical area, with so much shared history, this separation is likely to be more apparent than real.

Chapter 2 (pp. 34–45) gave some idea of the extent to which French policies are of necessity constrained and shaped by historical, geographical and political forces outside the borders of France. To help understand the intricacies of the context of the language policies of France, this chapter looks first in summary at the position of France and its language policies in the European context and then examines in greater detail four of the other member countries of the European Union: Germany, Italy, Spain and the United Kingdom, comparing relevant aspects of language policy and defence in those countries with policies in France.

The widely held impression that France is more concerned with actively defending its national language than other countries is to a large extent confirmed by the comparisons undertaken by various groups throughout the world interested in language policy. A quick way to compare the measures taken in different countries to defend languages is to consult one of the many encyclopedias available on the Internet. Wikipedia (an on-line encyclopedia in many languages, see web site list for different versions) for example has a widely copied, but probably not exhaustive, list of 60 languages having an official organisation.

Table 5.1 gives a selection of these. Such a list gives some idea of how important the issue of language is, both inside and outside Europe. (A

Table 5.1 Selection of Languages with an Official Organisation

Basque: *Euskaltzaindia, Euskerazaintza* (for dialects)
Czech: Czech Language Institute
Dutch: *Nederlandse taalunie* (Dutch Language Union)
Esperanto: *Akademio de Esperanto*
French: *Académie française* (French Academy)
Hebrew: Academy of the Hebrew Language (תירבעה ןושלל הימדקאה)
Hungarian: *Magyar Tudományos Akadémia Nyelvtudományi Intézete* (Research Institute for Linguistics of the Hungarian Academy of Sciences)
Indonesian: *Pusat Pembinaan dan Pengembangan Bahasa*
Malay: *Dewan Bahasa dan Pustaka*
Maori: Maori Language Commission
Mandarin (Republic of China): Mandarin Promotion Council
Norwegian (Bokmål and Nynorsk): *Norsk språkråd* (Norwegian Language Council)
Norwegian (Riksmål): *Norsk Akademi for Sprog og Litteratur* (Norwegian Academy)
Romanian (Romania): *Academia Române*
Romanian (Moldova): *Academia de Ştiinţe a Moldovei*
Slovene: Slovene Academy of Sciences and Arts
Spanish: *Real Academia Española* (Royal Spanish Academy)
Academia Norteamericana de la Lengua Española (American Academy of the Spanish Language)
Swedish: Swedish Academy

Source: http://en.wikipedia.org/wiki/List_of_language_regulators (15.11.2006)

more patchy coverage is given by other on-line encyclopedias, for example ThefreeDictionary web site.)

In most English-speaking countries, people are so secure in the predominance of their language that they feel no need to defend it against other tongues. Letters to the press and normative or humorous publications (Truss, 2003, for example) show nevertheless that there is genuine concern about the way the language is changing. In the United States, because of the increasing use of Spanish in North America, a growing number of Americans are worried about the situation of English. Agitated, if not always linguistically sophisticated, citizens of the US have set up a number of agencies to defend English against Spanish and, in order to contextualise their activities, they have done research into the position of official languages throughout the world (Calvet, 2004). The political tendencies of these agencies may give cause for concern, but their research is useful since it provides comparable data worldwide. The Internet site of the US English Foundation is one such example.

Using the same headings for each of the countries surveyed, the US English Foundation provides a frequently updated snapshot of the language situation in most countries throughout the world. The summary includes not only official and minority languages but also an outline of any legislation dealing with languages and background notes that may highlight relevant historical facts and current issues, and a useful list of references. The summary of the language situation in France, Germany, Italy, Spain and the UK shows that there are wide differences, particularly as far as legislation is concerned.

The official national language is, according to this site, spoken by 93.6% of the population in France, 91.5% in Germany, 94.1% in Italy, 74.4% in Spain and 81.5% in the United Kingdom. The majority language is enshrined only in the French and Spanish constitutions. Other legal provisions in France relate to the strengthening of the position of the national language. This contrasts sharply with the situation in Italy, Germany and Spain where references to language in the constitution and the law are designed to uphold and defend the linguistic and other rights of minorities. The situation in the United Kingdom is different. English is described on this web site as the 'non-statutory' official language, not mentioned in any law, and there are six minority languages, three of them: Welsh, Scottish Gaelic and Irish Gaelic are defended by law in the relevant constituent countries of the kingdom. In France (Chapter 2, pp. 29–34) there is ongoing and sometimes bitter opposition to the moves in Europe to give increased rights and protection to minority languages, with many people convinced that any such moves in France would be unconstitutional and a direct threat to the hard-won unity of the Republic (Dargent, 2004a: 8–9).

A more complete description of world languages is to be found on the site of the *Université Laval* (web site, *Université Laval*, <u>Index</u>). Naturally the section on French is more detailed than those for the other languages, but Laval gives very full descriptions of the languages of the world and the *géo-démolinguistique* [geographic, demographic, linguistic] and political contexts within which they function. The second part of the chapter returns to Laval for some of its detailed information.

Two other overviews, this time of the situation of languages in the European Union, are provided by the Council of Europe's European Centre for Modern Languages (ECML) and the 'independent' European

Federation of National Institutions for Language (EFNIL) (see respective web sites). Here the information provided by EFNIL, created in October 2003 in Stockholm, is examined. In this federation, each member country is represented by one, or at most two linguistic agencies. These can be either national institutions or other agencies for language, and collectively they are concerned to promote a multi-lingual Europe and to defend the equality of the national languages in the Union. Originally a French initiative, EFNIL arose from discussions between the DGLF, the Italian *Accademia della Crusca* and the *Nederlandse taalunie* (Dutch Language Union) in Mannheim in 2000 and in Florence in 2001. They were joined by the Spanish and then many other member countries expressed an interest in working together on an agenda where the French influence can be readily detected:

- promoting linguistic diversity in Europe;
- supporting the national languages in Europe;
- supporting national linguistic bodies;
- exchanging information and research findings;
- supporting the teaching, in each member state, of the national language and foreign languages and developing student and teacher exchanges.

The EFNIL site, still being developed, uses a grid to analyse linguistic policy in member countries, so providing the basis for realistic comparisons.

The list of the organisations making up the EFNIL is in itself revealing. France is represented of course by the DGLFLF, a government body and required to pursue official government policy. In contrast, the other member organisations are independent, not-for-profit organisations and many of them are research institutes. Their diversity is illustrated by the list of members from the countries discussed here: the *Institut für Deutsche Sprache* (Mannheim), the *Accademia della Crusca* and the *Opera del Vocabolario Italiano* (part of the national research council) in Florence, the *Real Academia Española* in Madrid and the *Oxford English Dictionary*. Thus here again the French stand out from the other member countries, most of whose representatives are research institutes with close ties to academics and universities.

The DGLFLF is building up for EFNIL an archive of linguistic informa-tion on all the EU member countries participating in its activities in favour of a multi- and pluri-lingual Europe (22 in March 2006) (web site, EFNIL Files). Less schematic in format than the various on-line encyclopaedias, this archive allows the member organisations to make relatively detailed comparisons of language policy in the Union and to plan future activities on a firm basis. The French perspective shaping the archive is possibly more revealing than the information it gives on the other countries and this perspective is apparent in the headings: legal context; institutional arrangements; disputes with the European Commission; official projects planned. Looking only at the introductory and concluding paragraphs for the countries of particular interest, shows at a glance what aspects of linguistic policy are of primary interest to the French. The EFNIL information for the other countries is summarised below (adapted from web site, EFNIL, <u>Files</u>).

Germany: There is in Germany no legislation aimed at protecting or promoting the national language. This absence of linguistic legislation is explained by history and the rejection of any measure which could be a reminder of the linguistic policy of the national socialists. There has been in recent years, especially from the opposition, a calmer relationship with German language and culture and a growing interest in the strong cultural and linguistic policies of other European states such as France and Poland.

Italy: There is no mention of the Italian language in the Constitution of the Italian Republic. On the other hand, Article 6 of the Constitution deals with the defence of minority languages. In spite of the interest the *Accademia della Crusca* and specialists in linguistics try to excite in the question of promoting the Italian language in Italy, there is little political activity. The idea of the 'defence of the national language' is difficult to promote in official speeches and texts for historical reasons.

Spain: The 'historical' autonomous communities have set up, over the last 20 years, institutional arrangements for the protection of the Basque, Catalan and Galician languages. These arrangements are supported by constantly increasing financial measures and the scope of their activities is widening. Beyond the declarations of the highest regional authorities, legislative activity and the initiatives by the autonomous administrations to promote the regional languages bear witness to the intention, ever more strongly expressed, of making Basque, Catalan or Galician the foundation of the autonomous communities.

The United Kingdom (England and Wales only – Scotland and Northern Ireland are omitted): In England there is no legislation concerning the use of languages in the areas of advertising, education or work. In the absence of a constitution, in these areas, as in many others, pragmatism takes the place of legislation.

Since 1993 Wales has introduced, in theory, equality between Welsh and English. A specific structure to promote the Welsh language reports directly to the Welsh National Assembly.

It is clear that the French, with their long history of centralised government and official responsibility for language policy, perceive the absence of a constitutional and legal framework for the defence and promotion of the national language as a serious problem for the future activities of the EFNIL. In addition, the determination of other member states of the Union to protect the rights, both political and linguistic, of minority groups, appears to be interpreted by the French almost as a deliberate and unnecessary obstacle to measures in favour of the national language.

Bearing these attitudes in mind, the following sections examine language policies and issues in four other European countries whose language is spoken throughout the world: Germany, Italy, Spain and the United Kingdom.

Germany: The Old Enemy, the New Ally

The language situation in the four countries is examined in turn, using the same headings for each: (1) Historical and political factors; (2) Official policy (government, the constitution and the law); (3) other linguistic agencies; (4) the European context (including minority languages); and (5) current issues and problems. It will not be possible to give an in-depth analysis of all the factors that arise in a consideration of the place of language in national life, nor to analyse in great detail the many-layered interactions between countries that have shared a long history and close geographical proximity for centuries. The purpose here is to tease out some of the background to the present-day linguistic situation of these near neighbours.

(1) Historical and political factors: Germany is probably at present France's closest European ally, but memories are long and both French and German citizens are watching the situation with some degree of scepticism. The history of Europe in the 19th and 20th centuries certainly justifies this. Some aspects of German history have shaped attitudes to language and continue to influence German, and to some extent European, language policy. A selection of these is discussed here.

While France has been accustomed to a single, highly centralised government for several centuries, the history of Germany is very different (Barbour, 2000: 162–166). Although there were trading, cultural and political contacts between the *Länder* now making up the Federal Republic, they did not come together to form one nation state until the second half of the 19th century. After the defeat of Napoleon at the conclusion of the bitter Franco-Prussian conflict, William was crowned in 1871 as the emperor of a group of states to make up the new united Germany. As if to add insult to injury, the coronation took place in the Hall of Mirrors at Versailles. The long-standing enmity between France and Germany was thus reinforced and the groundwork for future wars and a long period of mistrust was laid at this time.

The various states forming the new nation had a long history of independence or at least semi-independence and the kind of highly centralised government characteristic of France was not possible. In each *Land* people continued to speak the regional dialect and only gradually came to accept first written German and later spoken German as the common language (Wolff, 1986: 77–80; 511–515). The *Länder* had retained some of their independence in imperial Germany and that independence was enshrined in the constitution of the Weimar Republic when it was founded in 1918 after Germany's defeat in the First World War. Federalism continues to be a notable feature of the present Federal German Republic, which followed the fall of the Berlin Wall and re-unification at the end of 1989.

This historical background, so radically different from the history of France, has naturally led in Germany to attitudes to the national language – and to regional languages – quite unlike those in France. Nevertheless, German is now so strongly entrenched as the single official language in the Federal Republic that it is spoken by the vast majority of the population, it is the only language used in government, administration and the law by both federal and state governments, and there is no reference to it in the constitution. The unquestioning acceptance of High German as the standard official language is attributed by some commentators to the fact that it came to function as the more standardised written form of the language alongside the various regional dialects at the time of the invention of the printing press and then the reformation (Wolff, 1986: 108).

The spread of the Protestant religion relied to some extent on a widespread ability to read what Luther wrote and to read the Bible in the early 16th century (Walter 1994: 376; Wolff, 1986: 108). Luther also advocated the setting up of a state education system and encouraged the spread of education and of popular literacy, and although it was not until 1830 that schooling became obligatory, the importance of reading and writing was widely accepted in the German states long before the end of the 19th century when similar ideas were being put into practice in France. The German situation is therefore in sharp contrast to the position in France where all the pressure to create a virtually monolingual nation came from the top: first from the king and later from the highly centralised Republic. German, it appears, established itself as the single official language mainly through a bottom-up process with its roots in education and religion.

One more aspect of German history continues to influence attitudes to language and should be mentioned at this point: the close identification of language and patriotism. In the 19th century a largely anti-French form of extreme patriotism that elevated language to a powerful symbol of identity was propounded by figures such as Arndt. This 'union of language and fatherland, of brotherhood and blood, of vengeance and sword' (Kohn, 1967: 258) and the idea of the *Volk* as God's chosen people were to lead in the 20th century to the extremes of national socialism and the Holocaust. In their quest for German world dominance, the national socialists, seeking to control every aspect of German life, instituted language policies and legislation in the 1930s and 1940s echoing the 19th century attitudes.

The Nazi regime (1933–1945) politicised the language, insisted on a language purism that mirrored racial purism and imposed Germanisation in the occupied territories. Purism saw the removal of words, phrases and concepts from the language, if considered un-German or un-Aryan (including many famous French dishes). The politicised German from this period has been called '*Nazi Deutsch*' and its legacy is a lively mistrust in present-day Germany of official language policies. In the post-war period, the separation of Germany into two separate entities created divisions of a different kind and these were mirrored in the language differences that gradually developed during the period until re-unification in 1990. Sensitivity to these differences is still marked in Germany (Barbour, 2000b: 165–166; Wolff, 1986: 269). Another specifically German development at the end of the 20th century is the emergence of what is called *Gastarbeiter Deutsch* (immigrant worker German) and this has upset some purists (Schröder, 1993: 63).

With this history, with the continuing guilt and the legacy of the Holocaust and with constant reminders of post-war differences, it could be expected that attitudes to the national language in Germany are very unlike those in France. While the French associate their language with centralised national power and national and international prestige, the Germans have a more relaxed attitude since their love of their language is based on other aspects of their shared cultural experience and they have good reason to be wary of language legislation imposed by a central government.

(2) Official policy: Official language policy in Germany bears the marks of this historical and political background. It is a non-interventionist policy as the absence of any mention of language in the constitution testifies (web site, *Université Laval*, Germany). German is the only language used for public and administrative purposes, although there is an increasing tendency for English to appear, particularly in advertisements and the press. This is causing disquiet in some quarters, but for most German speakers the use of English does not pose a threat. Where there are laws, they refer to minority languages, and the *Länder*, rather than the federal government, have the responsibility for implementing this legislation

(3) Other linguistic agencies: While there are no official government bodies charged with defending and promoting the German language, there are a number of independent or semi-independent agencies. In the German *Länder* there has never been an equivalent of the *Académie française*, working inside the country to keep the language pure and having the final decision on linguistic changes. A standardising influence was to some extent exercised in the 16th century by the *Meistersinger* guilds and contests, and in the 17th century a number of academies were created. The most influential of these appears to have been the imaginatively named *Fruchtbringende Gesellschaft* (Fruitbearing Society) founded in Weimar, with the support and approval of the successive princes, in 1617 (web site, Wikipedia, *Fruchtbringende Gesellschaft*; Wolff, 1986: 489). The aim of the society was to fight against the 'watering down' of German by foreign influences and to restore the language to its *'uralte gewönliche und angeborne deutsche Reinigkeit'* (ancient, natural and inherent German purity). It is already clear that the French *Académie* was deeply concerned with the 'purity' of the language and it is a concept (albeit ill-defined) that not only recurs in the aims of other academies, but still has currency today in circles where would-be protectors of various languages gather. The *Fruchtbringende Gesellschaft* was short lived and did not really survive into the 18th century but its influence was extensive and it was an early model of a European language academy.

In 1838 the brothers Jacob and Wilhelm Grimm, linguists and philologists who are better known in the English-speaking world for their fairy stories, began work on their dictionary, an enterprise whose consequences for the German language were to be far-reaching. In its early form, the now revered DWB (*Deutsches Worterbuch*) or simply 'the Grimm' has been described as 'a collection of disconnected antiquarian essays of high value' (web site, Wikipedia, <u>Grimm</u>). It was not very far advanced when the Grimm brothers died, but this monument to the history and richness of the German language has since appeared in several editions. It was *'das erste Wörterbuch der Geschichte, in dem auch Schimpfwörter und <u>unfeine</u> Wörter . . . aufgenommen werden'* (the first dictionary in history to include swear words and <u>indelicate</u> words) (web site, Wikipedia, <u>Deutches Wör-terbuch</u>). It also included many of the dialect words of particular interest to the brothers and was based on usage rather than an ideal norm of the language. In its breadth and acceptance of regional varieties of German it was thus in sharp contrast to the purifying and codifying tendencies of other European dictionaries. It was not until the end of the 19th century that a normalising influence made itself felt, first with the *Duden* and then the 1901 official dictionary of German orthography, which formalised rules for written German. The role of the *Duden* as the arbiter in matters of spelling and punctuation throughout the German-speaking world was officially recognised in 1955.

The creation in 1925 of the *Deutsche Akademie* allowed the government to take active steps to promote German outside its borders. In 1951, after the Second World War, the Federal Republic replaced the *Akademie* with the *Goethe Institut* whose funding was provided by the Ministry of Foreign Affairs (web site, *Goethe Institut*). The smaller Goethe Societies were set up under the same umbrella. These were voluntary, non-profit organisations operating under local law, much as the *Alliances françaises* did. Both the institutes and the societies were obliged in effect to follow government policy and so acted (and continue to act) as semi-official government agencies for the defence and promotion of the German language and culture outside Germany. They are now under the aegis of the Ministry of Culture – in Germany, part of Foreign Affairs.

But government policies change and financial constraints increasingly limit cultural activities. This is shown by the fact that the sources of funding for the *Goethe Institut* now include the German Press Office, and by changes in the number and location of the institutes and societies to allow concentration of effort in areas where there are new political developments (in the new member countries of the European Union, for example) or emerging economic opportunities (Afghanistan and North Korea are recent examples).

In addition to these well-known and highly respected organisations, present throughout the world, there are other groups acting inside the country to defend and promote German. Some of these have set up defensive associations. Many of them are associated with universities and some cooperate with similar organisations in other countries: the *Verein deutsche Sprache* (see web site) works closely with the FFI and groups and individuals are active in e-mail groups such as *linguarum-democratia* for example. The German member of the EFNIL, the *Institut für deutsche Sprache* (see web site) in Mannheim, is an influential defensive group. The members of this association, created in 1964, are virtually all professional academic linguists.

Other defenders of German are the *Gesellschaft für deutsche Sprache* founded in Wiesbaden in 1947 (see web site) one of whose activities in defence of the language is its highly entertaining 'Non-Word of the Year' competition. The list of recent laureates (paparazzi, viagra, year 2000 compatible) provides a quick overview of the urgent, but frequently ephemeral concerns of the human species. Another original competition is the 'Language Defender of the Year' run by *Deutsche Sprachwelt* (see web site) battling in a determined but light-hearted way against Dr Pansch, the *Sprachpanscher* (Language Adulterator) who joyfully mixes

English and German. The *Verein deutsche Sprache* is also on the lookout for Dr Pansch. It runs a German Language Day and awards a number of prizes. In 2003, to assess the importance German-speakers attach to their language, it auctioned the German language on Ebay. The figure of €10,000 was quickly reached and the auction had to be halted (web site, *Deutsche Welle*). The number of such organisations seems to be growing: a group of senior citizens in Nuremberg (web site, Senior Citizens (Nuremberg)) has recently leapt into action against the increasing number of English words in advertisements and public announcements making life difficult for those who do not understand English.

(4) The European context and minority languages: In Europe the German policy is rather more interventionist than inside the country (web site, *Université Laval*, Germany, Section 1.2). Germany was one of the first countries to join EFNIL and it has been particularly active ever since re-unification in promoting the use of German in the various working bodies of the European Union: Commission, Parliament, Council of Europe. It made the most of the period from 1998–1999 when the presidency of the Union passed from Austria to Germany to strengthen the position of German and has since taken a stance similar to that of France, by insisting that its representatives on these bodies be able to work in their own language. German is now the third working language of the Union. The two countries working together may have more success than either would have alone.

It is in its attitudes to minority languages in Europe that Germany differs most markedly from France. At the federal level there are a number of legal texts defending the position of minorities and their languages in Germany. A 1955 bi-lateral treaty with Denmark; the 1990 treaty of re-unification; the 1994 version of the 'basic law', in effect since 1949 the constitution of the Federal Republic; Germany's willingness to sign and to ratify promptly both the European Convention on the Protection of Minorities (from 1998) and the European Charter on Regional and Minority Languages (from 1999) all bear witness to this. Thus the German determination to protect the language rights of minorities is clearly evident in legislation at federal level and is reinforced by the numerous similar laws enacted at state level. Although the legislation exists, it may not always be fully implemented. While international treaties take precedence over federal laws, linguistic legislation is put into effect (with greater or less conviction) by the *Länder*. Nevertheless, the contrast with language policy in France, where there was such a marked unwillingness to sign and ratify the European agreements (Chapter 2, pp. 38–40), could hardly be greater.

(5) Current issues and problems: As in France, the linguistic issues agitating Germans give rise to numerous web sites where concerned citizens try to

win support for their cause. The most distinctly German of these issues is anxiety about spelling reform. In France this is also a hotly disputed issue, with very strong, but frequently linguistically ill-informed, opinions on both sides. In Germany, where dissatisfaction with the spelling rules in force since 1901 was widespread, 10 years of work resulted in the introduction in 1996 of limited spelling reforms with a period of transition until July 2005. In spite of strident opposition and legal challenges, the new spelling reform (*Rechtschreibreform*) was implemented in most schools and by most publishing houses from 1998. Most of the media followed suit in 1999. Nevertheless the *Frankfurter Allgemeine Zeitung* reverted to the old spelling in 2000 and in 2004 the debate again hit the headlines when leading publishers announced they were reverting to the earlier spelling. The government has not retracted the reforms and they are now official policy, but this is an issue that will continue to disturb Germans and it distracts attention from other linguistic problems such as the influence of English.

The extent of concern over the invasion of German by English can be judged by the number of Google references (almost 157,000 in November 2006) to the problem of *Denglish* (or less frequently *Denglisch* or *Engleutsch*). Quoting some of the most extreme examples of incomprehensibility resulting from the use of English words in advertising, the media and in official publications and signs, these sites communicate an incipient hysteria reminiscent of some of the French language sites, but they are on the whole less virulently anti-American in tone. There seems though to be some good news on this front: the *Deutsche Welle* (see web site) reported early in 2004 that there may be a 'trend reversal'. It found there were signs that some companies were responding to protests about the pretentiously clever use of (sometimes approximate) English in their advertising campaigns. This seems to be a pragmatic rather than a linguistic response – people do not buy unless they can understand what they are being offered.

The linguistic climate prevailing in Germany is clearly different in important ways from the climate in France, although there are some shared anxieties. In the analysis of the other three countries, the pattern of language attitudes is revealed in a wider dimension.

Italy: Romance Neighbour

(1) Historical and political factors: The history of Italy and its language is again very different from French history. The factors that affected the Italian language show some similarities with the situation in Germany: recent unification and numerous dialects contrast with the intense centralisation in France and the early imposition by kings and successive governments of a single official language, the language of Parisian political

power. In Italy the route to the acceptance of present-day Italian as the official language of the whole country was different in important ways from the path followed by Germany. Italian was neither imposed from above by the political power as in France nor, as in Germany, accepted as the written language of communication by the ordinary people.

The history of love of language in Italy is at least as long as in France but in Italy the romance had literary rather than political roots and it was accompanied by the strong emotional attachment to regional dialects that continues today. The literary beginnings of modern spoken and written Italian go back at least to the 13th and early 14th centuries when Dante, writing in Florence, was looking at the various dialects and trying to find the form of common speech best suited to the production of serious and profound literary works. His conclusion was that the Tuscan dialect surpassed the others, and the powerful literary masterpieces he, Petrarch and Bocaccio produced in that dialect have meant that, since the 14th century, it has been accepted in Italy as the predominant form of the language for literary purposes.

The question of the most suitable standard form of the language had not been resolved for all time. In the 15th century Bembo, in an attempt to reach a definitive conclusion to the issue, addressed the *questione della lingua* (language question) (Migliorini, 1966: 212–225; Pulgram, 1958: 61–63). The disagreements and confrontations about language throughout the peninsula were reflected in the creation in 1583, well before similar concerns in France led to the setting-up of the *Académie française*, of the *Accademia della Crusca* with the remit of standardising and maintaining the purity of the language. What was known as the 'new language question' became a preoccupation in the middle of the 19th century when the writer Manzoni, a Milanese, again decided that the Florentine dialect – in its contemporary, cultivated form – was the one best suited to literary expression. By the end of the century there was finally a hard-won consensus that this dialect would be the language of the unified Italy. The literary prestige of Florence, its position in the centre of Italy, and its economic and cultural importance were vital elements in the acceptance of Florentine as the preferred written form by speakers of other dialects (Ruzza, 2000: 172).

It was during the 19th century that political moves (led by Garibaldi) to bring Italy under one government strengthened, and the Kingdom of Italy was declared in 1861. A long history of separate states and mutual mistrust meant that the unification was sometimes shaky and Italian history since 1861 has been marked by political instability and frequent changes of government. While Italian remains the official language, the vitality of the dialects is apparently scarcely diminished and indeed there are signs, with the increasing use of dialects in literary works and their popularity with young people, that they may be becoming stronger (Migliorini, 1966: 469). In any case, there is a considerable difference between attitudes to regional languages and dialects in France and in Italy. The Italians have never expected uniformity in their language. Typically, there is a broad tolerance of the different lexical and syntactic structures – a sign of the various dialects – and Italians enjoy this linguistic richness. They find it hard to understand the French desire to impose on all citizens a single 'correct' form of the written and spoken language (Walter, 1994: 178–179).

The present-day map of Italy, with its 15 'ordinary' regions and the 5 autonomous regions of Sardinia, Sicily, the Valley d'Aosta, Friulia-Venezia Giulia and Trentino-Alto Adige, is a testament to its varied linguistic history. Even the names of the latter two encapsulate a patchwork of history. The continuing relevance of this history is also highlighted by the number of separatist political parties active in Italy. While it is impossible to obtain a complete list, a recent catalogue (March 2006 – web site, *Alsace d'abord*) shows a total of 36 parties. Twenty-one of these are connected to separatist groups, most of which include linguistic demands in their manifestos.

Other aspects of Italian history explain to some extent the importance given to minority languages. At the end of the First World War, the territorial enlargement of Italy meant that there was now an increased number of speakers of other languages included within its borders: German-speaking inhabitants of the Tyrol, Slovenes, Croats and Yugoslavs (Bochmann, n.d.: 129). The severe policy of assimilation begun by the Italian state at this time was continued, for different ideological reasons, by the fascist government of Mussolini. These policies have been identified with the other language policies of the fascist regime and are now discredited: the strength of feeling for minority languages is proportionally all the greater.

In its history of fascist government in the middle of the 20th century, Italy therefore resembles Germany. A legacy of this period is a strong mistrust of overt nationalism and of policies imposed by the central government, particularly where language is concerned (Ruzza, 2000: 174–175). The government of Mussolini had an overall language policy that included the repression of Italian dialects in public and the replacement of foreign words (Bochmann, n.d.: 131; Migliorini, 1966: 468–469). Dialects were seen as a disgrace to the new, virile masculine culture and harmful to national purity and unity. The strong reaction after the war against the policies of the fascists has left Italians with a profound wariness when faced with centrally imposed language legislation and explains the fierce reactions to the various proposals to control language promulgated after the election in 2000 of right-wing Prime Minister Silvio Berlusconi. The suggestion in 2001 from *Forza Italia* (supported by Berlusconi) that the senate set up a

Supreme Council of the Italian Language has aroused concern and anger. This contrasts sharply with France, where the existence of the *Conseil supérieur de la langue française* is uncontroversial and its work is widely considered an essential tool in the protection of the language.

(2) Official policy: The Italian constitution of 1947 does not specify that Italian is the language of the republic but it does, in Articles 3 and 6, guarantee to respect the racial, linguistic and religious equality of all citizens. This proclamation was not formalised in national law until the presidential decree in 1991 called *Norme in matiere delle minoranze linguistiche* (Norms in the Area of Linguistic Minorities). Although somewhat tardy, this was a reflection of the historical context and a recognition of the importance of the various elements gathered together in the unified Italian republic, notably of the five autonomous regions.

Other laws protect minorities, including the newer law (No. 482) adopted in December 1999 relating to the norms for the protection of linguistic minorities. The first article of this law does, in the absence of any such statement in the constitution, state that the official language of the republic is Italian. The same law also states that the republic values and protects the linguistic and cultural heritage not only of Italian, but also of specific minority groups (web site, *Université Laval*, Italy, Section 4).

In the law courts Italian is used in virtually all situations and, for sentencing and judgments and in appeals, only Italian may be used. The administration communicates with its citizens exclusively in Italian, except in the autonomous regions where a language other than Italian may be used. The 1991 law allowed teaching in some minority languages, but the number of hours is fixed by the Ministry of Education. The 1999 law further extended the provisions for teaching in minority and regional languages (web sites, EFNIL; *Université Laval* Italy, Section 7).

In 1998 a proposal was put forward for a law to protect the Italian language (No. 4649) (web site, Italy, Government of, 1998 Proposal). This did not become law and the 2001 proposal (No. 933) from a *Forza Italia* senator for a *Consiglio Superiore della Lingua italiana* (Superior Council for the Italian Language) aroused fierce opposition ((1) above). The debate continues. So, although there seems to be a growing concern in Italy about the national language, even the right-wing Berlusconi government was unable to obtain general support for an official language policy or an official language regulator.

(3) Other linguistic agencies: The most important and best known of the organisations for the protection of Italian is the venerable and imaginatively named *Accademia della Crusca* (founded in 1583) (see web site). The *Crusca* and all its sections have names related to the making of bread from wheat, symbolising the purpose of the *Accademia*: to separate the

pure language – '*il piu bel fior nel coglie*' (the purest flour) (Petrarch) – from the *crusca* (bran), the impurities that have crept in. Florence, as the home of the national language, is naturally also home to the *Crusca*. The *Accademia*, although independent of the government, is the leading Italian member of the EFNIL. Some of its activities are similar to those of the younger *Académie française*, but the *Crusca* differs considerably from the French academy. Its powers are not sanctioned by the government and its members are not exclusively authors and personalities but, for the most part, academics and professional linguists. It supports research in Italian linguistics and philology, is the repository of knowledge on the history and development of Italian and collaborates with various foreign institutions, the Italian government and the European Union to promote multi- and pluri-lingualism (web site, EFNIL, <u>Italy</u>). The *Crusca* has a long tradition of conservatism in linguistic matters and its reputation as a stuffy old-fashioned body is well established. There are now signs, however, that things may be changing.

An example of this is the creation in 2001, in addition to the three existing centres in the *Accademia* (Philology, Lexicography, Grammar), of a fourth centre dealing with the contemporary language: CLIC (*Centro di consulenza sulla lingua italiana contemporanea*) (Centre for Consultancy on the Contemporary Italian Language) (see web site). This is composed of members of the *Crusca*, university scholars and professional linguists and its purpose is to study the contemporary language, to make the results of this research widely known, for example in the media, and to act as a pressure group for the national language in government circles.

The second Italian member of the EFNIL is the Florence-based OVI (*Opera del Vocabulario Italiano*) (Research on Italian Vocabulary) (web site, EFNIL, <u>OVI</u>; web site, OVI). This publicly funded body, part of the CNR (National Research Centre) was established in 1985. It works on the history of the vocabulary of Italian, and produces the dictionary *Tesoro della Lingua Italiana delle Origini*.

Italian is powerfully promoted by the Ministry of Foreign Affairs and by the *Società Dante Alighieri* (see web site). The Ministry of Foreign Affairs (web site, Italy, Government of, <u>Ministry of Foreign Affairs</u>) actively promotes Italian in the wider world. Its Office for the Promotion of the Italian Language within the Directorate General for Cultural Promotion and Cooperation is very active in teaching, publishing and the media. The 'Dante' was founded in 1889 to protect and promote Italian outside Italy. It is in many ways similar to the *Alliance française* but as well as running courses for foreigners in locally based organisations, it also has the remit – not shared by the *Alliance* – of teaching Italian to Italian emigrants in the extensive diaspora throughout the world.

Like France, and to a lesser extent Germany, Italy has its share of non-official and private organisations concerned to save the national language from destruction through the spread of American English or the activities of the Brussels bureaucrats. Italians are proud to call their language the *bella lingua* (beautiful language) and the *Associazione Bella Lingua*, created in 2000 by a group of politicians has been active in the defence of the language, issuing its *Manifesto in difesa della lingua* (Manifesto in Defence of the Language) in 2000. This was the second such manifesto: the first was issued in 1995 by two Lombard poets. According to the web site of the influential Dora bookshop, the 2000 *Manifesto* carried much more weight than the first. It was addressed to powerful people in business, industry and the administration, in an attempt to restore Italian to its earlier dynamism and expressive power.

The chat rooms of Dora (see web site) and other agencies interested in the language give an interesting picture of the attitudes of Italians to their language. One example is the July 2004 contribution to the web chat site *Assente* entitled *Salva la lingua* (Save the Language) (see web site). Like many such contributions it refers to the damaging and ongoing effects of the period of fascist government in Italy and vaunts the (supposed) merits of Esperanto as an international language. Fringe political elements such as the separatist parties in Lombardy (Ruzza, 2000: 186–169; web site, Lombardy League) and Liguria (web site, Liguria Independence League) and the 'independent' country of Padania (see web site) base much of their policy on the issue of language. The Italian Radical Party also makes an issue of language, at the same time promoting the apparently seductive merits of Esperanto (web site, Liguria Independence League, <u>Italian Radical Party</u>).

Outside the world of politics, the private, and uniquely Italian, Cassamarca Foundation (President: Dr Dino de Poli) (see web site) supports all aspects of the study of the humanities. Included in its many activities is strong support for the teaching, learning and defence of the Italian language throughout the world. Another non-political organisation was formed in 2003 by the association of Italian journalists (web site, *Ordine dei giornalisti*). Finding themselves at the forefront of the evolution of language in Italy, they recognise that they have a responsibility to ensure that the language of the media is clear and comprehensible and have thus decided, *'senza prevenzioni o sciovanismo'* (without prejudice or chauvinism), to examine closely the problem of the invasion of Italian by English terminology.

(4) The European context and minority languages: Italy is active, with other member states, in the defence of a multi- and pluri-lingual Europe. Its role in the discussions prior to the setting up of the EFNIL

is an indication of this. The history of Italy and its favourable attitude to minorities, particularly linguistic minorities, was not however reflected in a readiness to sign and ratify the European Charter on Regional and Minority Languages (1992). Italy, even more reluctant than France, finally signed in 2000 but there has been no ratification (Chapter 2, p. 38). This reticence is difficult to explain in view of the importance attached in Italy to these languages and of the troublesome political issues they create. As the *Université Laval* site comments (Italy, Section 8): 'the issue of linguistic minorities in Italy shows that there is many a slip between the cup and the lip, even when constitutional equality is assured and is enshrined in a battery of laws and decrees, and five regions of the country have been given their autonomy'.

(5) Current issues and problems: The prevalence of English terms, although a prevailing concern in Italy, arouses less hysteria than in France. Italians are more concerned with political issues such as increasingly strident calls for independence, particularly in the north ((4) above) and with questions of sovereignty in the developing European Union. The linguistic issues raising blood pressure in France – the increasing domination of English, feminisation, spelling reform etc. – do not on the whole excite Italians. Linguistic discussions are more likely to be about dialects and to have a positive rather than a gloomy defeatist tone. While there are Italians who are agitated by the increasing prevalence of *Italish, Italianglish, Engliano* or *Angliano*, Google produces fewer than 3000 references as compared with many thousands of similar references for German.

Compared with France, Italy seems a country largely at ease with its languages in spite of internal political overtones, and not overly preoccupied with the dominance of English. The situation in Spain (discussed in the next section) is different again, the history of the country having produced greater linguistic conflict and more divisive political fall-out.

Spain: Another Romance

(1) Historical and political factors: Looking at the history of Spain reveals yet another pattern in the formation of European nation states. Like France, Germany and Italy, modern Spain was formed from a number of constituent states or kingdoms in close interaction with one another since earliest times. In all four countries, a period of Roman domination gradually gave way to christianisation and to the formation of separate governments, finally unified into the modern nations, where linguistic confrontations and disagreements are a present-day reflection of the past. The timing was very different in the four countries: whereas unification

in Italy (1861) and in Germany (1871) is relatively recent, Spain (virtually with its modern boundaries, but at one time including Portugal) has been under one government, with the same official language – Castilian – since 1492. It was formed by the union of the crowns of Aragon and Castile and, unlike France, a republic since 1789, it has been a monarchy for the greater part of its history.

Spain alone of the four countries had a period of Arab rule and a strong Jewish presence both of which strongly influenced its language and its history. There were centuries of religious conflict as the Christians reconquered the peninsula. Spain had an extensive overseas empire and this is evident today in the large number of Spanish speakers throughout the world, mainly in the Americas. Deep religious and cultural differences persisted in Spain, even after the final defeat of the Moors at Granada in 1492, and they had ongoing repercussions on the Spanish language and on attitudes to regional and minority cultures and languages. Thus, although the Spanish nation state was one of the earliest, and for a long time the most powerful, in Europe, the specific conditions of its formation have produced a unique linguistic climate. In addition to the re-conquest of Granada, there are two other events marking the year 1492 as an important one in linguistic history: this was the year Columbus discovered America, so making it possible for Spanish to spread to the Americas where it is now the powerful second language of the USA (Ager, 1996: 9); it was also the year when what linguists regard as the very first grammar of a modern language – Castilian – was produced (Walter, 1994: 228). This might be regarded as the first measure to protect the official language of Spain.

In the 17th and early 18th centuries, Spain's great international power was declining and by 1700 a Bourbon king, Philip V (a grandson of Louis XIV) was on the Spanish throne. By the end of the war of the Spanish Succession in 1714, Spain was one of the weakest powers in Europe. Meanwhile in the intellectual sphere strong links had been developing between learned men throughout Europe and various private academies flourished. The *Real Academia Española* was founded (web site, *Real Academia Española, Breve historia, Origen y fines* (Short History, Creation and Aims)) in 1713 by a Spanish aristocrat. He already had his own small academy and had long admired the Italian *Crusca*, the Royal Society of London in Britain (founded in 1660, recognised by Charles II in 1662) and the French *Académie royale des sciences* (formed by Colbert in the name of Louis XIV in 1666).

Although Spain by the 19th century had a constitutional monarchy, it was beset by political instability and breakdowns of civil order. Periods of repressive government have characterised modern Spanish history and the creation of institutions capable of surviving the various stresses of Spanish society was difficult and painful (web site, US Library of Congress). The linguistic history of the country is a clear reflection of these tensions. As in Italy, the map of 21st century Spain, with its 17 regions, is an image of the past and an indicator of present-day linguistic territories. In only eight of the regions is Castilian Spanish the single official language (web site, *Université Laval*, Spain, Section 2; Wardhaugh, 1987: 119). In Aragon, Castile and Leon, Catalonia, Navarre, Valencia, Galicia, the Balearic Islands, the Basque Country and in Asturias the regional languages are also official. This highlights another difference between Spain and the other continental countries considered here. A number of fully developed languages has long been spoken by substantial regional minorities in Spain, as opposed to the presence mainly of dialects in France, Germany and Italy. The problems of managing Spain's linguistic diversity, from a political point of view, are considerably greater.

The civil war, from 1936–1939, dramatically divided Spain and Europe. It has no parallel in the other countries described here. The conflict revealed the deep fault lines in Spanish society – the profound religious, class, regional and linguistic differences. The government of the dictator General Franco, which came to power after the defeat of the left-wing republican forces at the end of the Civil War in 1939 and lasted until his death in 1975, did not seriously attempt to address these fundamental problems. Increasing militancy and terrorism characterised this period, posing a formidable problem for King Juan Carlos when the monarchy was restored. The period since the restoration of the monarchy and the establishment of a modern parliamentary democracy has seen an amazing change in the government of Spain but the country continues to face threats and violence from political parties and factions, most of which represent regional language groups.

As far as language was concerned, the period of the Franco dictatorship in Spain had very similar effects to the Hitler and Mussolini governments in Germany and Italy. The strongly integrationist policies of Franco's government aimed to produce a homogenised society where religious, ethnic and linguistic differences were suppressed in the interests of creating a strong nation. The 'nations within the nation', Catalonia, Galicia and the Basque Country, were particularly targeted and during the Franco period their anger at the wholesale destruction of their languages and cultures grew (Bochmann, n.d.: 134; Wardhaugh, 1987: 112–127). After the restoration of the monarchy in 1975, the governments in these regions achieved a degree of autonomy and immediately put in place policies to save their languages. This struggle continues and, as in all the countries in this sample, is closely allied to political movements for independence. In the case of the Basques it is marked by the terrorist activities of extremists, both in France and in Spain.

The political map of Spain (and Portugal), like the map of Italy, shows not only the deep historical, cultural and linguistic differences between its regions (Molinero, 2000: 83), but also portrays a form of government very different from the centralised political institutions of France. The strength of the Spanish regions is partly explained by their history. The example of Catalonia which, like the other autonomous regions, really needs a separate section (Molinero, 90–92; Wardhaugh, 121–123; web site, *Université Laval*, Spain, Catalonia) is a good illustration of the importance of history.

What is now the north-eastern part of Spain was itself the predominant power in the western Mediterranean in the 14th century. Although it was forced to a reluctant inclusion in the Spanish state in 1472, it took no part in Spain's colonial expansion and continued to develop separately, never accepting Spanish domination willingly, nurturing its own culture and language, sometimes turning to France rather than Spain as its ally. Since the mid-19th century the Catalans 'have developed a particularly strong national self-awareness' (Bochmann, n.d.: 134). At the outbreak of the Spanish Civil War Catalonia was autonomous and it submitted only with the greatest reluctance to the victorious forces of the dictator.

The repression in Catalonia during the Franco years, including legislation against the use of the Catalan language, was correspondingly severe, stimulating stubborn resistance. Although there was some relief from the worst of the repression after the Second World War, Catalonia did not obtain political autonomy and the re-instatement of its parliament until 1978. Since that time the Catalan government has done all in its power to strengthen and restore the Catalan language, first by trying to standardise modern Catalan, and second by a very active policy of promotion of the language. This was evident at the Barcelona Olympic Games in 1996, when speeches and announcements were made first in Catalan, then in Castilian and then in English. The decision by the Spanish government in January 2006 to devolve powers in the areas of education, culture, justice and the economy to the government of Catalonia is powerful evidence of the continuing political battle being waged and of the strength of the Catalan position.

Although Germany and Italy also had relatively short periods of fascist government, to some extent responsible for the linguistic issues of the 21st century, in Spain the bitter experience of the Civil War and the extended period of right wing dictatorship created conditions of deep resentment and battered pride far stronger than in the other two countries and these continue to shape the linguistic patterns and problems of Spain.

(2) Official policy: The Spanish constitution of 1978 specifies (Section 1) that Castilian is the official language of Spain and that all Spaniards have the duty to know it and the right to use it. Paragraph 2 of the constitution confirms that the other languages of Spain will be co-official in the different autonomous communities in accordance with their statutes. Castilian is the only language used in the *Cortes Generales* (the central governing body in Madrid), apart from occasional exceptions in the Senate (web site, *Université Laval*, <u>Spain</u>, Section 5), and it is therefore the language of the courts, services, official media and public signage. According to the constitution, only Catalan, Galician and Basque, of the regional languages, may, in certain circumstances, be used in public by the local administrations. Spain is therefore, by its constitution, a mainly monolingual country. The king speaks to his people in Castilian but, as a matter of political expediency, uses Catalan when he speaks officially in Catalonia.

The co-existence of two official languages in some of the Spanish regions does not always operate smoothly. A judgment in the Spanish equivalent of the High Court in 1986 ruled that in the communities with two official languages, citizens have the right to use either of them in communication with the devolved services of the Spanish state and in the law courts. This was enshrined in law in 1992 (Law No. 30/1992). The laws giving the autonomous communities the right to use two languages date from the 1980s (web site, EFNIL, <u>Spain</u>) and a guiding principle since then has been that civil servants working for the central government in one of the autonomous two-language communities must speak both the languages, although there appears to be no routine check on this and the principle is frequently not strictly applied. The 1992 law reinforces the ruling that the linguistic rights of the citizen take precedence over the rights of the employees of the state. In spite of all these protective measures, and references in many articles of the constitution to the equality of all citizens (Articles 14, 510, 511, 512, 515 for example), there is a considerable difference between the spirit and the application of such measures. The situation is worse for the Basque- and Galician-speaking minorities than for the Catalan speakers whose relatively high numbers and valuable contribution to the economy of Spain give them a high profile and greater political power.

(3) Other linguistic agencies: The royal decree of 1714 that sanctioned the creation of the *Real Academia Española* was an important indication of the determination in Spain to protect and promote Castilian. The interests of the *Academia*, in contrast to the Royal Society and the French *Académie royale des sciences*, were, like those of the *Crusca* and the *Académie française*, to be confined to purely linguistic matters. The

Spanish academicians, unlike the members of the *Académie française*, included linguists and philologists so that its pronouncements are usually treated with respect by professional linguists. Paradoxically it was Philip V who gave royal approval for the *Academia* in 1714, and he spoke only French. The *Academia* retained the word *real* (royal) in its title and, apart from the Franco years, it has had royal protection ever since. Its stated aims closely echo those of the *Crusca* and the *Académie française*: '*fijar las voces y vocablos de la lengua castellana en su mayor propriedad, eleganza y pureza*' (to fix the words and terms of the Castilian language in their greatest accuracy, elegance and purity) (web site, *Real Academia Española, Breve historia, Origen y fines (Short History, Creation and Aims)*). This royal support for Castilian has had a profound influence on its continuing acceptance as the official language of Spain.

With its long history and royal prestige, the *Academia* has continued to work, very much like the *Académie française* and the *Crusca*, to protect the national language. Like the other two academies, the *Real Academia Española* has a reputation for what is regarded by many as excessive conservatism and it is frequently criticised as being too centred, administratively and linguistically, on Madrid. It has, however, introduced grammatical and spelling changes from time to time and its main concern in the 21st century is less with the '*mayor propriedad, eleganza y pureza*' of the language than with adapting it to the demands of the modern world. Like the *Académie française*, its members (46) are mainly authors, each elected to a numbered seat for life.

In addition it has 'corresponding members' in Spain and abroad, a number of honorary members and close links with over 20 related academies for the Spanish language throughout the world (web site, *Enciclopedia Libre Universal en Español* (Free Universal Encyclopedia in Spanish)). In its early days it published the first edition of its dictionary (1726–1739), a definitive spelling guide (1741) and a grammar (1771). In addition to other publications, it continues to issue new editions of the dictionary. The twenty-first edition (2001) is available free on-line (web site, *Real Academia Español* <u>Dictionary</u>) and in a CD-ROM version. This is an indication of the way the *Academia* is adapting to the modern world.

It was not until 1991 that the other official organisation for the promotion and teaching of Spanish, the *Instituto Cervantes* (web site), was created. The Institute, like the *Alliance française*, the Goethe Institute and the Dante Alighieri Society, organises courses in Spanish, trains teachers, provides teaching materials, promotes Spanish at home and abroad and is involved in various cultural programmes. Its honorary president is the king and it is funded by the Ministry of Foreign Affairs and the Ministry of Education. A notable aspect of the work of the Cervantes Institute is its very extensive web site, the *Centro Virtual Cervantes* giving a comprehensive coverage of many aspects of Spanish language and culture, from up-to-date information on the triennial government-funded Spanish Language Congresses (the most recent was in September 2004) to the contents of the Prado Museum and advice on taking the pilgrim route to Santiago de Compostela.

In addition to these two national organisations, there are also, because of the particular importance of the regional languages in Spain, defensive and promotional institutions for Catalan, Galician and Basque. To take the example of Catalonia again, the Catalan government has a well-developed programme of language promotion. In collaboration with no fewer than 80 different associations (not all exclusively concerned with the language), it has launched a language volunteer programme to help new arrivals to learn Catalan and it actively promotes the use of Catalan in commerce and industry. Similar initiatives for Basque and Galician bear witness to a determination to make regional languages the fundamental cohesive force in the autonomous communities.

With all this language ferment in Spain, it is natural that there should also be numerous private and fringe groups engaged on what they may see as the language 'battlefield' where Castilian and the regional languages confront one another. Interestingly, many of the 'warriors' on both sides are located in Catalonia. Groups supporting the national language are worried, like similar groups in France, about the strength of support for the regional languages. They feel that these languages are a threat to national unity and diminish the rights of the majority – that is, the monolingual speakers of Castilian. One of the most vociferous of these organisations is the FADICE (*Federación de Asociaciones por el Derecho al Idioma Común Español* or 'Association Federation to have the right to use the common Spanish language [*sic*]' (see web site). It has its headquarters in the *Acción Cultural Miguel de Cervantes* in Barcelona. Another indication of the linguistic turmoil in Catalonia is the fact that the 1996 International Declaration of Linguistic Rights (see web site) originated with the Barcelona PEN Centre. The Declaration brought together an amazing collection of fighters for minority and regional languages, including such surprising names as Nelson Mandela, Yasser Arafat and Noam Chomsky.

Of the four countries, Spain is perhaps the closest to France in the degree of official support given to the national language. Mainly as a result of the very considerable autonomy of the Spanish communities, the regional languages, particularly Catalan, are much stronger and more closely entwined with national politics than is the case in France.

(4) The European context and minority languages: In Europe, Spain is one of 17 countries to have signed (1992), ratified (2001) and enforced

the legislation (2001) in the European Charter for Regional or Minority Languages. As in France, the strength of the regional languages to some extent obscures the problems with minority and immigrant languages in Spain. Apart from Basque, Catalan and Galician, mainly confined to specific geographic regions, with their own government and a considerable degree of political influence, there are other languages, some of them regional, some of them spoken by minorities distributed throughout Spain: Andalusian; Arabic; Aragonese; Asturian; Extremaduran; Judaeo-Spanish; Occitan (or Aranese); Rom, the language of gypsies. Although covered in theory by the provisions in the constitution, these languages do not receive the same attention and are considerably less well protected than the main regional languages (web site, _Université Laval_, Spain, Section 3).

A recent development, and one which is the fruit of ongoing political activity in favour of the regional languages of Spain, is the decision of the EU Committee of the Regions in November 2005 to allow Catalan, Basque and Galician to be used, for the first time, in a European institution. It remains to be seen if this will be extended to other European institutions. There are already concerns being expressed about the extra strain this will represent on scarce EU language resources.

Spain, through the _Real Academia Española_, is an active member of EFNIL, but it has not brought cases involving language to the European court and does not follow the French example of using the provisions of European law to protect its official language and ensure its use in European institutions. The strength of Spanish as a world language, its well-established network of academies throughout the world and its intense involvement in internal language policies mean that its language activities cover a wide area extending far beyond Europe.

(5) Current issues and problems: Although much of the available energy in Spain is expended on internal language questions, there are nevertheless signs that the dominance of English causes concern. In November 2006, _Spanglish_ (also the title of a 2004 film about Spanish in the US) had almost 3,000,000 Google responses and _Espanglish_ over 90,000. This arouses a considerable amount of largely wry comment, particularly in the Americas, but, unlike the French, Spanish speakers do not seem to judge it to be an issue for which they would go to the stake. Another hotly-debated issue in France, _la feminización de las profesiones_ (the feminisation of job titles), has met a more pragmatic reaction in Spain. Rather than calling forth the full repressive might of official language organisations, Spanish speakers throughout the world appear, after heated discussions, to have accepted the use of masculine and feminine job titles (except where the feminine form already had another meaning). In texting and in e-mails,

some Spaniards seem to have found a highly imaginative solution to this problem: the use of the now ubiquitous @ (arobase) symbol in the endings of words to replace both 'a' (feminine) and 'o' (masculine), so creating a new gender-neutral form (*L'Express*, 2004a).

In spite of sometimes bitter arguments about language and languages, the people of Spain give the impression that they are confident in their language and not anguished about its takeover by English. It is to English that we turn finally in the attempt to situate the French and their language in relation to their nearest European neighbours.

The United Kingdom and English: *vieux compagnons de route*

(1) Historical and political factors: Comparing France and the United Kingdom brings a new dimension to this chapter. Here it is not so much a question of comparing neighbour with neighbour as of looking at arch rivals whose long love/hate relationship is a matter of historical record (Baugh & Cable, 1993: 105–151). The English and French languages are, as Henriette Walter (1997: 217) says, old travelling companions and they have had a long and well-documented *histoire d'amour* (love affair) (Walter, 2001a: 11). Like very old friends or members of the same family, their long co-habitation means that they sometimes seem to take pleasure in even the bitterest of confrontations and their very public differences are enjoyed by many spectators. The battle has been transferred across the Atlantic and it finds its most extreme expression in the language politics of Quebec.

In England, from the time of the Norman Conquest in 1066, Anglo-French was the language of the court and the administration, and therefore effectively the official language (Baugh & Cable, 1993: 105), although the people in the countryside continued to use Anglo-Saxon and in church administration Latin was used. The English kings all spoke French until Henry IV (1399–1413), the first native speaker of English to rule the country, came to the throne. The Hundred Years War (1337–1453) was fought over French territory and the two opposing kings spoke French. Fiercely nationalist sentiment, exacerbated by the intervention of Jeanne d'Arc (Walter, 2001a: 12), developed on both sides during this long and destructive confrontation. By the end of the war in the mid-15th century Anglo-Saxon and Franco-Norman had merged in England to form the beginnings of modern English. This is a language that has shown a remarkable ability to absorb elements of other languages and still has parallel lexical strands derived from its main constituent languages.

The expansion of the territory ruled by the French/English king was gradual: Ireland had come under the authority of Henry II by 1171; England

and Wales have been united since 1542; the English and Scottish crowns were united in 1603 and the parliaments a century later in 1707. Meanwhile as an indication of the progress of English as the official language of the British Isles, the Statute of Pleading had established an early form of English as the language of the courts in 1362, the University of Oxford had taught in English from 1349 and from 1417 all the official correspondence of King Henry V changed suddenly to be written exclusively in English rather than French (web site, Webster's Dictionary, <u>Brief History (1989)</u>). The overpowering political dominance of England and the long history of shared government and a single language are largely responsible for the virtually unquestioned acceptance throughout the realm of a single dialect of English in administration and the law. Regional languages continued to be used in private and in unofficial circumstances.

In Britain, but to a lesser extent than in France, progress towards a single language was also hastened by attempts to annihilate the regional languages and dialects, particularly in Wales but also in Scotland and Ireland. The dominance of English was so complete that no government in London has felt threatened by the continued existence of other languages and dialects. Nevertheless resentment remains, as is shown by the strength of the Welsh Language Society, the strong support for political devolution and developments in the Scottish Parliament and the Welsh Assembly in favour of regional languages.

The next stage in the expansion of English came with the industrial revolution and the resultant economic power of Great Britain. This in turn led to the growth of the British empire whose greatest export was probably the English language. The emergence of English as the dominant world language in the 20th and 21st centuries came originally as the result of the might of the British empire, which established English in India, Africa and the Far East, so making it a world language (Baugh & Cable, 1993: 283–285). The dominance of English has since been confirmed and expanded by the vast economic and intellectual power wielded by Britain's former colony, the United States, and earlier sections have shown that American English is now the focus of most of the sometimes virulent anti-English language sentiments expressed in France today.

While Britain's imperial policy led to the spread of English throughout the world and ultimately the dominance of English as a world language, it also had, in the 20th century, a paradoxical linguistic outcome. With the influx of migrants from the former colonies into the United Kingdom came the problem of so-called 'ethnic (or immigrant) languages': Urdu, Hindi, Punjabi for example. Speakers of these languages now form vociferous minorities who seek official recognition for their languages. There is a similar problem in France, particularly with the immigrants from North Africa.

In spite of the present-day evidence of the fragmentation and impoverishment of English, those who speak it as their native language have never felt that it is threatened and are often unable to sympathise with its victims, with those who are convinced that English is destroying their language and their identity. Curiously it appears to be only in the United States that there is any perception that the dominance of English may be at risk and here Spanish is seen as the danger. It is interesting to observe that the various groups fighting in the US for 'English Only' legislation have, in their attitudes and confrontational language, much in common with some of the defensive groups in France.

(2) Official policy: Given the historical and political background briefly described above, it is understandable that there is no document establishing English as the official language in the United Kingdom. Without a written constitution and with a legal system relying on jurisprudence rather than legal codes, Britain differs markedly from the three continental countries in this chapter. There has been a number of laws relating to language passed in England and in Wales in the last 10 years (Barbour, 2000: 40–43; web sites, EFNIL; *Université Laval*, Wales, Section 3). As might be expected, since the official language is in no way perceived to be under threat, such language laws as are enacted in England deal not with English but with the situation in Wales, Scotland and Northern Ireland and they are confined to the regional rather than the ethnic languages. There is nevertheless a degree of government intervention in language matters, as evidenced by debates over the 'standard language' in the 1980s (Crowley, 1989: 269–274). Similarly the various parliamentary enquiries before the introduction of the national curriculum in England and Wales (Crowley, 2003) show that British politicians, like their French counterparts, are well aware of the power of language in 'reorganising the cultural hegemony' (Gramsci, quoted in Crowley, 1989: 274).

(3) Other linguistic agencies: The only official agency to promote English is the British Council. Founded in 1934, its original purpose was 'the promotion of British culture, education, science and technology in other countries, along the lines of existing French, German and Italian cultural organisations' (web site, British Council). Unlike these other organisations, the British Council did not refer explicitly in its founding statements to the promotion of the language. It was set up and partly funded by the Foreign Office so, from the beginning, was strongly influenced by government policy although it was technically responsible for its own policy and activities. It worked at first through British Embassies and High Commissions and then had its own offices. Like the *Alliance française* and the *Goethe Institut*, its development in recent years has mirrored shifts in foreign policy, with the current emphasis being on Eastern European

and Asian countries. Although set up in response to a perceived need to spread democratic values in the face of political developments elsewhere, particularly in Germany, it has inevitably become the international face of the British version of the English language and is associated in the minds of many with linguistic imperialism (Grillo, 1989; Phillipson, 1992). This fate has largely been avoided by the *Alliances françaises*: they have always been locally governed institutions and have retained, at least until recent times, a considerable degree of independence from the French government.

The much earlier moves in other European countries to control their language by setting up academies had not passed unnoticed in Britain. Throughout the 18th century discussion raged over whether or not there should be an Academy for English on similar lines to the *Académie française* (Baugh & Cable, 1993: 256–266). In 1712, Swift sent a pamphlet to the 'Lord High Treasurer of Great Britain'. Its title, 'A Proposal for Correcting, Improving and Ascertaining the English Tongue', is reminiscent of the aims of the continental academies (Crowley, 1991: 28, 31). No agreement could be reached and the English Academy was never formed (Ager, 1996; Baugh and Cable, 264–265). The great lexicographer Dr Samuel Johnson was against the creation of an academy, but when in 1755 he produced his famous dictionary, it was with virtually the same aims (Crowley, 1991: 42). Johnson has been described as a one-man English Academy (Walter, 1994: 483). The lexicographical tradition he began, one of openness to new words, encyclopedic knowledge and wit, continued in subsequent dictionaries, notably the *Oxford English Dictionary* (see web site) but also in other influential dictionaries of English such as the *Chambers Dictionary* (see web site) and, in a more conservative and repressive vein, the American *Webster's Dictionary of English Usage* (since 1843: *Merriam-Webster* (web site, *Webster's Dictionary*, <u>Merriam-Webster</u>)).

The *Oxford English Dictionary* was born as a result of an initiative of the Philological Society of London in 1857. In 1879 the Society came to an agreement with the Oxford University Press to begin work on a *New English Dictionary* (later to become the *Oxford English Dictionary*). The last volume of the first edition was published in 1928. After the publication of several supplements, the second edition appeared in 1989 and the CD-ROM version in 1992. It is 'an irreplaceable part of English [*sic*] culture'; it continues to demonstrate a 'commitment to the cultural values embodied in the dictionary' and is 'not only an important record of the evolution of [the] language, but also documents the continuing development of [. . .] society' (web site, *Oxford English Dictionary*). Although it is a commercial enterprise, its web site affirms that: 'At no period in its history has the *Oxford English Dictionary* been profitable commercially for Oxford University Press.'

Although, as Ager (1997: 43) points out, in most European countries the publishing industry is 'completely free of State influence, and it is the general consensus of the industry itself that maintains language norms, in much the same way that the speech community does', dictionaries exercise a normative function. In the absence of an accepted arbiter such as the *Académie française*, the role of dictionaries, particularly the *Oxford English Dictionary*, in celebrating, protecting and promoting the English language is extremely important (Crowley, 1989: 107–110). It is also apparent in Germany that the role of a national dictionary can be crucial. This is perhaps less obvious in the countries where an official body takes decisions on language change.

Other organisations have been set up from time to time to protect or promote the English language (Wardhaugh, 1987: 128–140). Notable among these are the Society for Pure English (1913–1946) whose tracts were influential and whose aims were less conservative than the title suggests, and the English-speaking Union (founded in 1918). The aims of this government-supported organisation were originally confined to the 'English-Speaking democracies', and to improving understanding between the British Commonwealth and the United States. Since 1975 it has also taken an interest in speakers of English as a second language. It is now active in Hungary, Belgium and France for example and states that its mission is to 'promote international understanding and human achievement through the English language' (web site, English-Speaking Union). The BBC (both radio and television) also has considerable importance in spreading and in protecting the language.

Like other European languages, English has also aroused fervent, if sometimes linguistically naive, support from a number of fringe purist groups but it is probably fair to say that, apart from the *Oxford English Dictionary*, the role of guardian of the language is played by letters to *The Times* and other newspapers, where there is frequent, heated and not always irrelevant debate on matters related to the use of English. Journalistic language is subject to a degree of control through the newspapers' style guides and through the frequently uninhibited criticism of readers.

(4) The European context and minority languages: The growing dominance of English in Europe and in the institutions of the European Union means that there is no obvious need for the United Kingdom to participate in the various groups defending the use of a variety of official languages in the Union. The United Kingdom was nonetheless an early member of EFNIL. The organisation representing English in that body is the *Oxford English Dictionary* and this confirms the important, although non-official, role of the dictionary as the arbiter of the language.

As far as regional and minority languages are concerned, the United

Kingdom, because of the activities of the IRA, waited until after devolution in 1998, and signed the European Charter on Regional and Minority Languages in 2000. In 2001 it both ratified and legislated for the provisions of the Charter. The absence of acute concern about this matter is in stark contrast to the French reaction. Rather than seeing the recognition of regional and minority languages as a threat, the British were not convinced that there was any urgency about the question.

The regional languages of Wales, Scotland and Northern Ireland have nevertheless been an increasing problem for the Westminster government. This is borne out by the list of laws enacted, beginning with the Welsh Courts Act in 1942 and culminating in the granting of greater autonomy to Scotland (1997), Wales (1998) and Northern Ireland (1998). All three have seen, notably since the Second World War, mounting pressure for independence or at least an increased degree of self-government and this has involved moves to defend and promote the regional languages. There has been a degree of violence involved in all these independence movements and all have, to a greater or lesser extent, made claims for increased use and protection of the traditional languages. The degree of devolution is different in each of the three countries, but all are now free to enact language policies appropriate to their particular situation. The languages involved go far beyond the 'indigenous minority languages' to include 'ethnic minority languages' and sign languages. The enactment by the United Kingdom of the European Charter on Regional and Minority Languages has, as many of the French fear it would do in France, given a new impetus to the activists; in the constituent countries of the kingdom it has aroused a new pro-European stance and support for a Europe of the Regions. It has encouraged an increasing appreciation of the political possibilities of defending linguistic diversity through European legislation in all member countries.

In Wales, although Welsh has been a second official language since the Welsh Language Act of 1993 (web site, Wales, <u>Welsh Language Act</u>), the Assembly is now considering strengthening the provisions of the Act. There are moves in the Scottish Parliament (see the 2003 report of an inquiry into the languages of Scotland (web site, Scotland, <u>Languages</u>)) to legislate for a wide-ranging language policy that differentiates between Gaelic and Scots (not described as minority languages) and (ethnic) minority languages. In Northern Ireland the government Department of Culture, Arts and Leisure (web site, Northern Ireland, <u>Languages</u>) has an active programme to promote all the languages other than English spoken in the province.

The unspoken background to all this activity is the unquestioning acceptance of English as the single language of the majority of the citizens of the whole kingdom.

(5) Current issues and problems: There is very little sign that speakers of English in the United Kingdom are seriously concerned about the proliferation of amalgams of English with the various European languages, but *le franglais* in particular is a frequent source of amusement in the press. Native speakers of British English are more likely to become agitated about the fate of the apostrophe (Truss, 2003) than about the invasion of their language by a neighbouring tongue. The versions of English used on the web – Globish or Netlingo – may provoke wry comment, but most English speakers are almost entirely, even arrogantly, unaware of the possibility of any threat to their language. They may be overly confident in the unshakeable position of English as the dominant world language. Many linguists and commentators (for example Graddol, 2004, 2006; Leclerc, 2005; Schmid, 2004) point out that there are signs that English is 'past its sell-by date', that it is fragmenting and that it cannot remain forever in its present powerful position. Speakers of English are on the whole quite unprepared to envisage this possibility and are thus at the opposite end of the spectrum from those French speakers who are prone to see threats to their language at every turn.

Conclusions

So how do these neighbour countries shape up in the examination of the historical and political factors that have influenced their languages and language policies? In spite of a number of striking similarities, particularly between the continental countries, there are very clear and in some cases dramatic and telling differences between them (Table 5.2, below). Their shared past has produced individual histories. These differ sharply and the passing similarities between them are outweighed by their distinctive and proudly cherished individuality, not only in matters of language.

In some ways France, in its attitude to its language, sets itself apart from the other four countries. It has the longest tradition of highly centralised government and by far the longest history of state intervention in language matters. Its history has not favoured the emergence of strong regional distinctions within the centralised state and this distinguishes it from all the others. The French language has been consciously used as a political force at least since the time of François Ier and as the French cherished and perfected it, it became the pride and glory of those who spoke it, the evidence – at least in the 17th and 18th centuries – of their cultural and intellectual superiority and the guarantee of the unity of the nation. Such attitudes do not necessarily disappear when circumstances change, and so it is plain that the history of the French and their language goes some way towards explaining present-day attitudes and expectations.

Table 5.2 Language Protection and Promotion in Europe: Comparison between France, Germany, Italy, Spain and the United Kingdom

	Academy	Date	Other official agencies	Date	Protective law	EFNIL member/s	ECRML Signed	Ratified	Law
France	*Académie française*, Paris	1647–	*Alliance française* CTT HCLF ACCT Francophonie DGLF(LF)	1881 1933 1966 1970 1986 1989	*Loi Deixonne* 1951 *Loi Bas–Lauriol* 1975 *Loi Toubon* 1994	DGLFLF	1999		
Germany	*Fruchtbringende Gesellschaft*, Weimar	1617-1700?	*Goethe Institut*	1947		IDS	1992	1998	1999
Italy	*Accademia della Crusca*, Florence	1582–	*Società Dante Alighieri*	1889		*Crusca* OVI	2000		
Spain	*Real Academia Española*, Madrid	1713–	*Instituto Cervantes*	1991		RAE	1992	2001	2001
UK			British Council	1934		OED	2000	2001	2001

Notes:

ACCT	*Agence de coopération culturelle et technique* (Paris)
Crusca	*Accademia della Crusca* (Florence)
CTT	*Commission de terminologie technique* (Paris)
DGLFLF	*Délégation générale à la langue française et aux langues de France* (Paris)
ECRML	European Charter for Regional and Minority Languages
EFNIL	European Federation of National Institutions for Language
HCLF	*Haut comité de la langue française* (Paris)
IDS	*Institut für Deutsche Sprache* (Mannheim)
OED	Oxford English Dictionary (Oxford University Press, Oxford)
OVI	*Opera del Vocabolario Italiano* (Florence)
RAE	*Real Academia Española* (Madrid)

The plethora of official pronouncements, laws and decrees relating to the language in France has no parallel in the other four countries. The official language is enshrined only in the constitutions of France and Spain and none of the other countries has anything to compare with the *Loi Toubon*. From time to time the groups trying to protect the official language in other countries (but not of course in Britain) speak longingly of the need for such a law but, as for example in the case of Italy, most people are very wary about state intervention in language protection. The massive and convoluted structure of agencies in France involved in the implementation of the *Loi Toubon* is therefore unique. There is no parallel for the multiple and far-reaching activities of the DGLF or the CSLF.

La Francophonie, the worldwide geo-political group based on shared values through language and similar cultural and political aspirations has some similarities with groups for speakers of English, of Spanish and of Portuguese, and with the more politically oriented Arab League. Other groups of nations in the world, for example in Africa, South America and the Asia-Pacific region, do not share a language but seek increased strength based on geographical proximity. *La Francophonie* may not be unique, but the extent of official French government involvement and investment is not paralleled in the other countries. (The close grouping of the Spanish academies across the world is a non-political structure, devoted mainly to the study and protection of the Spanish language.) It is in the area of official, legal and constitutional protection of French that the difference between the countries is greatest.

The closest similarity between them is probably in the various cultural institutes set up by each of these countries throughout the world. The *Alliance française*, the *Goethe Institut*, the *Società Dante Alighieri*, the *Instituto Cervantes* and the British Council work in broadly similar ways and there is usually no spirit of competition between them. Indeed, they are increasingly to be found working together in cities where several of them are present. In the case of the recent close collaboration between the *Alliance française* and the *Goethe Institut*, this reflects the closer relations between the French and German governments in the 21st century. Cynics might say it also reflects the increasing intervention of governments as the paymasters in the policies and activities of their cultural institutions.

All these countries (except the United Kingdom) are pro-active in the promotion of linguistic and cultural diversity in the European Union and are concerned to promote the use of their language in the various working groups in Brussels and Strasbourg. The French though are most likely to take initiatives – EFNIL for example – and resent more bitterly than the others the decreasing use of their language in the Union. As far as minority and regional languages are concerned, only Germany, Spain and the

United Kingdom have enacted the provisions of the European Charter for Regional and Minority Languages. In all five countries minority language groups, particularly separatist groups, having agitated with such determination for the Charter, have been quick to gain whatever advantage they can from its provisions. In this the United Kingdom does not differ from the other countries. Only in France has there been a continuing legal struggle leading to a decision by the courts that the terms of the Charter are contrary to the constitution. But the degree of opposition in France to the Charter has perhaps been exaggerated by the publicity given to the legal action. Opinion polls have consistently shown that a majority – even an increasing majority – is in favour of the enactment in France of its provisions. Opponents see this as proof of fecklessness and naivety and insufficient concern for the future of the threatened French language, and indeed the Republic, but this view is not universal.

Since speakers of French, German, Italian and Spanish all feel to some degree threatened by the spread of English, it is predictable that there will be, in the four non-English-speaking countries, a shared mistrust of English and of those who speak it, particularly on the other side of the Atlantic. To varying degrees they are concerned at the invasion of their language by English words, at the development of interface languages such as Denglish or Spanglish and at the loss of diversity and richness that would follow a total domination by English. In Germany, Italy and Spain the linguistic issues most likely to preoccupy average citizens are those related to their own language. Nevertheless the increasing perception that the disappearance of languages constitutes a damaging impoverishment of the human species is behind much of the united effort to ensure a pluri- and multi-lingual future for Europe. Here again France is more sharply outspoken than other countries, apparently seeing no contradiction between leading the struggle for the maintenance of the languages of Europe while lagging behind other countries in the preservation of its own minority and heritage languages.

So the answers to the questions: 'Are the highly developed structures and strategies for the defence of French unique?' and 'Do they really exist in isolation from language policies in the rest of Europe?' are not entirely straightforward. The comparison has shown that it is true to say that the linguistic structures and strategies for the defence of French are unique and sometimes dramatically different from those to be found in neighbouring countries. The existence of the *Loi Toubon*, of the DGLFLF, of the *Commissions de terminologie*, all support the view that France has taken a different route from the other countries. In answer to the second question, these activities do not and could not exist entirely in isolation from the policies in other European countries. A shared history going back over the centuries has shaped the languages of Europe and resulted in a network of linguistic and political influences. Recent developments in the European Union and the heightened awareness of the political potential of languages have brought the member nations closer together as they seek to ensure a future for their languages in a multi- and pluri-lingual Europe, part of a globalised world. The creation of the group of francophone countries is certainly a uniquely French achievement but in the European Union the linguistic activities of France depend to a very considerable extent on the support and understanding of old and valued neighbours.

Chapter 6

Problems and Paradoxes; Interference and Interaction

Cross-currents in the Resistance Movement

In considering how French is defended, various potential problems and apparent contradictions have emerged. This is not necessarily surprising, since France is a nation that prides itself on its fierce individuality and prizes independence of thought and action. The French also typically hold strongly argued and hotly defended positions on language. For pragmatic Anglo-Saxons the problem with these is their impracticality. Is the language really best protected by a variety of defenders at odds with one another? Does the full gamut of weaponry, from traditional government *dirigisme* to Internet chat rooms, achieve any of its multiple aims or do the many different forms of defence actually work against one another, limiting their effectiveness and making the future of the language more rather than less uncertain?

Before coming to any conclusions about these and other questions (such as whether there is in fact a crisis or any need for linguistic resistance in France), this chapter looks more closely at some of the problems and contradictions already uncovered and assesses their importance. Which of the many areas of conflict are to be taken seriously? Are some of the activities of the linguistic resistance founded on myths or are they, as the activists proclaim, a noble response to a real threat, one the French nation ignores at its peril? All of these questions (and many more) have been raised in sometimes heated and always passionate discussions with friends, colleagues and specialists in France, the United Kingdom and Australia during the writing of this book.

Two important areas where there are obvious paradoxes are French policies on regional and minority languages (Chapter 2, pp. 29–43, Chapter 4, pp. 90–94) and attitudes to European Union policies on languages (Chapter 2, pp. 34–45). The Introduction recalled that many of the confrontations over language are binary, and divide and polarise the defenders: tradition and modernity seem to be opposite poles, state inter-ventionism and free development divide the nation, the French tradition of government by the élite appears to conflict with the commitment to democracy. The first of these confrontations is examined in more detail in the next section of this chapter. Developing some of the trains of thought from Chapter 4, the third section then deals with some of the political ambiguities in the area of language policy and at the end of this chapter, in the fourth section, comes the vital but very difficult question: What is the relationship between the French language and French identity?

A number of other important questions could be the subject of a complementary study. Many of them are linguistic. Reference has already been made, for example, when speaking about the *Commissions de terminologie* (Chapter 3, p. 64), to the tendency for defenders of French to equate language and vocabulary. As long ago as Du Bellay's *Deffence et illustration*, words were being taken as a reliable indicator of the state of the language. The *Académie* concentrates almost exclusively on its dictionary to the exclusion of other, and arguably more important work on the structure of the language. A glance at the lengthy list of legal measures concerning the language passed in France in the 20th century shows that virtually all of them refer only to words. The massive effort put into official attempts to create French terminology bears witness to a widespread belief, in France as elsewhere, that a language is essentially a collection of words. Public pronouncements about the language also tend to make the words = language equation, for example in François Mitterrand's famous adaptation of Mistral: *'un peuple qui perd ses mots n'est plus un peuple libre'* (a people that loses its words is no longer a free people) (Dargent, 2004a: 7). Many of the articles aired on *Voxlatina* make the same assumption and Dargent gives it strong endorsement in his editorial in *Libres No. 2*, the journal of the Gaullist organisation *Cercle Jeune France*. This issue of the journal is entitled *Géopolitique de la langue française* with Dargent's editorial headed: *Retrouver nos mots, rester libres* (Retrieve our words, remain free) (Dargent, 2004a: 7). There is no doubt that it is easier, particularly for non-linguists, to observe and document changes in words than in syntax or other aspects of a language and this may explain why it is that worries about the French language are almost always restricted to the way the vocabulary is changing.

Linguists are necessarily aware that a language is much more than its words. Changes are to be expected and even welcomed in the word base of a language: *'un emprunt . . . constitue toujours un enrichissement'* (a borrowing is always an enrichment) (Walter, 1994: 505). The structural changes, the moves in syntax, in the underlying patterns of a language, are much more insidious and difficult to observe, but they reveal far more about the health of a language. Calvet (1999: 258) points out that concentrating exclusively on words leads to a '*croisade contre les emprunts*' (a crusade against borrowings) and gives a delusion of protective action which is almost certainly self-defeating. To go to battle over words is to mistake the symptom for the disease: '*si maladie il y a*' (if disease there be) and he questions, as we all must, the wisdom and the efficacy of the cumbersome government terminology agencies. It is certainly not obvious that official efforts to impose a French (as opposed in most cases to an Anglo-American) terminology have seriously stemmed the tide of borrowing. Further, all this energy could probably be better used in defending, or in promoting the language in other ways.

Another aspect of the language it would be interesting to explore is the tension between the language of culture and the popular language. This is reinforced (Bengtsson, 1968: 10) by the widening gap between the written and the spoken forms, very strongly marked in French. Martinet (1962) and Gilder (1993) both note this phenomenon, but draw radically different conclusions for the future of French. This tension is closely related to the *marché aux langues* (language market) (Bourdieu, 1982; Calvet, 2002(a); Schiffman, 2000). Then there are the intricate questions of intrinsic and extrinsic factors in language change, decline and death. For some defenders of French, still under the spell of the 18th century and Rivarol (Chapter 1, p. 6; Chapter 3, p. 55), French has a universal humanising, civilising mission and possesses intrinsic qualities distinguishing it from other languages. According to this view, the French language is, by its very nature, destined to play a role in world events and any attempt to undermine it must be vigorously opposed. Linguists take a different view and see, as they observe changes in language patterns in the world, that the influence of any language at a particular stage in world history has less to do with its intrinsic qualities than with other aspects of human history, notably political and economic power. Martinet (1962) makes this case powerfully as does Calvet (1999). This leads back to the ideas of Bourdieu and Schiffman and the concept of an interplay of sociological, economic and political forces having very little to do with the nature of language but everything to do with the way nations and societies operate.

There is yet another worrying puzzle in relation to language. Many of the defenders, not only those on *Voxlatina*, state explicitly that what worries them most about the dominance of English, apart from the effect this will have on French, is the concomitant imposition throughout the world of one culture and one world view. The assumption is that all those who speak a language necessarily share one point of view and one culture (Calvet, 2004: 35). Therefore, if English dominates the globalised world, this will be an intellectually and culturally impoverished world where it will no longer be possible for differences of opinion to exist or be expressed. *Voxlatina* furnishes many expressions of this idea. The most extreme of these attribute to the United States an explicit and aggressive single language policy, an arm of its political aim of world dominance. To take just one example by one of the most outspoken of the anti-American defenders, Durand (2002) writes in his book *La Manipulation mentale par la destruction des langues* (Mental Manipulation by the Destruction of Languages): 'the push for the use of a single language . . . promotes the rise of a single mode of thought which has the potential, eventually, to become a single power, that is, a dictatorship'.[70]

This prompts some further reflections. How do comments such as these sit with the long-standing French policy of a single national language? While there is some evidence that speakers of a language do tend to share a common set of values, it is surely simplistic to assume that their thought patterns are inevitably identical in all respects. Do the people who promote the one language one culture idea really believe that all speakers of French are conditioned or condemned to share a single point of view? How, if that is so, is it possible to explain one of the outstanding features of French culture – the love of argument and verbal confrontation? If a language condemns all its speakers to a single mindset, how is it possible to explain the sometimes bitter disagreements between speakers of English in the United States and those in the United Kingdom or between different political groups in those countries? How can democracy operate in any country if, because there is one language, there is no possibility of opposing points of view?

The French historian and philosopher Ernest Renan, in his influential lecture: *Qu'est-ce qu'une nation ?* (What Is a Nation?) at the Sorbonne as long ago as 1882, explicitly refuted the idea that a language imposes a single pattern of thought on all its speakers. Arguing for a pluri-lingual France he turns the one language one mindset argument on its head and asks: '*Ne peut-on pas avoir les mêmes sentiments et les mêmes pensées, aimer les mêmes choses dans des langues différentes ?*' (Can one not have the same feelings and the same thoughts, love the same things in different languages?) (Renan, 1882).

Finally among the language problems is the question of what the defenders mean when they talk of saving 'French'. Those who cling to the idea of the universal mission of French are, it seems, unlikely to entrust this fore-ordained task to the French spoken in the *cités*, to *verlan*, to the French of the media, of rap, reggae, the Internet and texting. There are many defenders who feel that the present-day French language is a proof that the rot has set in, so far has the language strayed from the purity of its golden age and the 'perfection' of the 18th and 19th centuries. In this view, the language to be defended and imposed whatever its speakers may think is not a living language but an ideal. It alone is perfect, while all its realisations (particularly the modern ones) are simply imperfect shadows (Hobsbawm, 1990: 57).

On the other hand, many French people celebrate the vibrancy, the energy and the creativity of their language in the 21st century. They show little sign of a desire to join the resistance. The *résistants* bewail the lack of young people in their ranks but this is scarcely surprising when they are so critical of the present-day language, particularly the many forms of the spoken language used by the young. The gulf between the traditional and the modern forms of the language, between the spoken and the written language seems to be widening, and the resultant linguistic, cultural and generation gap is increasingly difficult to bridge. Identity (pp. 153–160), like the language, is not a monolithic, unchanging entity, the same for everyone who thinks of themselves as French. By assuming, as they seem to do, that a single French language and a single French identity are necessary in order to unite all citizens of the Republic, some of the defenders of the language are alienating the very people who can ensure its future. The *émeutes* (riots) of November 2005 have made this alienation very apparent.

The interplay between modernising forces and the weight of tradition, closely entwined with these questions of identity, is the subject of the next section.

Tradition and Modernity

The tension between the strength of tradition and the attraction of modernity is very marked in all European countries but nowhere more so than in France. All the features of French identity, including attitudes to the national language, are prey to this tension. Curiously, the attraction of the past, as both inspiration and model, is very clear in the most modern form of defence of the language, the Internet, and in particular on *Voxlatina*. As the Introduction and other sections have shown, the constant reference to past glories is almost a mantra intended no doubt to motivate modern speakers of the language by persistent references to a shared and glorious past. The importance of the past is emphasised by Flynn (1995) who entitles the first section of his book 'The weight of history in France today'. Citron (1991) takes issue with the overweening importance given by French historians to what she describes as a largely mythological vision of the past. But the continuing strength of the view she criticises is illustrated by Alfred Mignot (2001), founder of *Voxlatina*, web site of the FFI, speaking of *'une résistance digne des grandes heures du passé'* (a Resistance worthy of the great moments of the past) and the writer Alfred Gilder (2001), also on *Voxlatina*, evokes *'les grandes heures de notre passé'* (the great moments of our past). Such references occur constantly on *Voxlatina* and in the publications of the defensive organi-sations, as witness these extracts (Fleutot, 2005) from the *Tribune libre* of *Voxlatina* in January 2005:

> Our politicians should be aware that, for a people to be in touch with its roots, two essential things must be taught: its history and its language.[71]

> French, the French language, our common language, as good King Francis 1st wanted it to be, is now in grave danger![72]

Tradition, a proud history, awareness of past greatness, these exercise a powerful attraction on the French, especially in relation to their language. The linguistic pull of the past is not, however, a uniquely French phe-nomenon. The history of linguistics bears ample witness to the power apparently always exerted by the languages of the past. The European idea of an original, perfect language of which all later languages are but a flawed reflection, has been explored by Eco (1994) among others. It recurs in the work of many linguists (for example Calvet, 1999: 27), philosophers and would-be intellectuals and feeds a dissatisfaction with the present and a hunger for an earlier, more perfect world. Much of modern histori-cal linguistics is founded on this turning towards the past to explain the Babel of modern tongues. In a similar way, speakers of modern languages frequently hark back to a golden age when their language was unspoiled by the 'degeneracy' evident in modern times.

For the French, this tendency to refer to the linguistic glories of the past is particularly potent since there is ample evidence (Fumaroli, 2001, for example) that in earlier centuries the influence of French, mainly in Europe, was indeed widespread. The use of French throughout Europe by the cultivated élites of many nations, the formidable body of great litera-ture and powerful philosophical, political and scientific thought in French that dominated western thinking for so long, constitute a precious inher-itance and this cannot fail to have an impact on present-day users of the language.

But there is a price to pay for this awareness of former glory. It can also be a burden (Flynn, 1995), reinforcing feelings of failure and inadequacy. In this situation, the language, although it is only one of many forces in establishing the power and influence of a nation, can become a symbol for national prestige almost to the exclusion of other contributing factors. The symbolic status accorded to the national language is both a symptom and a cause of deep divisions in society. Looking back at the glories of their language, the French are reassured and comforted by the incontrovertible evidence of its greatness and tempted to think that the language in its modern form is unable to carry the burden of their lost grandeur. This in turn leads to wholesale condemnation of the modern forms of the language and renewed calls for 'purity', the catchword of language conservatives and academies throughout the ages.

This view, this return to a golden age, is found in many fields. It creates a potentially highly productive tension with another strong trend in French society – the modernising forces making France one of the most technologically advanced countries in the world. In the field of language, the tension has been less productive. Henriette Walter (1988: 341) sees the *Académie française* as the traditional pole and the advertising industry as the modernising, inventive pole in this unresolved binary tension. Harking back to the past specifically in terms of language is in direct opposition to the views of descriptive linguists, whose preoccupations with language are professional rather than political. For linguists language cannot be reduced to an historical artefact, a symbol of national identity. Its relationship to political realities or its usefulness as a diagnostic tool for the problems of the nation are not their main field of enquiry.

For both historical linguists and those concerned with the present state of the language, changes in language are a sign of life, an indication that the language is healthy enough to respond to the challenges of new developments in society. Descriptive linguists observe the changes in the French language with a good deal of pleasure and even pride, rejoicing in its vitality and resilience. They take the view that 'it [the language] will adapt or it will perish',[73] (Walter, 1988: 341). Other French commentators take the same view. Dargent (2004b: 56), for example, affirms that '[t]o maintain the 'purity' of the language is the best way to finish it off'.[74]

This point of view is echoed by Calvet (1999), Chaurand (1999), and many others. For defenders of French to hope that the language will not change and that a former state of linguistic glory can be somehow reinstated (and with it the power and influence of the nation) is entirely counter-productive. First, it is impossible to choose a specific state of the language, acceptable to all its defenders as the standard bearer of national identity and sovereignty. Second, it is the very ability of the language to change and adapt that will ensure that it survives. Atrophy is not an option. Even the much maligned *Académie française* has always, whatever its critics may say, admitted the inevitability of language change.

It may be a measure of the extent to which the language has been transformed in the thinking of the *résistants* from a living entity into a symbol of national identity that linguists are so rarely involved in the resistance movements, either as participants or consultants. Not only are they sometimes not included in the defensive work of government and other agencies, they can also be the target of bitter criticism from the *résistants* for their failure to nail their colours to the mast and publicly espouse the defensive cause. The tension between tradition and modernity inherent in all aspects of French society reveals itself here as two opposing attitudes to language: the purists and more outspoken defenders proclaim that adaptation is death while the linguists, rather less stridently, affirm the necessity for change if the language is to remain healthy. Sadly this does not seem to be a productive confrontation. It prevents cooperation and causes scarce resources to be wasted on a battle that need never be fought. Could it be time for a joint effort to establish what Gallo (2004) describes as *'la liaison organique, l'échange permanent entre Histoire et avenir'* (the organic connection, the permanent exchange between History and the future)?

Political Ambiguities

Among the many areas where language controversies arise in France, the political domain is, as Chapter 4 showed, a major locus of conflict. Problems with regional languages and in Europe have already been commented on. In both these cases the potential differences of opinion on language are largely political. There are (at least) three other more general problem areas where there is a potential for political disagreement on the subject of language, where conflicts between traditional attitudes and the imperatives of a modern European state can make defence of the language more difficult and can undermine it:

- state *dirigisme* and democracy;
- centralisation and devolution;
- élites and popular consensus.

The official solution proposed for each of these problems has been, as far as language is concerned, to promote a strongly defended centralist policy of monolingualism in direct conflict with modern efforts to make France a less highly centralised pluri- and multi-lingual state. The political fall-out in France from the government volte-face on the European Union Charter on Regional and Minority Languages (Chapter 2, p. 36; Chapter 4, p. 95) illustrated all three of these closely related tensions. Continuing battles over the role and the place of the regional languages show that the conflict still rages. The conflicting policies of *dirigisme* and democracy serve as an example of these confrontations.

State *dirigisme*, centralisation and government by élites all represent specifically French solutions to the difficulties of government. They have been arrived at over at least four centuries of centralised rule whether by a royal dynasty or a republic. The incompatibilities between these policies and modern political trends like democracy, decentralisation and consensus politics can, like the tension between tradition and modernity, be very productive in some fields. In others such as language policy they prevent an objective approach to language planning, frustrate the articulation of unambiguous policies, create confusion and foster an impression of muddle and uncertainty.

The long tradition of state intervention in language development and use has been described in earlier chapters, and the Introduction cast some doubt on its efficacy as a defensive measure. In the 21st century one of the main factors inhibiting its usefulness is the ever more pervasive influence of democratic ideals. While the kings, the revolutionaries and the republic (Chapter 4, pp. 82–90) could all plausibly defend their involvement in language defence and support for a single national language, the citizens, particularly those who speak more than one language, increasingly tend to see things in a different light. The stated purpose of the 1994 *Loi Toubon*, according to the DGLFLF and those whose job it is to interpret it and bring legal actions against offenders, is to ensure inclusiveness and prevent monolingual French citizens from being excluded from communications in a language other than French. The law therefore insists that a translation into French be provided for all public announcements in another language. On the face of it this is an admirable provision.

Nevertheless, in a democratic state citizens demand the right of free expression and this may include the use of other languages, particularly where cultural heritage and traditions are highly valued, where commercial interests are involved and where academic reputations are at stake. Personal interests (*liberté*) may be put ahead of *égalité* and of the interests of the state, and government intervention in language use is often resisted and resented. The lack of effective sanctions and the relatively low level of the fines it is possible to impose under the *Loi Toubon* are indications of the limited scope of government action (Chapter 1, p. 17; Chapter 2, pp. 26–28). Another indication of this is the decision by the *Conseil constitutionnel* that, as passed by the *Assemblée nationale*, the law can be applied only in certain areas of public life. It is possible, for example, for the government to insist on compliance with the law in its own departments but many other areas of language use, including the private media, are outside its control.

The carefully worded and extremely measured 'recommendation' issued in February 2005 by the CSA to all those involved in public and private broadcasting (web site, CSA French language) is a another indication of the limits of government action. Although this recommendation is hailed by *Voxlatina* as a 'denunciation of *franglais* in the media' it reads like the most tentative of suggestions. Even within the government, strict compliance with the *Loi Toubon* depends on the enthusiasm of heads of departments and this varies greatly. Furthermore it is virtually impossible to enforce the vast array of legal measures meant to ensure government control of language. There is a stark contrast between the extent of the legal measures available for the defence of the language and their success in stemming the tide of change.

Chapter 5 gave other examples in Europe of direct state intervention in language policy: in Germany, in Italy and in Spain. In those countries, and in others throughout the world, the governments which felt it necessary to elaborate and enforce strict controls on language have usually been extremist regimes of the far right. No doubt successive French governments have been able to argue that their involvement in language is justified since it is designed to ensure the 'conduct of government'. Hobsbawm (1990: 112) sees any government-imposed language policy as a form of 'social engineering' and Thody (1995: 68) finds uncomfortable parallels between government language policies and extremist regimes.

But it is not only pragmatic and laissez-faire Anglo-Saxons who have been critical of government manipulation of language. At the time of the passage of the *Loi Toubon*, there was considerable concern expressed. Both the French press and the opposition parties in the *Assemblée nationale* saw dangers in a law allowing so significant an increase in government intervention in language matters. This was also expressed for example by Calvet (1999: 260–262) who felt that the arguments of many (although of course not all) of those who wanted stronger government intervention in 'saving' the language had *'des tonalités gênantes'* (disturbing overtones). While it is evident to any observer that a country where a Le Pen is dismissed by a very large majority of the population can in no sense be described as totalitarian, for Calvet, as for many others, it is nevertheless a fact that *'l'intervention directe de l'État sur la langue dans l'intention de la "purifier"'* (direct state intervention in language with the intention of 'purifying' it) has been a feature *'dans la majorité des pays fascistes'* (in most fascist countries). Thus, he says, that although it would not be accurate to describe French language policy as fascist, it is *'chauvine à l'évidence et surtout, hélas, vouée à l'inefficacité'* (obviously chauvinist and also, alas, certain to be ineffective) (1999: 262).

There is an ambiguity about strong government involvement in language and many French people are not happy with the situation, seeing it as repressive and overly interventionist, but also, and more importantly, unlikely to be successful in ensuring the strength and survival of the language. These differences of opinion are mirrored in the different ideas of French identity that both unite and divide the nation. The next section looks at this paradox.

Language and Identity

For many of the *résistants* language and national identity are virtually indistinguishable and there is a tendency to think of the language as a powerful symbol of what it means to be French. A language crisis is an identity crisis. Consciousness of national identity is a long-standing preoccupation of the French, never more so than in this new century. In the context of the European Union, particularly as discussions over the future of the Constitution continue, the interface between national sovereignty and European control is hotly contested. To some extent the idea of a national identity has been hi-jacked by the far right who constantly refer to it as their special concern. On the other hand, many who do not share their political views also feel that the issue of identity is crucial in 21st century France. As the validity of other symbols of national identity is increasingly questioned, language may be seen as a constant, a rallying point for defenders of the nation and its sovereignty. Chapter 4 (pp. 98–106) looked at some of the results of this. But national identity cannot be reduced to a shared language, greatly loved and enshrined in the national consciousness though that language may be.

The French, like many Europeans, are aware of a deep concern about their identity in the increasingly Europeanised and globalised world. Changing political and economic realities are forcing them to ask themselves uncomfortable questions. Awareness of this led *Le Figaro* in the summer of 2004 to commission a series of articles based on the question: *Qu'est-ce qu'être français aujourd'hui ?* (What does it mean to be French today?) (*Le Figaro*, 2004). The length of the series (there was an article almost daily from 8 June until 9 August), the stature of those who were asked to respond and the variety of political opinions expressed all bear witness to the topicality and seriousness of the issue of national identity in France. Not all the respondents gave a preponderant place to language, but many referred to its central place in their definition of French identity. Some had harsh things to say about the defence of the language, judging it inefficient and ineffectual. These included the only professional linguist among the writers, Claude Hagège (30.06.2004) and also Daniel Hervouet (9.07.2004). Others, notably René Girard (10.06.2004), attacked the concept of French identity defined by the anti-Americanism so prevalent in France. This is particularly prevalent among the *résistants*. Girard describes it as misguided and ill-judged.

The close connection between language and identity has been commented on by various writers, but in France a classical and frequently quoted contribution to the debate is Renan's 1882 lecture (mentioned earlier in this chapter). Speaking of the role of language in defining the nation, he argues strongly against limiting the definition of national identity to the sharing of a single language: 'Concentrating exclusively on the language has . . . its dangers, its unwelcome effects. If we exaggerate [the importance of the language] we enclose ourselves in one particular culture, we shut ourselves in.'[75]

The breadth of the debate can be judged from this more light-hearted, but nevertheless entirely serious list of essential features of national identity as given by Theisse (2001: 14):

> [A] history which establishes continuity with great ancestors, a series of heroes who are paragons of the national virtues, a language, cultural monuments, a folk tradition, important towns and a typical countryside, a special mentality, official symbols – a national anthem and a flag – and typical picturesque features – costume, special foods or a symbolic animal.[76]

In this list, the national language is not the most obvious symbol of identity. Nor do the French lack the other symbols, particularly historical continuity. Language is readily accepted as the main symbol of identity in France not because other features are lacking or threatened, but because of the unique role played by language in creating and maintaining a unified nation.

The literature on identity in France is marked, like so much else in French life, by opposing views of what it means to be French. The classical study by Braudel sees French identity as '*un résidu, un amalgame, des additions, des mélanges*' (a residue, an amalgam, additions, mixtures) (1986: 17). French identity is essentially an entity, the product of various inputs making up the whole. The idea of national unity is never far away: '*Toute identité nationale implique, forcément, une certaine unité nationale*' (Any national identity necessarily implies national unity). Although Braudel is aware of the dangers of simplification, insisting that it is vain to '*ramener la France à un discours, à une équation, à une formule, à une image, à un mythe*' (reduce France to a single way of speaking, a single equation, a single formula, a single picture, a single myth), he nevertheless posits the existence of something he calls '*la vraie France*' (the real France) which survives all the changes of history.

This is very different from the French identity described for example by Le Bras and Todd (1981), Mordrel (1981) or Citron (1991), the titles of whose books reveal their resolutely non-traditional viewpoints. Citron sets out to show that the 'religion' of France taught in schools and unquestioningly adhered to by generations of historians promotes a false image of national identity. She traces the development of a different identity, a multi-faceted reality, recognising and welcoming multiple historical and ethnic roots. This, unlike the traditional construct, is an identity where all today's French people can recognise themselves and their different pasts.

Citron shows how the imposition, through the education system, of the politically approved idea of a single indivisible national identity creates and fosters the experience of exclusion. Her words, written in 1989, are prophetic. As continuing political unrest in France, particularly the national upheaval in November 2005, has shown, the experience of exclusion, of rejection by 'the real France' is at the heart of many of the political problems in the 21st century. Linguistically, *'la francisation par en haut'* (the top-down imposition of French) (Citron, 1991: 231) has led to the exclusion of all those who speak other languages. There is only one real 'Frenchness' and it is confined to those who speak *le beau langage* (the beautiful language). *Verlan* is the popular, resolutely non-'beautiful', counter-cultural and widely used French slang of many of the young who feel dispossessed in today's France. It is an example of the importance of language in the identity debate. Doran (2004) shows how *verlan* can act to counter the top-down imposition of identity and create a breathing space between culture of origin and monolithic French culture. The Conclusion (Chapter 7) returns to this question.

If there are problems in reducing identity to a single construct, there are also difficulties in making language the one emblem of that identity. For Hobsbawm (1990: 98) the predominance given to language as a defining feature of identity, in France as in some other countries, is probably due to the fact that aspects of it can be 'objectively counted and tabulated' rather than to its inherent power. In a comment that is obviously applicable to France and those who defend its language, he warns (1990: 57) against 'the mystical identification of nationality with a sort of platonic idea of the language, existing behind and above all its variants and imperfect versions' and suggests that what he aptly calls French 'philological nationalism' is not beneficial either for the language or for France. Other scholars have described the same phenomenon in different terms. For Gordon (1978: 210), 'language is only one factor among many others constituting the personality of a people' and the 'virtual cult, . . . mystique, of the French language' (1978: 3) inhibits rather than encourages the acceptance of what is necessarily an ever-changing definition of identity.

While commentators in English, however admiring of France, might understandably tend to be wary of a tradition so very different from their own, it is less easy to dismiss the comments of the French themselves (for example Calvet, 1999; Dargent, 2004a and b; Hagège, 1996, 2004). Analysts on both the left and the right have taken the view that identity cannot be reduced to one factor. Without denying the importance of language, they propose a dynamic, multi-layered model of identity, not limited by the past but responding to changing circumstances in a flexible and creative way. This view of identity includes not only the traditional elements: nationality, history, geography, ethnicity, culture and language, but also an essential temporal dimension so that there are both constant and emerging aspects in people's view of what makes them who they are. This is similar to the view expressed by the sociologist Alain Touraine (2003) in his debate on identity with Elisabeth Badinter for the *Nouvel Observateur*:

> For my part, I would find it inappropriate, excessive, even dangerous to define myself principally by my nationality. Each one of us has very dispersed identities, cultural, political or economic, and each of us is also trying to construct an identity as a citizen.[77]

In this definition, identity is moving, growing, *éclatée*, multiple. For each individual it is a process and not a static concept. It is healthy for people to adjust some elements of their idea of who they are according to the time or place they find themselves in.

Admittedly not all the defenders insist on a single, exclusive, totally unchanging definition of French identity, nor do they all discuss the question of identity solely in terms of language. But many appear to be convinced that the best and most obvious way of strengthening the national identity (and the Republic) is to strengthen and purify the language (Ager, 1999: 238). While one can sympathise with this view, it has led to a largely inward-looking defensive movement, a monolithic entity, unchanging over time. For Calvet, Dargent, Hagège and other commentators such efforts are based on a failure to understand the nature of language and its relationship with national identity. They have not only been ineffective, but they have, in addition, been a waste of scarce resources. A harsh judgement, but it shows the extent to which those for whom the French language is an essential feature of national identity have become polarised and locked in unproductive polemic.

Finally the discussion of the question of identity returns briefly to the three aspects looked at elsewhere:

- regional and minority languages;
- the European Union;
- globalisation.

If the French are finding it difficult to define their identity in the modern world, it is largely a result of these forces from both within and outside the country. These, although they have little direct connection with language, affect the role French speakers attribute to it. From inside France there are increasing pressures for greater recognition of the regional, minority and immigrant languages (Chapter 2, pp. 29–43; Chapter 4, pp. 90–98). This immediately poses the question of how those who demand the right to use these languages as well as or instead of French in their daily lives perceive their identity. After centuries of government action, forging the kingdom, the empire or the Republic on the basis of a single shared language, any diminution in the role of that consciously nurtured unifying force appears to many as a threat. This is the point made, for example, by Dargent (2004a: 8):

> We must be specially careful as far as the promotion of regional and minority languages are concerned, since although they are also part of the national identity, they should not be developed to the detriment of French which alone is the basis of our unity.[78]

The increasing politicisation of the language issue at regional level is encouraged by membership of a European Union where similar demands are being made in other member states. Many people in France, feeling that Union policies on minorities threaten the Republic, now question the enthusiasm they have always shown in embracing the idea of Europe and are reassessing what they have always seen as their leading role in its construction. On the other hand, the realignment of linguistic policy, beginning in the 1990s with Catherine Trautman and the European Charter on Minority and Regional Languages, is seen by some, possibly a majority, as a welcome sign of openness, a healthy return to grass roots, a strengthening of French identity by extending it to embrace openly some of its constituent elements.

Apart from the Charter, another aspect of membership of the Union is causing grave concern over identity in France. The failure to agree on the Constitution (text at web site, European Union, Constitution) sharply divided the nation, but not along traditional political lines. The fact that it was on the 18 June 2004 that the Council of Ministers, meeting in Brussels, first approved the Constitutional Treaty will not have been lost on the French with their sensitivity to historical references: it was on 18 June 1940 that General de Gaulle made his radio appeal from London and it was on the same date in 1429 that Joan of Arc won her first victory over the English at Patay. This time the implications of that date were for many quite different and signalled a frightening loss of French sovereignty. In the preparation for the 2005 referendum in France, both right and left were split. Unsurprisingly it has not escaped the notice of some French opponents of the Constitution (who are virtually all strongly opposed also to the entry of Turkey into the Union) that 29 May, the date the referendum on the Constitution was held in France, was the date Constantinople fell to the Turks in 1453 (web site, *Europe, Une, Libre, Grande,* <u>Constitution Date</u>). Memories are long and elements of the mythical national identity (Citron, 1991) are still unhesitatingly exploited.

The defenders of the language have opposed the Constitution since it was first mooted. They saw the role of their own former President Giscard d'Estaing as the President of the Convention (web site, European Union <u>Convention</u>) set up to prepare the Constitution as a betrayal of France, French sovereignty and French identity. As the unwelcome evidence of support for the Constitution from both right and left in France emerged, the calls for a 'No' vote at the May 2005 referendum became more urgent. Immediately after the signature of the treaty Albert Salon, President of the FFI, published (on 11 November 2004, another important date) an article on *Voxlatina*. His view was that a 'No' vote in France, rejecting the Constitution, would give the country a valuable chance to '*recouvrer son entière souveraineté*' (regain its full sovereignty) and, at the same time, to '*relancer fortement la construction de la Communauté francophone*' (give a strong new impulse to the construction of the francophone community) in a Europe '*qui promeut le plurilinguisme*' (which promotes plurilingualism [possibly the sense here is official multi-lingualism rather than personal pluri-lingualism]) (Salon, 2004b). The stalemate after the 'No' vote has apparently not had the electrifying effect he hoped for.

On the other hand there are those who take a more sanguine view of the place of France in Europe:

> Europe may be seen by many French citizens as a threat to the identity of France. It represents, very much to the contrary, a challenge, a hope, an opportunity.[79] (Moisi, 2004)

Thus the confrontation between those who saw in the Constitution a chance for France to affirm its identity and exercise its influence in a more powerful and united European Union and those who argue for a return to 'full sovereignty' continues to mobilise and polarise forces on both sides of the language debate.

Globalisation constitutes what the language defenders see as the greatest external threat to French identity and therefore to the French language. It is often referred to in France as Americanisation and is frequently linked, in the discourse of the defenders, to Europeanisation (or 'Brusselisation'), as specially coined words such as *Euro-ricains, Euraméricanie* from *Voxlatina* attest. The French also use the term *mondialisation* to signify a more benign form of globalisation, one fostering cultural, economic, political and linguistic diversity. The awareness of an external threat (allied to a bitter disenchantment with the failure of the French governing élite) is at the root of the very strongly pro-Francophonia policies argued with such passion by Salon and others in the private defensive associations.

He and his fellow authors Arnaud and Guillou (Arnaud *et al.*, 2002: 260) are at pains to make the distinction between *mondialisation* and *globalization*, a distinction it is difficult to make in English. *Mondialisation* is, they claim, a neutral process involving the extension to the whole world of modern techniques, modern methods and content of communication and the interaction of ideas and behaviours. French battles at the UN for cultural and linguistic diversity are based on this idea of interaction. *Globalization* (for which they deliberately retain the American spelling) is the use by the United States and the English-speaking countries of the process of *mondialisation* in the service of their own interests and of the expansion of their concept of the world, their commercial empire, their culture and their language. The many Cassandras who bewail the extent of globalisation and the deleterious effects it is having on France and its language and identity might be surprised to read the views of the North American authors Barlow and Nadaud (2004), the title of whose book, *Sixty Million Frenchmen Can't Be Wrong*, is not entirely ironic. They report with some admiration (282) that the French have found, in *la mondialisation*, a typically subtle Gallic way of dealing with globalisation and suggest that the word globalisation, although apparently the same in both English and French, is actually a *faux ami*.

Several of the writers in the *Figaro* series on identity mention the way the French, as they face up to globalisation, have a tendency to focus on the Anglo-Saxon, particularly the American world as the source of all their problems and this is certainly true of the language defenders. More objective observers mistrust this concentration on an evil external force, accused of pursuing an explicit anti-France and anti-French language campaign. Widely held as the anti-American view is, it is refuted by most Anglo-Saxons and also by Girard (2004), by Hagège (1996: 169) and by Calvet (1999: 269) who is convinced that: 'it is nevertheless true that overall the United States have never, it seems, had as a priority the spreading of their culture . . . and their language'.[80]

Girard (2004), Dargent (2004b: 56), D'Ormesson (2004) and other commentators suggest that constant attacks on the United States (and other Anglo-Saxon countries) are inhibiting. They prevent France both from actively confronting the changes brought about by globalisation and from benefitting from them: 'we must get out of this destructive game of comparisons between France and other countries'.[12] (Girard, 2004). The negativity of such an approach is, he argues intellectually and culturally stultifying and ultimately non-productive. Calvet (1999: 262) also argues against looking outside France for a scapegoat: '*On ne changera rien à la puissance des pays anglo-saxons, en particulier des États-Unis, en luttant contre les emprunts à l'anglais'* (We will in no way change the power of the Anglo-Saxon countries, particularly the United States, by fighting against borrowings from English).

The battlefield is bigger than this and the issues are broader. The economic, cultural and political forces now dominating the world cannot be countered by a language (and cultural) policy, however strongly defended. Globalisation does indeed appear to pose a serious threat to different cultures, languages and identities, but that threat will not be removed by fighting for languages. The defence of languages requires other weapons (Fishman, 1991). Progress could perhaps come from embracing multilingualism (Edwards, 1984, 1994) and welcoming and managing the process of constructing the *identités éclatées* in our globalised world.

Chapter 7

Conclusion

Earlier chapters have looked at the long history in France of passionate and powerful devotion to the national language and observed how alive that devotion is in the 21st century. The extent of government commitment, the intense involvement of private and semi-private associations and the extensive political ramifications of French language policy have added extra dimensions to the picture. Putting the situation in France in the context of what is happening to language in neighbouring countries has shown that the French situation is in many ways unique. Along the way there have been confusing and puzzling problems, many arising in the context of the heightened concern over national identity in an expanding Europe, itself part of an increasingly globalised world.

One problem area is the different ways the language is defended by two very unequal groups of protagonists. The government agencies, vast and powerful, are sharply contrasted with the private associations, small and struggling. The differences between the two are brought into focus by Tables 7.1 and 7.2, adapted from Cooper (1989: 98). These tables make it possible to give a brief description of the main points distinguishing the two sets of language defenders.

Language and cultural policies are so closely entwined that it is virtually impossible to disentangle them. The description of linguistic policy must reflect the very close relationship between these two aspects of government action. The official agencies are described in Table 7.1.

(1) The actors here are mainly formally constituted élites, the constituent agencies of government (Ager, 1996: 54). They include three of the most powerful ministries and the revered *Académie française*. Subsidiary actors who influence policy are the defensive associations and the many private and semi-private operators involved in the implementation of government policies on language and culture. Private involvement is extensive, difficult to control and to measure.

(2) The behaviours these agencies aim to influence cover a very wide spectrum, both inside and outside France. Structural behaviours related directly to language: correctness of French; maintenance of linguistic

Table 7.1 The Defence of French – Government Agencies

1	**Actors** (who?) MCC; DGLFLF MAE; DGCID Ministry of Education *Académie française* Private associations and independent operators
2	**Behaviours** (what?) Correctness of French; terminology National language; regional languages; world languages Social cohesion Political partnerships Economy; trade; aid Acceptance of French values, ideals
3	**People** (to whom?) French nation; Europe; *La Francophonie*; United Nations Government departments; media; business; advertising Education system; researchers
4	**Ends** (why?) Maintain French power, prestige, image, identity, security Convey "universal values" Achieve internal social cohesion Promote linguistic diversity; pluri-lingualism; multi-lingualism
5	**Conditions** (where? when?) In the *Assemblée nationale*; *Sénat*; courts; media At summits and meetings of *La Francophonie* In Brussels; United Nations; UNESCO In international meetings, discussions Permanently; as need arises
6	**Means** (how?) Authority; force; law; promotion; persuasion Education system; commissions of terminology; *Académie française* International treaties and alliances; *La Francophonie* *Alliances françaises*; approved associations; defensive associations; private operators
7	**Decision-making process** Policy statements of ministries, OIF; structures for "enrichment", acceptance of new terminology Goals vague Means not always a limiting factor (funded by ministries)
8	**Effect** "Measured" in annual reports of DGLFLF, OIF, reports commissioned by government, publications; statistics Difficulty of relating cause and effect; cost and benefit

Source: Adapted from Cooper (1989: 98)

'standards'; and terminology are indeed part of their concern but most of their work (in so far as it is concerned with language) is devoted to status, acquisition and diffusion planning. The purposes for which the desired behaviours are to be used are extremely varied, covering internal and external political, social and economic structures.

(3) These actors seek to extend their influence over the linguistic and cultural behaviours of the widest possible range of people, in France, in Europe and throughout the world. They target, either directly or indirectly, individually or through another agency, all the people of France, all inhabitants of the European Union, all members of the UN. Their intermediary targets include the private operators on whom they rely for implementation of some aspects of policy.

(4) The overt ends of government language policy, the specifically language-related activities, are increasingly subsumed in the latent ends, and the satisfaction of interests takes precedence over the linguistic goals. Ager has analysed the motivations for this massive government effort and finds that considerations of identity, security and image are paramount, but the desire to promote a strong national image internally and externally is possibly inspired by pride at least as much as by fear (Ager, 1999: 217).

(5) Given their variety, it is apparent that the activities of these government agencies will take place under a number of different conditions. Although, both inside and outside France, language and cultural policy may be a response to a particular situation or crisis event (invasion of English computer terminology; World Trade Organisation discussions; enlargement of the European Union, for example) it usually addresses the long term. Political structures are the main operators and political considerations take precedence over economic and social structures. Influences from outside the system (EU, UN etc.) have considerable impact. Much of the activity of the DGLFLF for example is devoted to accumulating the information required by the planning process, but the difficulty of acquiring accurate data in this area is notorious and decisions are necessarily sometimes based on less than adequate information.

(6) The means used to implement government policy within France are usually top-down. Authority and legal force are the foundations of the policy, but increasingly it seems that persuasion is also used by government agencies (Judge, 2000: 78). Outside France, reminders of existing agreements and treaties in the EU or the UN are regularly issued but diplomatic means are also favoured for the promotion of French and France. The non-government operators involved in policy implementation do not embody the full force of government and so must use promotion and persuasion.

(7) The last two questions reveal some of the problems with official policy-making and its implementation through a decision-making process. Successive government reports (Table 3.7) have criticised imprecise policy formulation and vaguely expressed and frequently repeated goals. This is exemplified by the main points of the 'language policy statement' of the Minister of Culture and Communication on taking office in October 2005:

- raise awareness in the general public of what is at stake for French by mobilising the main forces of economic, social and cultural life;
- guarantee the right of citizens to receive information and to express themselves in French;
- promote activities allowing the French language to be used for social cohesion;
- improve the efficiency of work on enriching the French language;
- build a Europe that respects the linguistic diversity of its citizens.

The very extensive ramifications of the government language and cultural policy-making machine, and the involvement of numerous private sector operators make precise articulation of goals virtually impossible and so weaken the decision-making process. Exceptions to this are the responses already mentioned to specific challenges.

Discussion of the financial means to be used takes place in an annual budget round. Considerable financial support is available, but it is possibly not sufficiently focused to obtain maximum benefit.

(8) The measurement of effect is virtually impossible in such a field as this. The collection of statistics by the DGLFLF, for example, does not readily enable the making of a cost benefit analysis, as these few examples from the 2005 report to the parliament show:

- in 2005 10,026 actions were undertaken by the Department for the Repression of Fraud for infractions of government language policy (23% more than in 2003);
- the Department pursued 8.9% of these infractions, the lowest figure for 10 years;
- 223 new terms (including *courriel* for e-mail) were published in the *Journal Officiel*;
- 26% of the documents at the European Commission were in French in 2004, compared with 40% in 1997.
- 5,800 civil servants from the new member states of the EU did a course in French.

It is in fact doubtful if a strict calculation of cost effectiveness, or indeed a clear statement of the effect of its policies, would be in the government interest. In any case, there are far too many intangibles involved for such a calculation to be made. The necessity for government action in the joint areas of language and culture has not been questioned in France for centuries. It does not appear likely that any French government in the near future will be prepared for a radical re-examination of the structures underlying that action, unsatisfactory though they may appear in some respects.

Set against the mighty apparatus of the state, the activities of the non-official organisations appear extremely limited (see Table 7.2).

(1)   Here the actors are not formal élites, but rather what Cooper calls influentials and counter-élites. They range from language defence associations and groups to individuals. Some of the latter are prominent personalities while others are ordinary citizens. Among groups who are involved as actors on the margins are some of the small political groups and regional and sovereigntist activists.

Compared with the vast numbers of government employees who are involved directly or indirectly in official defence actions, the numbers of private defenders seem to be limited to several thousands. In 2003, the ALF, one of the largest groups, claimed to represent 'directly or indirectly' 6000 people. It had obtained a total of 1100 signatures to the two petitions launched in 2001. The membership documentation of the DLF in 2006 refers to 3000 members. It is possible that many of these actors are of an older generation and that at least some of them are not vigilant and dynamic language defenders. Much of the activity in the non-government sphere is due to the work of a small number of dedicated individuals.

(2) The behaviours these actors seek to influence overlap to a considerable extent with those targeted by the official agencies: correctness of French; terminology; and use of French nationally and internationally. There is however a greater emphasis on the purity of the language and on an anti-English language and anti-American crusade. The private organisations observe all aspects of government action related to the language and take official agencies to task when they fail to implement official language policy. Like the government agencies, the private defenders have seen the expediency of supporting pluri-lingual and multi-lingual policies where these may serve the cause. The private agencies are more likely to have explicitly linguistic aims than the government.

(3) The private groups seek particularly to influence the people who are their fellow citizens – but one might be tempted to ask: Who is listening? They also try to bring pressure to bear on government agencies to take a more pro-active stance in the national and international defence of French, notably in relation to *la Francophonie*. The complaints collected by the accredited associations in relation to infringements of the *Loi Toubon* are

Table 7.2 The Defence of French – Non-government Actions

1	**Actors** (who?) Associations; individuals; prominent and influential people Politicians; pressure groups; fringe political groups
2	**Behaviours** (what?) Correctness of French Use of French nationally and internationally Replacement of terms borrowed from English Operation of government language policies Multi-lingualism; teaching of French as a foreign language
3	**People** (to whom?) Mainly inside France; links with Quebec; throughout *La Francophonie* All speakers of French Government; politicians; media; business; advertising
4	**Ends** (why?) Restore prestige, power of French and France Maintain language purity Oppose English
5	**Conditions** (where? when?) As need arises; meetings; campaigns Web sites; Internet; e-mail; chat rooms *Assemblée nationale; Sénat*
6	**Means** (how?) Demonstrations; articles; media appearances Persuasion; promotion Petitions, propositions for the *Assemblée nationale* Guilt; emotional rhetoric; republican sentiments Allies: regional language groups; fringe political groups
7	**Decision-making process** Reactive; crisis response Umbrella groups
8	**Effect** Annual reports of organisations; statistics Difficulty of measuring

Source: Adapted from Cooper (1989: 98)

directed mainly at publishers, the media and advertisers whose linguistic behaviours the private groups seek to change.

(4) Like the government, the private groups have both overt and latent ends. They state that they want to restore the purity, the prestige and the power of their language, to fight against English and the American form of globalisation (language-related behaviours), and that by doing so they aim to strengthen the Republic (non-language related behaviours). The

outcomes of their actions perhaps reveal covert motivations: exclusion of speakers of other languages (including regional languages), and a Jacobine, sovereigntist agenda in internal and external politics. Fear of difference and resistance to change (whether linguistic or not) may be underlying incentives for their actions.

(5) The private groups operate under very different conditions from the government agencies. Their official power is limited to seeking to bring prosecutions. They must try to acquire a high public profile to increase their chances of bringing pressure to bear on the official agencies. They have limited recognition from the DGLFLF and in the structures of *la Francophonie* but otherwise they operate under the same restrictive conditions as other lobby groups. They attempt to exert pressure to have their point of view put in the *Assemblée nationale,* they have constant contact with the media and they make considerable use of the Internet.

Their activities are largely sporadic, in response to perceived crises, and may take place in public or in the corridors of power. They are subject to environmental influences from both inside and outside France but do not have an adequate infra-structure to allow them to gather all the detailed information they require. Nevertheless much of their activity is connected with the collecting of information they can use when the need arises.

(6) Because of recurrent funding problems, they must seek less costly means than the government to forward their aims. Thus they use persuasion, emotional rhetoric and accusation to raise their profile. Activities such as demonstrations, publications, media coverage, use of the Internet and links with other groups who appear to share their aims allow them to spread their message. The *Guide de l'usager* of the ALF (ALF, 2003) sets out the linguistic rights of citizens in various situations and encourages them to defend those rights by protesting and by filling in the complaints form provided. A similar form provided for members of the DLF also gives private citizens the means to take their complaints further.

(7) The private actors do not have direct access to the official decision-making process for language policy and their power to influence it is very limited. They must try to use indirect influence and enlist the help of sympathetic members of parliament. The larger private groups formulate proposals for laws, for example, and try to create a climate of public opinion capable of influencing policy decisions. Because their means are limited, their goals are sometimes more precisely articulated than those of the government and they work for fixed small-scale objectives: a march and demonstration at Villers-Cotterêts to promote the restoration of the *Château* as a centre for *la Francophonie* (October 2005); actions to promote the setting up of a government inquiry into the defence of the

language (November 2005); action against the Constitution or the London Protocol.

(8) It is not possible to measure the effect of the defensive activities of the private organisations, but some of their small-scale campaigns can have measurable effects – the opposition to the ratification of the *Protocole de Londres* for example. The annual report of the ALF presents a certain number of statistics and these give some idea of the effectiveness of their work. The 2003 report reveals that the association forwarded 276 complaints under the *Loi Toubon*; that there were 27 conferences held in France where the only language used was English; and that more than 50 of the French government Internet sites were in French and English only (in conflict with the stated government policy of multi-lingualism).

The comparison of the two tables in this chapter highlights some of the very obvious differences between government and non-government defence. Official action, well supported politically, relatively well funded and adequately staffed is weakened by lack of focus, an enormous spread of activities and agencies, reliance on private operators for the implementation of some of its policies and by failures in detailed planning. All this makes it impossible to assess the effects of government policies with any accuracy. Non-government groups struggle against prevailing public indifference, possibly engendered by centuries of reliance on the government to protect the language. These groups have small memberships, are poorly funded and depend to a large extent on the commitment of a small number of highly motivated individuals.

There is, and has long been, such widespread acceptance of the government's role in defending and promoting the language, and so pervasive is the assumption that these activities are the responsibility of government that a culture of dependence and even apathy has resulted. Dissatisfaction with the results achieved has not led to a mass movement or to extensive popular support for the non-government defensive agencies, who sometimes appear to be fighting a rearguard action. There is little sign of the *'puisssant vouloir humain'* (powerful human will) Hagège (2006: 235) identifies as the main requirement for success in defending languages, a strong motivation for the recovery of Hebrew in Israel for example. The *'vaste programme d'information des masses de locuteurs'* (huge programme of information for all [French] speakers), necessary as a first step to reversing the decline of French (Hagège, 2006: 237), is not part of government planning and the strong political and social forces required to stem language decline (Fishman, 1991) are not apparent in France today.

Looking now to the future and attempting to assess the prospects for the French language, it is time to try to answer some of the questions arising from the description of the way linguistic resistance in France operates. Is there a crisis? Is it really necessary, or even possible, to defend French? If so, how should it be done?

The history of defending languages unfortunately provides very few examples of success (Crystal, 1997, 2000; Fishman, 1991; Hagège, 2002a; Janse & Tol, 2003; Nettle & Romaine, 2000) and these occur only where special social, political and psychological conditions are met. Nevertheless, in the interests of maintaining a rich and stimulating human environment, every language, every instance of human diversity is worth defending. If the French believe their language is in crisis and is worth defending, and if they are prepared to go to such lengths to do so, it is necessary to accept that the effort is an existential necessity for them. Although there is not any immediate proven threat of the disappearance of French, it is, like many other languages in the world, endangered by the enormous economic, political and cultural strength of the United States – whose language happens to be English.

Perhaps we can take heart from the history of powerful languages, a history showing convincingly that no language will remain in the dominant position forever. No-one knows which language will replace English, but it is certain that it will eventually be dislodged from its present position, for political, economic, cultural or other reasons, by another world language (Graddol, 2004, 2006). Indeed, observers of English report a growing fragmentation of the language, possibly the precursor of its decline. Even in the all-powerful United States there is growing concern over the strength of Spanish, perceived as a threat to the national language. Those who, like the French, live with a constant and heightened awareness of history and historical precedents, may be encouraged by signs such as these.

Another aspect of linguistic history that is important for the future is the convincing evidence of pluri-lingualism as the norm for most of the world's people and multi-lingualism as the norm for most countries. This recognition of 'linguistic pluralism' (Edwards, 1984; Maiden, 2002), as well as now being acknowledged as expedient in France, is of growing importance in Europe. The Council of Europe, with the Europass, the Common European Framework of Reference for Languages, the European Language Portfolio and other developments planned for coming years has strongly espoused pluri-lingualism for the citizens of the Union. The European Commission set up in November 2005 a Strategic Framework for Multilingualism and has a comprehensive plan for the development of language variety in the Union. Calvet's comments (1999: 43), referred to in the Introduction, also suggest that acceptance of many languages, rather than concentration on preserving a monolingual state, is the way of the future.

For French, this involves accepting the co-existence of many living languages and finding an appropriate way of managing their co-existence. To put this another way:

> [T]he problem, therefore, is in the area of sociolinguistics. ... It is not by acting on the language [itself] but by acting on the situation within which it operates, and to which in part it contributes, that we may possibly be able to find a solution.[82] (Calvet, 1999: 265).

This emphasis on the changing social conditions affecting language goes against the traditional approach to language in France, where the national language has been to some extent constructed independently of society and where a strongly conservative monolingual culture has evolved in response to the largely political problems posed by a variety of languages (Lapacherie, 2004: 97). Is it impossible to imagine what an increasing number of commentators in France are suggesting: that some of the traditional attitudes to language can be changed and a realistic assessment of the sociolinguistic situation accepted as a basis for future action? This means, in du Bellay's terms, concentrating energies on *Illustration* rather than *Deffence*, engaging in positive rather than negative action and having faith in the language and those who speak it.

So how do the efforts of the resistance movement fit with this perspective? The defenders of the language have found it advisable to support multi- and pluri-lingual policies, but their underlying motivation remains the defence, promotion and strengthening of the dominant national language. Spurred on by incontrovertible evidence that the influence of French in the world, particularly in Europe, is weakening, the defensive movement emphasises decline and withdrawal and is concerned at the 'degeneracy' of the modern forms of the language. Its defensive efforts are aimed at re-establishing French as a powerful world language through *la Francophonie*, at reinforcing the position of French in Europe and at restoring the language to its former glory. The picture they paint is not rosy and the limited degree of success they have met with is commented on by both the *résistants* themselves and by outside observers.

Like the *Académie française*, the more strident defenders of French are an easy target for mockery, particularly in the Anglo-Saxon press. They are nevertheless clear-sighted enough to see that their valiant efforts have, to date, met with relatively little success (see, for example, Salon, quoted in Arnaud *et al.*, 2002: 55). Other French commentators, sympathetic to the defence of the language, and from the political left as well as the right, have also remarked on how little has been achieved and on the general air of pessimism among the defenders. Dargent (2004b: 55) comments that '*on n'arrête pas l'océan avec des digues de papier*' (you can't keep back the ocean with walls of paper) and Hervouet entitles his contribution to the *Figaro* (2004) debate on identity:

'*Halte au narcissisme mélancolique !*' (Stop this narcissistic gloom!). Calvet (1999: 257) feels that the negativity of the defenders, the constant moaning about the position of French, the condemnation of others and the reliance on '*textes punitifs*' (punitive [legal] texts) is self-defeating.

Other observers comment critically on those who speak about 'defending' the language, particularly those who take a strong republican or Jacobine line, noting that they can create the very climate of crisis, gloom, fear and panic that actually prevents their activities from being effective. Lipiansky (1991: 266) concludes his book on *L'Identité française* by calling this '*une réaction protectrice et appauvrissante, une forme de résistance au changement et à l'ouverture*' (a reaction which protects and impoverishes, a form of resistance to change and openness). Similarly Hervouet (2004) is convinced: 'The defence of the language . . . is a sign of retrenchment, of lost initiative.'[83] These writers and many others are convinced that the attribution of blame, the search for culprits outside France, is completely misguided.

While it would possibly be helpful for the language if there were changes at an international level, it is essential, as a first step, to look at the situation in France and '*responsabiliser les locuteurs plutôt que de les culpabiliser ou vouloir les protéger malgré eux*' (give the speakers [of French] responsibility [for the future of their language] rather than making them feel guilty or wanting to protect them whether they want protection or not) (Calvet, 2002a: 212). For Dargent, the situation is plain: 'The reality is that if French is in decline, if it is retreating, being lost, the responsibility for this is in the first instance French'[84] (2004b: 59).

There is in France a strong and growing body of opinion seeking, like Dargent, to find solutions to the problem of language by looking inwards rather than outwards, by affirmative rather than punitive action, by concentrating on the many positive strengths of the nation rather than by focussing on negative and pessimistic assessments.

And now the question of how best to defend French. Calvet's statement that 'the history of language, which is one of the aspects of the history of the world, is to a large extent concerned with managing plurilingualism'[85] (1999: 43) provides a starting point for this dynamic management of a constantly evolving situation. As French identity evolves and as the language evolves, its speakers must look forward rather than back with confidence rather than pessimism.

Among those who advocate positive, 'illustrative' action within France and abandoning the *chasse aux sorcières* (witch hunt), the *croisade* (crusade), the *guerre de tranchées* (trench warfare) to *responsabiliser les locuteurs* (give the speakers ownership [of their language]) are Calvet, Touraine, D'Ormesson, Dargent and Hervouet. While they may agree that French is best defended by example, by those who speak it as their native language, they have a variety of suggestions as to how this might be done. All agree that there is a problem of motivation and this was tackled, in the broader context of national identity, by the issue of *L'Express* (2005) in a *dossier* (special report) entitled *Et si on décidait d'avoir le moral ?* (What if we decided things are good?). Deliberately going against the prevailing pessimism and quoting sources from Horace onwards, the report gives many reasons for the French to feel good and to face the future with confidence rather than giving way to despondency. Many speak of the need for an imaginative political or linguistic project, a bottom-up initiative involving ordinary citizens, who would be motivated by the fact that their contribution is valued. This, as the analysis of Tables 7.1 and 7.2 showed, has been notably lacking in relation to the language.

For Dargent the project for the language must be educational. New pride and confidence in their language can be instilled in children at school and he makes an impassioned plea for his 'project':

> Our friends the defenders of French, all those who love it so much, must understand that it is that fight, the fight for the teaching of the French language to the youth of France, which is the most important, infinitely more important than the fight which consists in arguing for or against making English words more French, for or against feminising the names of the professions, more important too than to fight in a derisory fashion and quite uselessly against the Anglo-Saxon hegemony by promoting a fuzzy kind of Francophonia, more important too than to fight, perhaps in error, in obedience to an ideological reflex, against the free expression and the free development of the regional languages.[87] (2004b: 61)

Brave words (echoed by Gambotti (2004: 14–15)), arising from confidence rather than pessimism, they are likely to strike a chord in many French people who, faced with constant criticism and doom-laden predictions, will be glad to hear this call for positive action.

But this suggestion for a new, exciting and empowering way of teaching French to French children is not a complete response to the problem. Indeed if it means using older methodologies and teaching them to go back to older (purer?) forms of the language it too is doomed to fail. By closing his book with provocative interviews with media specialists and rap stars, Hagège (1996: 163) seems to propose a more iconoclastic course of action involving the management of a different kind of plurilingualism: the *'superposition de plusieurs langages : langages de banlieue, verlan, expressions américaines, qui vont avec la mode vestimentaire, mais aussi la manière d'écrire'* (a layering of several 'languages': the languages of the suburbs, slang (*verlan*), American expressions, which go with fashions in clothes, but also the way of writing). This foreshadows Doran's work in 2004 on the mediating role of *verlan* in identity construction. Ten years later Hagège (2006) advocates a more traditional programme but this too is directed at changing conditions in society. If the French realise how important their language is, they can begin to value and encourage its constantly developing multiplicity of linguistic forms. They can affirm and cherish these signs of vitality. French will then have a strong chance of survival because the social conditions for its long-term protection will be in place.

It may be that these are the timid beginnings of another way of defending French, not dependent on the one hand on writing lengthy diatribes against a supposed enemy, making impassioned speeches to the faithful or, on the other, on a call for ever stronger government measures, a rearrangement of the structures of existing official organisations (OIF, *Alliance française*) and demands for enhanced legal protection for the (classical) language. In this new climate, there might be more prizes of an affirmative kind, rewarding confidence, invention and vitality. The OIF and the DLF have a number of such prizes and they contrast sharply with the kind of prize involving crowing over the apparent defection of well-known personalities (for example in the awards for the annual *Carpette anglaise* (English Doormat) prize (see web site)).

In a celebration of creativity, some of the more innovative raps by French musicians like those whose talent is praised by Hagège (1996: 164) deserve to be promoted just as much as more traditional songs such as those by earlier songwriters (Yves Duteil: *La langue de chez nous* and Léo Ferré: *La langue française* for example) showcased on the *Langue française* web site. Other new developments in the spoken language, for example in incorporating words and modes of speech from immigrant communities, show that French continues, as it always has done, to tell the story of the people who speak it. In contrast to the many serious, defensive Internet sites, there is no lack of lively sites like *D*lires* (see web site) encouraging all those who love French to celebrate its vitality.

The increasing number of Internet sites in French and the growing proportion of sites in languages other than English are in fact very encouraging signs that language dominance is not permanent. The speed with which French has (almost in spite of the Commissions for Terminology) produced new, unique and specifically French written registers to handle technological innovations, for writing e-mails, for chat rooms and for text messaging is yet another sign of a healthy and vigorous language and a cause for delight rather than gloom. The Marso (2004, 2005) sites teaching SMS and PMS reveal a confident, playful and creative attitude to French owing nothing to English. They are testimony to the fact that French is a language with the confidence to confront the future. These new kinds of language will continue, for as long as they are necessary, to exist alongside the more traditional forms providing a rich, robust linguistic environment.

Bernard Pivot's (2004a and b) television programmes and *dictées* mobilised language lovers of all generations. His ongoing campaign, promoted by *L'Express* (web site, *L'Express*, Interview with Bernard Pivot, 2004), to save words has made the subject of language attractive and exciting to likely and unlikely people, and arguably done more to illustrate and defend the French language in the 20th and 21st centuries than many a wordy defensive article, solemn government declaration or new law. The growth of the *Clubs d'orthographe* (see web site; *L'Express*, 2006a), with many young people among their members, is ongoing testimony to the success of Pivot's work. Publicity and gratitude should be showered on creative writers such as Erik Orsenna of the *Académie française* who, with his books *La Grammaire est une chanson douce* (Grammar is a Sweet Song) (2001) and *Les Chevaliers du subjonctif* (The Knights of the Subjunctive) (2004), has shown that there are positive and engaging ways of celebrating the language, enjoyable ways of 'illustrating' and defending it. Jean-Christophe Bailly, Pierre Merle, Boris Seguin, Faïza Guère and Jean-Pierre Goudailler are others who have found innovative and amusing ways of illustrating what is happening to the language and showing how it is responding to modern challenges in the street, on the Internet and in the housing estates.

To an outside observer it seems possible that all these developments are signs not of a crisis but of an important change. Political regimes since François 1er have been crafting and polishing the French language. It is still, in spite of all their attempts at constraint, a living, growing tool of communication. By dint of extraordinary efforts they have controlled it, kept it caged (Laurent, 1988) for centuries. Now, as external and internal pressures on the language mount, it is escaping from the straitjacket of the past. French is a language at last loosening the bonds of the powerful élites and becoming a democratic channel of communication for the whole francophone community. The increasing evidence of the power of new forms of oral French is a reminder that the gulf maintained for so long between the spoken and the written language is an artificial one. *Résistants* and linguists alike may be observing a language liberating itself, becoming more democratic, and thus mirroring some of the political upheavals that have shaken the world in recent times. It may be that rather than a crisis, a sort of language rebellion is taking place. If so, there are painful but interesting times ahead.

As long as French can take words and expressions from English and make them its own, can crunch them up into a *franglais* puzzling to most English-speakers, as long as it can respond with flexibility and creativity to the changing needs of its speakers, it will not die. Its future is likely to depend not on crisis management or on an impressive panoply of defensive measures but on those who speak it. The French language is not an ailing invalid, *un être fragile*. Its vital signs are good, in spite of the prevailing climate of dependence on government action. Although it seems unlikely that the strong popular movement needed for a return to a golden age is imminent, it is not impossible that the language in its modern, evolving form, could inspire today's speakers to a new, more democratic *Deffence et illustration*. The future of French, the national language of a pluri-lingual France at the heart of a multi-lingual Europe, will then be assured.

Notes

(Original French of longer quotations)

Chapter 1

1 *Afin qu'il n'y ait cause de douter sur l'intelligence desdits arrêts, nous voulons et ordonnons qu'ils soient faits et écrits si clairement qu'il n'y ait ni puisse avoir aucune ambiguïté ou incertitude.*

2 *Ainsi la vie publique du pays était-elle indissociablement liée à l'emploi scrupuleux … du « langage maternel français ».*

3 *Deux dialogues du nouveau langage françois italianizé et autrement desguizé, principalement entre les courtisans de ce temps.*

4 *Enfin Malherbe vint, et le premier en France,*
Fit sentir dans les vers une juste cadence.

5 *offre d'abord l'image d'un objet de <u>prestige</u>, préservé et surveillé avec un soin jaloux, aux dépens de sa part d'expression variable et libre.*

6 *C'est à Richelieu que nous devons la première, principale et emblématique confusion entre autorité politique et force interne de la langue.*

7 *notre langue est un être fragile qu'il faut sans cesse surveiller et régler.*

8 *donner à l'unité du royaume forgée par la politique une langue et un style qui la symbolisent et la cimentent.*

9 *Le cardinal Richelieu s'était proclamé protecteur de l'Académie. À sa mort, cette protection fut exercée par le chancelier Séguier, puis par Louis XIV et, par la suite, par tous les rois, empereurs et chefs d'État successifs de la France.*

10 *où les Français sont partout chez eux, où Paris est la seconde patrie de tous les étrangers, et où la France est l'objet de la curiosité des Européens.*

11 *donner des règles certaines à notre langue, la maintenir en pureté, lui garder toujours capacité de traiter avec exactitude tous arts et toutes sciences, et assurer ainsi les caractères qui lui confèrent l'universalité.*

12 *dans une démocratie, laisser les citoyens ignorants de la langue nationale, incapables de contrôler le pouvoir, c'est trahir la patrie.*

13 *Ces jargons barbares et ces idiomes grossiers qui ne peuvent plus servir que les fanatiques et les contre-révolutionnaires.*

14 *Combien de dépenses n'avons-nous pas faites pour la traduction des lois des deux premières assemblées nationales dans les divers idiomes de France ?*

15 *Dans toutes les parties de la République, l'instruction ne se fait qu'en langue française.*

16 *Par tous les moyens possibles, favoriser l'appauvrissement, la corruption du breton … Il faut absolument détruire la langue bretonne.*

Chapter 2

17 *rechercher les meilleurs moyens de favoriser l'étude des langues et dialectes locaux dans les régions où ils sont en usage.*

18 *chaque fois qu'ils pourront en tirer profit pour leur enseignement, notamment pour l'étude de la langue française.*

19 *La promotion des identités régionales sera encouragée, les langues et cultures minoritaires respectées et enseignées.*

20 *Chaque fois, ils [les immigrés] ont représenté pour elle [la France] un acquis, un profit, quelque chose de plus et non pas quelque chose de moins. … Chaque fois, cela a signifié quelque chose de plus.*

21 *Peut-on vraiment attendre du système scolaire la revitalisation d'un patrimoine qu'il a contribué à détruire par le passé ?*

22 *Le français vient couronner cet héritage ; il ne l'abolit pas.*

23 *La langue française est bien installée ; la République n'est pas menacée ; l'unité nationale n'est pas remise en cause.*

24 *les langues de France contribuent à la créativité et au rayonnement culturel de notre pays. … elles sont notre bien commun et une partie du patrimoine de l'humanité.*

25 *La pluralité des langues est une donnée de mieux en mieux perçue et reçue en France, comme représentation du passé mais aussi comme projet d'avenir.*

26 *Le site des Nations sans État, des minorités nationales, culturelles et linguistiques, des peuples autochtones, des groupes ethniques, des territoires à forte identité et à tendances fédéralistes ou séparatistes en Europe.*

27 *Nous avons bien conscience que le front principal sur lequel l'avenir du français va se jouer, c'est le front européen.*

28 *Pourquoi veulent-ils tuer le français ? Les fonctionnaires pour faire carrière, les hommes d'affaires pour gagner de l'argent, les chercheurs pour gommer leur nationalité, les politiciens par soumission aux prétendues lois du marché.*

29 *Le protocole de Londres entérinerait définitivement la mort de la diversité culturelle et linguistique qui a fait … la richesse de l'Europe.*

30 *avec l'aide constante des fonctionnaires de l'Angleterre blayrienne, l'éviction, non seulement du français, mais également de toutes les autres langues de l'Europe.*

Chapter 3

31 *travailler, avec tout le soin et toute la diligence possibles, à donner des règles certaines à notre langue et à la rendre pure, éloquente et capable de traiter les arts et les sciences.*

32 *Les doléances et les plaisanteries que suscitent les lenteurs du <u>Dictionnaire</u> sont presque aussi anciennes que l'Académie elle-même.*

33 *Aucune révision ne peut être publiée sans l'accord de l'Académie française.*

34 *elle agit pour en [de la langue française] maintenir les qualités et en suivre les évolutions nécessaires.*

35 *Plus précisément l'américain, qui tend à envahir les esprits, les écrits, le monde de l'audiovisuel.*

36 *une institution qui maintient les mots est en même temps gardienne des valeurs qu'ils expriment.*

37 *défendre les mots, c'est aussi sauver les idées qu'ils contiennent.*

38 *La langue [française] a atteint la plénitude de ses qualités, qui en fait depuis deux siècles le langage des élites du monde entier.*

39 *la langue française, analytique et d'une richesse syntaxique incomparable, mérite de*

demeurer langue de référence pour tout ce qui exige, à commencer par les traités internationaux, une impérieuse précision de la pensée.

40 *Nous sommes là pour définir et rappeler les <u>permanences</u>, et par là être les premiers serviteurs des valeurs suprêmes de notre civilisation.*

41 *Les langues, les cultures et la civilisation sont ce qu'elles sont, et occupent, dans le monde, les places que l'Histoire leur a données et qu'elle n'a jamais cessé de réduire ou d'élargir à son gré. Si telle langue paraît un jour plus utile que d'autres, ou même plus apte à l'expression de certains aspects de la civilisation, que nous importe ? Demain, les choses auront changé et seul l'esprit a chance d'être éternel.*

42 *La langue française donne des habitudes françaises; les habitudes françaises amènent l'achat de produits français. Celui qui sait le français devient le client de la France.*

43 *L'Alliance est favorable <u>au respect de la civilisation</u>. Non pas seulement la civilisation française, qui n'en est qu'une forme, mais des diverses civilisations. Aussi entend-elle pratiquer le dialogue des cultures.*

44 *L'association dite « Alliance française » ... a pour mission d'enseigner la langue française dans le monde, d'organiser des manifestations culturelles, de rassembler à l'étranger les amis de la France.*

45 *les hautes valeurs ne subsisteront pas dans une psychologie outrée de nationalisme intellectuel. ... c'est par de libres rapports spirituels et moraux, établis entre nous-mêmes et les autres, que notre influence culturelle peut s'étendre à l'avantage de tous et qu'inversement peut s'accroître ce que nous valons.*

46 *du fait de sa structure associative et de son insertion dans les pays d'accueil, elle [l'Alliance française] est particulièrement bien placée pour encourager le dialogue des cultures et développer les valeurs d'échange, de partage de d'amitié.*

47 *Elle [l'Alliance française] est étrangère à toute préoccupation politique ou religieuse.*

48 *étudier les mesures propres à assurer la défense et l'expansion de la langue française, d'établir les liaisons nécessaires avec les organismes privés compétents, notamment en matière de coopération culturelle et technique, de susciter ou encourager toutes initiatives se rapportant à la défense et l'expansion de la langue française.*

49 *une politique favorable au développement et au rayonnement de la langue française ... aider son progrès.*

50 *l'emploi de la langue française en France et à l'étranger ... le respect du français, langue d'organisations internationales ... anticiper l'ouverture de l'Europe ... promotion du français dans le cadre du nécessaire plurilinguisme européen et mondial.*

51 *[travailler] pour le plurilinguisme ... à l'intérieur des frontières.*

52 *La DGLFLF contribue à préserver et valoriser les langues de France, à savoir les langues autres que le français qui sont parlées sur le territoire national et font partie du patrimoine culturel national.*

53 *le feu sacré s'éteint, étouffé par la question de la réforme de l'orthographe.*

54 *ce qui change aujourd'hui, c'est que pour la première fois depuis que l'État s'est préoccupé de langage, un organisme [la DGLFLF] tente de mener à la fois une politique en faveur de la langue nationale et en faveur des autres langues. Jusqu'alors, pour des raisons historiques regrettables, ... on a conçu les deux activités comme distinctes, voire opposées. ... Aujourd'hui, il s'agit de penser les deux approches en même temps.*

55 *un débat animé, au coeur duquel s'inscrit la volonté de doter les langues de France d'un véritable statut et d'une protection juridique.*

56 *Nous n'avons trouvé qu'une stratégie virtuelle, une juxtaposition d'actions et de politiques, mais non pas une stratégie réelle ni une politique d'ensemble ...*

Chapter 4

57 cette mainmise des instances dirigeantes sur la langue n'a été que la première d'une série d'interventions qui se poursuivra jusqu'à nos jours.

58 L'État a donc constamment pesé sur l'évolution de la langue française depuis le Haut Moyen Âge.

59 il était bien-séant ... que les hommes plus notables ... eussent, comme en robe, ainsi en parole quelque prééminence sur leurs inférieurs.

60 mettre fin à cette étrange inégalité : la langue de la Constitution et des lois y sera enseignée à tous; et cette foule de dialectes corrompus, dernier reste de la féodalité, sera contrainte de disparaître.

61 La monarchie avait des raisons de ressembler à la tour de Babel; dans la démocratie, laisser les citoyens ignorants de la langue nationale, incapables de contrôler le pouvoir, c'est trahir la patrie. ... Chez un peuple libre, la langue doit être une et la même pour tous.

62 Le fédéralisme et la superstition parlent bas-breton, l'émigration et la haine de la République parlent allemand; la contre-révolution parle italien et le fanatisme parle basque. Cassons ces instruments de dommage et d'erreur.

63 Depuis les années soixante, c'est en toute connaissance de cause que la France a choisi d'utiliser son influence linguistique comme un instrument de domination lui permettant de pérenniser son influence économique et politique.

64 Le legs de la pensée linguistique révolutionnaire est double. D'une part elle impose l'identification de l'unité politique à l'unité linguistique, identification à laquelle aucune politique linguistique ne peut échapper jusqu'à nos jours. D'autre part, elle institue le modèle d'une langue bien faite, construite sur les principes de l'analogie qui se substituerait aux langues capricieuses et historiques en éradiquant tous les germes d'une possible diversification.

65 ... la France est une fois de plus en péril ...
Le temps est venu d'un soulèvement partisan ...
Ainsi, le FFI se constituera sur la base d'une Nouvelle résistance, non plus seulement française, mais de toute la Francophonie. Une résistance digne des grandes heures du passé, mais porteuse d'une vision d'avenir.

66 la France est menacée de disparaître et sa voix dans le monde s'éteint.

67 Ce dépérissement de la souveraineté nationale et populaire s'intègre dans le mouvement plus vaste du mondialisme, autre nom de l'américanisation, dont le recul du français dans le monde au profit de l'anglais, les atteintes au contenu de notre langue, les progrès de la colonisation culturelle sont les conséquences logiques.

68 9° La sauvegarde de la langue française est enfin un autre domaine, non moins important, où se pose le défi de l'indépendance. En effet, la langue n'est pas un simple instrument de communication. Elle est un creuset dans lequel s'est forgé au cours des siècles l'unité nationale, non seulement sur le plan d'une identité culturelle, mais aussi sur le plan politique.

69 Cet élément de notre souveraineté et de notre identité paraît négligeable à beaucoup parce qu'il constitue une habitude acquise, qui ne paraît devoir changer. Son importance doit néanmoins être soulignée face à la menace que constitue l'invasion des vocables anglo-américains, accompagnée du déclin de notre langue sur le plan international. Tous phénomènes résultant eux-mêmes de la domination économique, voire politique acquise par les Etats-Unis.

Chapter 6

70 *la poussée vers l'usage d'une langue unique … favorise l'émergence d'une pensée unique ayant le potentiel, à terme, de se transformer en pouvoir unique, c'est-à-dire en dictature.*

71 *Nos politiciens devraient savoir que deux enseignements sont essentiels à l'enracinement d'un peuple : celui de son histoire et celui de sa langue.*

72 *Le français, la langue française, notre langue commune, comme l'a voulu le bon roi François Ier, est ici en grave danger !*

73 *elle [la langue] s'adaptera ou elle périra.*

74 *Maintenir la « pureté » de la langue est le meilleur moyen d'en finir avec elle.*

75 *Cette considération exclusive de la langue a … ses dangers, ses inconvénients. Quand on y met de l'exagération, on se referme dans une culture déterminée ; on se limite, on se claquemure.*

76 *une histoire établissant la continuité avec les grands ancêtres, une série de héros parangons des virtus nationales, une langue, des monuments culturels, un folklore, des hauts lieux et un paysage typique, une mentalité particulière, des représentations officielles – hymne et drapeau – et des identifications pittoresques – costume, spécialités culinaires ou animal emblématique.*

77 *Pour ma part, je trouverais incongru, excessif, voire dangereux de me définir centralement par ma nationalité. Chacun de nous a des identités très éclatées, de nature culturelle, politique ou économique, et chacun tente aussi de se construire une identité citoyenne.*

78 *il s'agit d'être particulièrement prudent face à la promotion des langues régionales et minoritaires, car si ces dernières participent également de l'identité nationale, elles ne doivent pas se développer au détriment de la langue française qui, seule, fonde notre cohésion.*

79 *L'Europe peut être perçue par de nombreux citoyens français comme une menace pour l'identité de la France. Elle constitue, bien au contraire, un défi, un espoir, une chance.*

80 *il demeure que globalement les États-Unis n'ont semble-t-il jamais eu pour objectif prioritaire de diffuser leur culture … et leur langue.*

81 *il nous faut sortir du jeu délétère des comparisons entre la France et les autres pays.*

Chapter 7

82 *le problème, donc, est d'ordre sociolinguistique. … Ce n'est pas en agissant sur la langue qu'on pourra éventuellement le résoudre, mais en agissant sur la situation dans laquelle se meut la langue et dont elle témoigne en partie.*

83 *La défense de la langue … est un indice de retranchement, d'initiative perdue.*

84 *La réalité est que si le français décline, recule, se perd, la responsabilité en est d'abord française.*

85 *l'histoire linguistique, qui est l'un des aspects de l'histoire du monde, est en grande partie constituée par la gestion [du] plurilinguisme.*

86 *Que nos amis défenseurs de la langue française, que tous ceux qui l'aiment tant, comprennent que c'est ce combat-là, celui de l'enseignement de la langue française aux jeunes Français, qui est le plus important, infiniment plus important que celui qui consiste à entretenir des débats pour ou contre la francisation de mots anglais, pour ou contre la féminisation des noms de professions, plus important aussi que de lutter de façon dérisoire et en pure perte contre l'hégémonie anglo-saxonne en promouvant une francophonie encore évanescente, plus important aussi que de combattre, peut-être à tort, pour obéir à un réflexe idéologique, la libre expression et le libre développement des langues régionales.*

Bibliography

Books and articles (print and Internet; classified alphabetically by author or name of publication)

Ager, D.E. (1996) *Language Policy in Britain and France. The Processes of Policy.* London: Cassell.

Ager, D.E. (1997) *Language Community and the State.* Exeter: Intellect Ltd. Available at http://www.intellectbooks.com/europa/number5/ager.htm (accessed 29.03.2005).

Ager, D.E. (1999) *Identity, Insecurity and Image. France and Language.* Clevedon: Multilingual Matters Limited.

ALF (2003) *Guide de l'usager.* Paris: ALF. Available at http://www.avenirlangue-francaise. org/ (accessed 06.04.2006).

Arnaud, S., Guillou, M. and Salon, A. (2002) *Les Défis de la francophonie – pour une francophonie humaniste.* Paris: Alpharès.

Ball, R. (1997) *The French-speaking World. A Practical Introduction to Sociolinguistic Issues.* London: Routledge.

Barlow, J. and Nadeau J.-B. (2004) *Sixty Million Frenchmen Can't Be Wrong.* London: Robson Books.

Barbour, S. (2000) Britain and Ireland: 'The varying significance of language for Nationalism'. In Barbour and Carmichael (2000) (pp. 18–43).

Barbour, S. and Carmichael, C. (2000) *Language and Nationalism in Europe.* Oxford: Oxford University Press.

Baugh, C. and Cable, T. (1993) *A History of the English Language.* Englewood Cliffs, NJ: Prentice Hall.

Becquer, B., Cerquiglini, B., Cholewka, N., Coutier, M., Frécher, J. and Mathieu, M.-J. (1999) *Femme j'écris ton nom . . . , Guide d'aide à la féminisation des métiers, titres, grades et fonctions.* Paris : Centre National de la Recherche Scientifique and Institut National de la Langue Française. La Documentation Française. Available at http://atilf.atilf.fr/gsouvay/scripts/feminin.exe (accessed 29.03.2005).

Bengtsson, S. (1968) *La Défense organisée de la langue française.* Uppsala: Almquist and Wiksells.

Blaise, A. (2001) *L'Alliance Française, une association institutionnalisée. Thèse de fin d'études, 2000–2001.* Available at http://doc-iep.univ-lyon2.fr/Ressources/Documents/Etudiants/Memoires/detail-memoire.html?ID=743 (accessed 31.10.2006).

Bochmann, K. (n.d.) *Racism and/or Nationalism: Minorities and Language Policy under Fascist Regimes.* Leipzig: Leipzig University. Available at http://www.stm.unipi.it/Clioh/tabs/libri/7/09-Bochmann_127–138.pdf (accessed 29.03.2005).

Boileau-Despraux, N. [1674] (1998) *L'Art poétique ; épîtres ; odes ; poesies diverses et épigrammes.* Paris: Flammarion.

Bourdieu, P. (1982) *Ce que parler veut dire*. Paris: Fayard.

Braudel, F. (1986) *L'Identité de la France. Espace et Histoire*. Paris: Arthaud-Flammarion.

Bruézière, M. (1983) *L'Alliance française, 1883–1983. Histoire d'une institution*. Paris: Hachette.

Bruneau, C. (1955) *Petite Histoire de la langue française*. Paris: Armand Colin.

Brunot, F. (1932) *Observations sur la grammaire de l'Académie française*. Paris: Droz.

Buffon, H.L. de (2003) *'Le français une langue pour l'Europe'*. In *Paris Match* No. 2799 (9.01.2003). Available at http://www.presse-francophone.org/GAZETTE/gazette_109lavenir.htm (accessed 29.03.2005).

Busnel, F. (2004) *'100 mots à sauver. Luc Ferry : Ce que je veux pour la langue française'*. In *Lire*, March 2004. Available at http://www.lire.fr/enquete.asp/idC=46375/idR=200 (accessed 2.11.2006).

Calvet, L.-J. (1999) *La Guerre des langues et les politiques linguistiques*. (2nd edn). Payot: Paris

Calvet, L.-J. (2002a) *Le Marché aux langues : Les Effets linguistiques de la mondialisation*. Paris: Plon.

Calvet, L.-J. (2002b) *Linguistique et colonialisme* (4th édn). Paris: Payot.

Calvet, L.-J. (2004) *'Une langue qui meurt, c'est une vision du monde qui disparaît'*. In *L'Express*, 22.11.2004 (pp. 33–35). Interview with Marianne Payot. Available at http://www.lexpress.fr/info/monde/dossier/francophonie/dossier.asp?ida=430558 (accessed 29.03.2005).

Caput, J.-P. (1975) *La Langue française. Histoire d'une institution. Tome II. 1715–1974*. Paris: Larousse.

Castle, S. (2004) *'New members will push EU translators' bill to £700m'*. In *The Independent*, 5.02.2004. Available at http://news.independent.co.uk/europe/article67620.ece (accessed 2.11.2006).

Cerquiglini, B. (1999) *Les Langues de la France*. Available at http://www.culture.gouv.fr/culture/dglf/lang-reg/rapport_cerquiglini/langues-france.html (accessed 06.04.2006)

Cerquiglini, B. (2000) (ed.) « *Tu parles ?* » *Le français dans tous ses états*. Paris: Flammarion.

Cerquiglini, B. (2002) *Bien dans nos langues*. Interview. Available at http://www.culture.gouv.fr/culture/dglf/entretien-BC.htm (accessed 29.03.2005).

Cerquiglini, B. (2003) *Le français, une religion d'état ?* Available at http://www.culture.gouv.fr/culture/dglf/politique-langue/article_francais.html (accessed 30.01.2006).

Cerquiglini, B. (2004) *Faut-il avoir peur des langues régionales ?* Café Géo au Flore 30.03.2004). Available at http://www.cafe-geo.net/article.php3?id_article=301&var_recherche=cerquiglini (accessed 2.11.2006).

Certeau, M. de, Julia, D. and Revel, J. (1975) *Une Politique de la langue. La Révolution française et les patois*. Paris: Gallimard.

Chaurand, J. (ed.) (1999) *Nouvelle histoire de la langue française*. Paris: Seuil.

Citron, S. (1991) *Le Mythe national. L'histoire de la France en question*. Paris: Les Éditions ouvrières.

Clanché, F. (2002) *Langues régionales, langues étrangères : de l'héritage à la pratique*. INSEE PREMIÈRE No. 830, February 2002. Available at www.insee.fr/fr/ffc/docs_ffc/IP830.pdf (accessed 29.03.2005).

Colin, J.-P. (1997) *D'une langue à l'universel*. Reims: *Université de Reims*. Available at http://www.univ-reims.fr/Labos/CERI/francophonie.htm#I.%20La%francop honie%20et%201a%20France (accessed 20.03.2005).

Comité Valmy (2003) *Communiqué : La mondiacolonisation et l'Empire-vampire* (11.04.2003). Available at http://www.voxlatina.com/vox_dsp2.php3?art=1677 (accessed 29.03.2005).

Cooper, R.L. (1989) *Language Planning and Social Change*. Cambridge: Cambridge University Press.

Crowley, T. (1989) *The Politics of Discourse: The Standard Language Question in British Cultural Debates*. London: Macmillan.

Crowley, T. (1991) *Proper English?: Readings in Language, History, and Cultural Identity*. London: Routledge.

Crowley, T. (2003) *Standard English and the Politics of Language*. (2nd edn) London: Macmillan.

Crystal, D. (1997) *English as a Global Language*. Cambridge: Cambridge University Press.

Crystal, D. (2000) *Language Death*. Cambridge: Cambridge University Press.

Dargent, R. (2004a) *'Retrouver nos mots, rester libres'*. In *Libres* No. 2 (pp.7–9). (Editorial.) Paris: Office de l'Édition Impression Librairie.

Dargent, R. (2004b) *'L'État et la langue française'*. In *Libres* No. 2 (pp. 51–61). Paris: Office de l'Édition Impression Librairie.

Decaux, A. (2002) *'L'Avenir de la langue française'*. In *Revue de l'AMOPA* No. 155. Available at http://www.amopa.asso.fr/decaux_principale.htm (accessed 30.03.2005).

Désirat, C. and Hordé, T. (1976) *La Langue française au 20ᵉ siècle*. Paris: Bordas.

Diouf, Abdou (2006) *Voeux du Secrétaire générale*. Available at http://www.francophonie.org/doc/dernieres/Discours_sg_2006_01_16.pdf (accessed 06.04.2006). (See also web site, OIF.)

Doran, M. (2004) 'Negotiating between *Bourge* and *Racaille*: *Verlan* as youth identity practice in suburban Paris'. In Pavlenko and Blackledge (eds) (2004) (pp. 93–124).

D'Ormesson, J. (2004) *'Mourir pour renaître'*. In *Le Figaro* (12.07.2004). Série: Qu-est-ce qu'être français aujourd'hui ?, p. 10.

Downes, W. (1988) *Language and Society*. Cambridge: Cambridge University Press.

Druon, M. (1995) *Académie française: Statuts et règlements. Note préliminaire. Juillet 1995*. Available at http://www.academie-francaise.fr/role/statuts.html (accessed 29.03.2005).

Du Bellay, J. [1549] (1892) *La deffence et illustration de la langue francoyse* (E. Person, ed.). Paris: Le Cerf.

Durand, C.-X. (2002) *'La Manipulation mentale par la destruction des langues'*. Article No. 19, *Dossier. Mondialisation et Démocratie linguistique* (14.09.2002). Available at http://www.voxlatina.com/vox_dsp2.php3?art=1573 (accessed 29.03.2005).

Eco, U. (1994) *La Recherche de la langue parfaite*. Paris: Seuil

Edwards, J. (1984) *Linguistic Minorities, Policies and Pluralism*. London: Academic Press.

Edwards, J. (1994) *Multilingualism*. London: Routledge.

Étiemble, R. (1964) *Parlez-vous franglais ?* Paris: Gallimard.

Express, L' (2004a) *'@robase politiquement correcte'*. No. 2759 (17.05.2004). Available at http://www.lexpress.fr/services/archives/special/consultation.asp?fiche=014062X (accessed 29.03.2005).

Express, L' (2004b) *'Mais à quoi sert la Francophonie ?'* No. 2786 (22.11.2004).

Available at http://www.lexpress.fr/services/archives/special/consultation asp?fiche=018600X (accessed 29.03.2005).

Express, L' (2005) '*Et si on décidait d'avoir le moral ?*' *Dossier*. No. 2796 (31.01.2005) (pp. 12–21).

Express, L' (2006a) '*Les dictées à la page*'. No. 2854 (16.03.2006). Available at http://www.lexpress.fr/services/archives/special/consultation.asp?fiche=064988F (accessed 08.04.2006).

Express, L' (2006b) '*Patriotisme linguistique*'. No. 2856 (30.03.2006) (p. 48).

FFI (*Forum français international*) (2001) *L'Appel de Villers-Cotterêts* (7.10.2001). Available at http://www.voxlatina.com/petition4.php3 (accessed 29.03.2005). 55

Figaro, Le (2004) *Qu-est-ce qu'être français aujourd'hui ?* (*Série*.) Available at http://www.lefigaro.fr/series/20040908.FIG0361.html (accessed 29.03.2005).

Fishman, J.A. (1972) *Language in Sociocultural Change*. Stanford, CA: Stanford University Press.

Fishman, J.A. (1991) *Reversing Language Shift. Theoretical and Empirical Foundations of Assistance to Threatened Languages*. Clevedon: Multilingual Matters.

Fleutot, F.-M. (2005) '*La république française doit-elle quitter l'Organisation Internationale de la Francophonie ?*' *In Franche Contrée*, No. 19. Available at http://www.voxlatina.com/vox_dsp2.php3?art=1838 (accessed 29.03.2005).

Flynn, G. (1995) *Remaking the Hexagon. The New France in the New Europe*. Boulder, CO, San Francisco, Oxford: Westview Press.

Fumaroli, M. (2001) *Quand l'Europe parlait français*. Paris: Éditions de Fallois.

Gallo, M. (2004) '*La fragmentation délétère de la nation*'. *In Le Figaro* No. 18617 (15.06.2004) (p. 13).

Gambotti, C. (2004) '*Situation de la langue française sur le territoire de la République et dans le monde*'. *In Libres* No. 2 (pp.13–21).

Gilder, A. (1993) *Et si l'on parlait français ?* Paris: Le Cherche Midi.

Gilder, A. (2001) '*Culture mondialisée ou monde des cultures ?*' *In Revue des deux mondes* Novembre-Décembre 2001. Available at http://www.voxlatina.com/vox_dsp2.php3?art=1075 (accessed 29.03.2005).

Girard, R. (2004) '*Le prestige des intellectuels*'. *In Le Figaro* (9.06.2004). *Série: Qu-est-ce qu'être français aujourd'hui ?*, p. 65.

Gordon, D.C. (1978) *The French Language and National Identity (1930–1975)*. The Hague: Mouton.

Graddol, D. (2004) '*The future of language*'. *In Science* Vol. 303 (27.02.2004) (pp. 1329–1331).

Graddol, D. (2006) *English Next*. London: British Council. Available at http://www.britishcouncil.org/files/documents/learning-research-english-next.pdf (accessed 3.10.2006).

Grau, R. (1981) *Le Statut juridique de la langue française en France*. Quebec: Publications du Conseil supérieur de la langue française. Available at http://www.cslf.gouv.qc.ca/Publications/PubD108/D108P1–1.html (accessed 30.03.2005). Also at http://www.infotheque.info/ressource/4988.html (accessed 31.03.2005).

Griesmar, D. (2001) *Contre l'usage de l'anglais en droit français* (29.6.2001). Available at http://www.voxlatina.com/petition2.php3 (accessed 29.03.2005).

Griesmar, D. (2006) *Protocole de Londres : le retour des suicidaires !* Available at http://www.voxlatina.com/vox_dsp2.php3?art=1916 (accessed 01.03.2006).

Grillo, R.D. (1989) *Dominant Languages. Language and Hierarchy in Britain and France*. Cambridge: Cambridge University Press.

Grin, F. (2003) *Language Policy Evaluation and the European Charter for Regional or Minority Languages*. Basingstoke: Palgrave Macmillan.

Hadoux, M. (1997) *La langue française: Heurs et malheurs (1986–1997)*. Available at http://www.langue-francaise.org/Articles_Dossiers/Heurs_malheurs.php (accessed 29.03.2005).

Hagège, C. (1987) *Le français et les siècles*. Paris: Odile Jacob.

Hagège, C. (1996) *Le français, histoire d'un combat*. Paris: Éditions Michel Hagège.

Hagège, C. (2002a) *Halte à la mort des langues*. Paris: Odile Jacob.

Hagège, C. (2002b) '*Nous laissons l'anglais dominer, par fatalisme ou servilité*'. Interview. *In Enjeux* (11.05.2002). Available at http://www.langue-francaise.org/Articles_Dossiers/Dos_Entretien_Hagege_mai_02.php (accessed 31.03.2005).

Hagège, C. (2002c) '*Le français progresse comme jamais*'. Interview with Hervé de Saint-Hilaire. In *Le Figaro* (19.07.2002).

Hagège, C. (2004) '*L'identité par la langue*'. Interview. In *Le Figaro* (30.06.2004). *Série : Qu'est-ce qu'être français aujourd'hui ?*, p. 32.

Hagège, C. (2006) *Combat pour le français*. Paris: Odile Jacob.

Héran, F. (1993) *L'Unification linguistique de la France*. *Population et Sociétés* No. 285. Available at http://www.ined.fr/fichier/t_publication/481/publi_pdf1_pop_et_soc_francais_285.pdf (accessed 2.11.2006).

Héran, F., Filhon, A. and Deprez, C. (2002) *La dynamique des langues en France au fil du XXe siècle*. *Population et Sociétés* No. 376. Available at http://www.ined.fr/fichier/t_publication/65/publi_pdf1_pop_et_soc_francais_376.pdf (accessed 2.11.2006).

Hervouet, D. (2004) '*Halte au narcissisme mélancolique !*' In *Le Figaro* (9.07.2004). *Série : Qu'est-ce qu'être français aujourd'hui ?*, p. 15.

Hobsbawm, E.J. (1990) *Nations and Nationalism since 1870. Programme, Myth, Reality*. Cambridge: Cambridge University Press.

Janse, M. and Tol, S. (2003) *Language Death and Language Maintenance*. Amsterdam and Philadelphia: John Benjamins Publishing Company.

Judge, A. (1993) 'French: A planned language?' In Sanders (1993) (pp. 7–26).

Judge, A. (2000) 'France: One state, one nation, one language?' In Barbour and Carmichael (2000) (pp. 44–82).

Judge, A. (2002) 'Contemporary issues in French linguistic policies'. In Salhi (ed.) (2002) (pp. 35–72).

Judge, S. (2002) 'Language as a human right: A legal problem for France'. In Salhi (ed.) (2002) (pp. 73–106).

Kessler, M.-C. (1999) *La Politique étrangère de la France. Acteurs et processus*. Paris: Presses de Sciences Po.

Kohn, H. (1967) *Prelude to Nation-states. The French and German Experience 1789–1815*. Princeton, NJ: D. van Nostrand Company, Inc.

Lambert, R.D. and Shohamy, E. (eds) (2000) *Language Policy and Pedagogy. Essays in Honor of A. Ronald Walton*. Philadelphia: John Benjamins Publishing Company.

Lapacherie, J.-G. (2004) '*Les élites et la langue française : le grand délaissement*'. In *Libres* No. 2 (2004) (pp. 89–100).

Laurent, J. (1988) *Le français en cage*. Paris: Bernard Grasset.

Le Bras, H. and Todd, E. (1981) *L'Invention de la France. Atlas anthropologique et politique*. Paris: Pluriel.

Lecherbonnier, B. (2005) *Pourquoi veulent-ils tuer le français ?* Paris: Albin Michel.

Leclerc, J. (2005) *Histoire de la langue française*. Available at http://www.tlfq.ulaval.ca/axl/francophonie/histlngfrn.htm (accessed 29.03.2005).

Leparmentier, A. (2004) '*Avec l'élargissement, l'usage du français recule dans les institutions européennes'*. In *Le Monde* (17.02.2004). Available at *Langue française*: http://www.languefrancaise.net/news/index.php?id_news=130 (accessed 2.11.2006).

Lepschy, A.L. and Tosi, A. (2002) *Multilingualism in Italy Past and Present*. Oxford: Legenda.

Libres (2004) No. 2 *Géopolitique de la langue française*. Paris: Office d'Édition Impression Librairie.

Lipiansky, E.M. (1991) *L'Identité française. Représentations, mythes, idéologies*. La Garenne-Colombes: Éditions de l'Espace Européen.

Lodge, R.A. (1993) *French from Dialect to Standard*. London and New York: Routledge.

Maiden, M. (2002) 'The definition of multilingualism in historical perspective. In Lepschy and Tosi (2002) (pp. 331–46).

Marso, P. (2004) *Pa Sage a TaBa : Le 1ᵉʳ livre en langage SMS*. Accessed at http://www.profsms.com.compasage.htm (19.03.2005, no longer accessible).

Marso, P. (2005) *L*. Available at http://profsms.com/comL.htm (accessed 17.03.2005).

Martinet, A. (1962) '*Le français tel qu'on le parle'*. In *Esprit* No. 311, November (pp. 620–631).

Migliorini, B. (1966) *The Italian Language* (T.G. Griffith, ed.). London: Faber and Faber.

Mignot, A. (2001) *Création du FFI – Forum francophone international* (3.07.2001). Available at http://www.voxlatina.com/vox_dsp2.php3?art=910 (accessed 5.04.2005)

Mignot, A. (2002a) *La francophonie, un devoir de résistance* (05.2002). Available at http://www.voxlatina.com/vox_dsp2.php3?art=1460 (accessed 29.03.2005).

Mignot, A. (2002b) *Francosphère – Info ou intox ?* (21.07.2002) Available at http://www.voxlatina.com/vox_dsp2.php3?art=1492 (accessed 29.03.2005).

Mitterrand, F. (1981) *Propositions*. Available at http://www.psinfo.net/entretiens/mitterrand/110.html (accessed 30.03.2005)

Mitterrand, F. (1983) Speech (accessed 2004, no longer accessible).

Moisi, D. (2004) '*La célébration d'un art de vivre'*. In *Le Figaro* (26.06.2004), *Qu-est-ce qu'être français aujourd'hui ?*

Molinero, C. (2000) 'The Iberian peninsula: Conflicting linguistic nationalisms'. In Barbour and Carmichael (2000) (pp. 83–104).

Mordrel, O. (1981) *Le Mythe de l'hexagone*. Paris: Jean Picollec.

Nettle, D. and Romaine, S, (2000) *Vanishing Voices. The Extinction of the World's Languages*. Oxford: Oxford University Press.

Offord, M. (1994) 'Protecting the French language'. In Parry *et al.* (1994) (pp. 75–94).

Orsenna, E. (2001) *La Grammaire est une chanson douce*. Paris: Stock.

Orsenna, E. (2004) *Les Chevaliers du subjonctif*. Paris: Stock.

Ostler, N. (2005) *Empires of the Word. A Language History of the World*. New York: HarperCollins.

Parry, M.M., Davies W.V., and Temple R.A.V. (eds) (1994) *The Changing Voices of Europe*. Cardiff: University of Wales Press.

Pavlenko, A. and Blackledge, A. (eds) (2004) *Negotiation of Identities in Multilingual Contexts*. Clevedon: Multilingual Matters.

Petnkeu Nzepa, Z. (2003) '*Espace francophone et politiques linguistiques: glottophagie ou diversité culturelle ?' In Présence francophone* No. 60 (pp. 80–97).

Phillipson, R. (1992) *Linguistic Imperialism*. Oxford: Oxford University Press.

Phillipson, R. (2003) *English-only Europe? Challenging Language Policy*. London: Routledge.

Pivot, B. (2004a) *100 mots à sauver*. Paris: Albin Michel.

Pivot, B. (2004b) '*Saint Bernard des mots'*. Interview. In *L'Express (8.03.2004)*. Available at http://www.lexpress.fr/concours/100mots/ (accessed 23.11.2006).

Poignant, B. (2003) *'Trois questions à . . . Bernard Poignant'*. In *Le Monde* (3.10.2003). Available at http://www.mondeberbere.com/presse/20031004_lemonde_poignant.htm (accessed 30.03.2005).

Price, G. (1971) *The French Language: Present and Past*. London: Edward Arnold.

Pulgram, Ernst (1958) *The Tongues of Italy*. Cambridge MA:, Harvard University Press.

Renan, E. (1882) *Qu'est-ce qu'une nation ?* Lecture at the Sorbonne (11.03.1882). Available at http://ourworld.compuserve.com/homepages/bib_lisieux/nation01.htm and other sites (accessed 30.03.2005).

Rickard, P. (1989) *A History of the French Language*. London: Unwin Hyman.

Rivarol, A. de (1783) *Discours sur l'universalité de la langue française*. Available at http://homepage.univie.ac.at/manuel.chemineau/Texte/rivarol-univ-lf.htm (accessed 31.03.2005).

Ruzza, C. (2000) 'Language and nationalism in Italy: Language as a weak marker of identity'. In Barbour and Carmichael (2000) (pp. 168–182).

Saint Robert, M.-J. de (2000) *La Politique de la langue française*. Paris: Presses universitaires de France.

Sanders, C. (ed.) (1993) *French Today. Language in its Social Context*. Cambridge: Cambridge University Press.

Salhi, K. (ed.) (2002) *French In and Out of France. Language Policies, Intercultural Antagonisms and Dialogue*. Bern: Peter Lang.

Salon, A. (2003) *Une pétition pour la défense de la Francophonie* (8.07.2003). Available at http://www.voxlatina.com/vox_dsp2.php3?art=1726 (accessed 30.03.2005).

Salon, A. (2004a) *'Francophonie et Internet'*. Interview. In *Fête de l'Internet* (27.02.2004). Available at http://www.fete-internet.fr/article43.html (accessed 23.03.2004, no longer accessible).

Salon, A. (2004b) *Esquisse d'une nouvelle politique étrangère de la France après une victoire du « Non » au référendum* (11.11.2004). Available at http://www.voxlatina.com/vox_dsp2.php3?art=1819 (accessed 30.03.2005).

Schlieben-Lange, B. (2000) *Sprache et Gesellschaft in Frankreich um 1800. Brigitte Schieben-Lange en tant que dix-huitièmiste*. Available at http://www.neccessaire.com/exposition/menue2.htm (accessed 21.03.2006).

Schiffman, H.F. (2000) *French Language Policy: Centrism, Orwellian dirigisme, or Economic Determinism?* Available at http://ccat.sas.upenn.edu/~haroldfs/540/handouts/french/dirigism/DIRIGISM.html (accessed 30.03.2005).

Schmid, R. (2004) 'English dominance 'past sell-by date''. In *The Guardian Weekly. Learning English (TEFL) Supplement* (March 2004), p. 1.

Schröder, K. (1993) 'Languages'. In Shelley and Winck (eds) (1993) (pp. 113–64).

Shelley, M. and Winck, M. (eds) (1993) *Aspects of European Cultural Diversity*. London: Routledge.

Spolsky, B. (2004) *Language Policy*. Cambridge: Cambridge University Press.

Spolsky, B. and Shohamy, E. (2000) 'Language practice, language ideology, and language policy'. In Lambert and Shohamy (2000) (pp. 1–41).

Theisse, A.-M. (2001) *La création des identités nationales. Europe XVIIIe–XXe siècle* (2nd edn). Paris: Seuil.

Thody, P. (1995) *Le Franglais. Forbidden English Forbidden American. Law, Politics and Language in Contemporary France. A Study in Loan Words and National Identity*. London: The Athlone Press.

Touraine, A. (2003) *'Une France plurielle . . . ou éclatée ? Un débat entre Elisabeth Badinter*

et Alain Touraine'. In Le Nouvel Observateur (19.06.2003). Available at http://perso.
wanadoo.fr/sacw/fund/touraine_badinter_june2003.html (accessed 30.03.2005).
Truss, L. (2003) *Eats, Shoots and Leaves. The Zero Tolerance Approach to Punctuation.*
London: Profile Books.
van Dixhoorn, L. (2002) *Entrevue avec . . . Bernard Cerquiglini, Délégué général à la
Langue française et aux langues de France* (March 2002). Available at http://www.
rfi.fr/francais/languefr/articles/072/article_234.asp (accessed 2.11.2006).
Vaugelas, C.F. de [1647] (1970) *Remarques sur la langue françoise utiles à ceux que
veulent bien parler et bien escrire.* Paris. Facsimile Edition: Geneva: Slatkine.
Vinatier, J. and Xvolt, F. (2002a) *'Pour en finir avec la Francophonie'.* In *Le Figaro*
(8.08.2002). Available at http://www.presse-francophone.org/GAZETTE/gazette_
107pour%20en%20finir_htm (accessed 03.10.2006).
Vinatier, J. and Xvolt, F. (2002b) *Pour en finir avec la Francophonie.* Available at
http://www.voxlatina.com/vox_dsp2.php3?art=1524 (accessed 30.03.2005).
Walter, H. (1988) *Le Français dans tous les sens.* Paris: Laffont.
Walter, H. (1994) *L'Aventure des langues en occident.* Paris: Laffont.
Walter, H. (1997) *L'Aventure des mots français venus d'ailleurs.* Paris: Laffont.
Walter, H. (2001a) *Honni soit qui mal y pense L'incroyable histoire d'amour entre le
français et l'anglais.* Paris: Laffont.
Walter, H. (2001b) *'Nous sommes trop timides'.* In *Lire* No. 294 (pp. 50–51). Available at
http://www.lire.fr/enquete.asp?idC=34254&idTC=15&idR=200&idG=8(accessed
30.03.2005).
Wardhaugh, R. (1987) *Languages in Competition.* Oxford: Basil Blackwell.
Wolff, G. (1986) *Deutsche Sprachgeschichte.* Frankfurt am Main: Athenäum.
Wiltzer, P.-A. (2004) *'L'avenir de notre langue se joue sur le front européen'.* In *L'Express*
(15.03.2004) (p. 32).

Internet sites (dates most recently accessed in brackets)
ABC de la langue française, L' (30.03.2005) http://www.languefrancaise.net
Aigreurs francophoniques: http://www.languefrancaise.net/news/index.php?id_
news=195
Barère: http://www.languefrancaise.net/dossiers/dossiers.php?id_dossier=
64
Chronologie: http://www.languefrancaise.net/dossiers/cat.php?idcat=53
Grégoire: http://www.languefrancaise.net/dossiers/dossiers.php?id_dossier=66
Montbret: http://www.languefrancaise.net/dossiers/dossiers.php?id_dossier=28
Publications: http://www.languefrancaise.net/dossiers/dossiers.php?id_
dossier=28
Académie française, L'. (30.03.2005) http://www.academie-francaise.fr/
Dates: http://www.academie-francaise.fr/histoire/index.html
Defence: http://www.academie-francaise.fr/role/index.html
History: http://www.academie-francaise.fr/histoire/index.html
Language: http://www.academie-francaise.fr/langue/index.html
La Francophonie (OIF): http://www.academie-francaise.fr/langue/index.html
Lefrançais, langue de la nation: http://www.academie-francais.fr/langue/index.
html
Preface, 9th edition: http://www.academie-francaise.fr/dictionnaire/index.html
Questions courantes: http://www.academie-francaise.fr/langue/index.html
Statutes: http://www.academie-francaise.fr/role/statuts.html

Accademia della Crusca (30.03.2005) http://www.accademiadellacrusca.it/CLIC http://www.accademiadellacrusca.it/Info_CLIC.shtml
Acción Cultural Miguel de Cervantes (30.03.2005) http://www.ctv.es/USERS/fadice/acmc.htm
Action française (21.04.2006) http://www.actionfrancaise.net/
Adminet (30.03.2005) http://www.admi.net/index_fr.html
  Decree 85–1006: http://www.admi.net/jo/dec85–1006.html
  Decree 96–602: http://www.adminet.com/jo/19960705/MCCB9600333D.html
Agence Intergouvernementale de la Francophonie (AIF) (30.03.2005) http://agence.francophonie.org/
  European Union: http://www.parlez-francais.com/
  French language: http://www.francophonie.org/actions/francais/index.cfm
AIMF (*Association internationale des maires francophones*) (30.03.2005) http://www.aimf.asso.fr/
ALF (*Avenir de la langue française*)(6.04.2006) http://www.avenirlanguefrancaise.org/
Alliance française (30.03.2005) http://www.alliancefr.org
  Chirac: (2.11.2006) http://www.elysee.fr/ (Speech: 27.01.2004)
  Daugé: http://www.assembleenationale.fr/rap-info/i2924.asp
  de Gaulle: Available on PowerPoint
  Mission: Available on Powerpoint
  PowerPoint: (2.11.2006) http://www.alliancefr.org/html_fr/pdf/extranet/diaporama_france.ppt
  Viot: Available on Powerpoint
Alliance pour la Souveraineté de la France (30.03.2005) http://www.souverainete-france.org/
  Movements: http://www.souverainete-france.org/php/pages/choix.php?menu= 20300
Alsace d'abord (30.03.2005) http://www.alsacedabord.org /
An Arvorig (30.03.2005) http://www.anarvorig.com/
Assemblée nationale see France, Government of
APF (*Assemblée parlementaire francophone*) (30.03.2005) http://www.apf.francophonie.org/
APROBI (*Association des professionnels de la traduction des brevets d'invention*) (30.03.2005):
  (a) http://www.aprobi.asso.fr/AccordLondres.html
  (b) http://www.aprobi.asso.fr/PositionsAprobi.htm
ASGPF (*Association des secrétaires généraux des parlements francophones*) (30.03.2005) http://www.asgpf-francophonie.org/
ASSELAF (*Association pour la sauvegarde et l'expansion du français*) (22.04.2004, no longer accessible)
AUG (*Agence Universitaire de la Francophonie*) (30.03.2005) http://www.auf.org/
Avenir France République (2005) see *Europe, Une, Libre, Grande* and *Alliance pour la Souveraineté de la France*.
  European Charter (a) http://persoweb.francenet.fr/~languefr/asselaf/lettres25-P3.htm (no longer accessible)
  (b) http://www.perso.wanadoo.fr/.escoles/CHARTE.htm (no longer accessible)
British Council (30.03.2005) http://www2.britishcouncil.org/history/
Canada, Government of (29.03.2005) *Les Langues et les cultures minoritaires en France : une approche juridique contemporain.* Quebec: *Publications du Conseil supérieur de*

la langue française, No. D118 (1985). http://www.cslf.gouv.qc.ca/publications/PubD118/D118P1T1ch1.html.

CSLF (30.03.2005) http://www.cslf.gouv.qc.ca/Publications/pub.htm

Carpette anglaise, la (30.03.2005) http://www.languefrancaise.net/news/index.php?id_news=193

Cassamarca Foundation (30.03.2005) http://www.fondazionecassamarca.it/home. html

Catholiques pour les Libertés économiques (6.04.2005) (newsletter) http://www.libeco.net/lettres0.htm

Centre national de recherche scientifique (CNRS) (2.11.2006) http://www.cnrs.fr/_Raffarin Circular (dated 14.02.2003):_ http://www.dsi.cnrs.fr/bo/2003/05-03/431-bo0503-cirdu14-02-2003.htm

Chambers Dictionary (30.03.2005) http://www.chambersharrap.co.uk/chambers/

CLIC _(Centro di consulenza sulla lingua italiana contemporanea)_ (30.03.2005) http://www.accademiadellacrusca.it/Info_CLIC.shtml

Club d'orthographe (8.04.2006) http://guterrien.free.fr/partenariat-club-orthographe-INPG.html

Confédération des écologistes indépendants (29.09.2006) http://www.cei-msr.com
Aims: http://www.dfait-maeci.gc.ca/foreign_policy/francophonie/perm_sectoral-fr.asp#laconferencedesministresdeleducationdespaysayantlefrancaisenpartage

CONFEJES _(Conférence des ministres de la Jeunesse et des Sports des pays francophones)_ 30.03.2005) http://www.confejes.org/

CONFEMEN _(Conférence des ministres de l'éducation nationale des pays francophones)_ (30.03.2005) http://www.confemen.org/

Conseil constitutionnel see France, Government of

Council of Europe (30.03.2005)
Charte européenne des langues régionales et minoritaires (voted 5.11.1992) (text) http://conventions.coe.int/Treaty/EN/Treaties/Html/148.htm

Courrier Sud (30.03.2005) http://courriersud.free.fr/historique.htm

CSA _(Conseil supérieur de l'audiovisuel)_ (30.03.2005) http://www.csa.fr/index.php
French language: http://www.csa.fr/infos/langue/langue_francaise.php

DLF _(Défense de la langue française)_ (30.03.2005) http://www.langue-francaise.org/
Voisin text: http://www.langue-francaise.org/Textes_politiques/Voisin_28_04_2003. php

de Gaulle, Charles (www.charles-de-gaulle.org) (30.03.2005) http://212.234.185.8/

DGLFLF _(Délégation générale à la langue française et aux langues de France)_ see France, Government of

D*lires (30.03.2005) http://cetnia.blogs.com/d_lires/

Deutsche Sprachwelt (31.03.2005) http://www.deutsche-sprachwelt.de/

Deutsche Welle (31.03.2005) http://www.dw-world.de/english/

DGCCRF _(Direction générale de la concurrence, de la consommation et de la répression des fraudes)_ see France, Government of

Dora bookshop (31.03.2005) http://www.italialibri.net/

Droit de comprendre (30.10.2006) http://perso.orange.fr/avenirlf/DDC/Presentation.htm

ECML (European Centre for Modern Languages) (03.10.2006) http://www.ecml.at

EFNIL (European Federation of National Institutions for Language) (31.03.2006) http://www.eurfedling.org/
Files: http://www.eurfedling.org/ll/files/
Italy: http://www.eurfedling.org/ll/files/italie.pdf

<u>OVI</u>: http://www.eurfedling.org/ita/ovi.htm
<u>Spain</u>: http://www.eurfedling.org/ll/files/.
Enciclopedia Libre Universal en Español (30.10.2006) http://enciclopedia.us.es/
index.php/Enciclopedia_Libre_Universal_en_Espa%F1ol
English-Speaking Union (31.03.2005) http://www.esu.org/
EUROPA A Constitution for Europe (8.12.2005) http://europa.eu.int/constitution/
index_en.htm
Europe, Une, Libre, Grande (17.03.2005) http://www.argent.fr/
<u>Constitution Date</u>: http://www.argent.fr/reunions.htm
European Charter for Regional or Minority Languages (31.03.2005) http://conventions.coe.int/Treaty/EN/Treaties/Html/148.htm (5.11.1992)
European Patent Office (31.03.2005) http://www.european-patent-office.org/news/info/2003_04_30_f.htm
European Union (31.03.2005) http://europa.eu
<u>Constitution</u>: http://ue.eu.int/ueDocs/cms_Data/docs/pressData/en/misc/81109.pdf
<u>Committee of the Regions</u> (30.10.2006) http://www.cor.europa.eu/en/index.htm
<u>Convention</u>: http://european-convention.eu.int/
Europe politique. Le portail francophone de la vie politique en Europe: (31.10.2006) http://elections.online.fr/
Express, L' http://www.lexpress.fr
<u>Interview with Bernard Pivot</u> (8.03. 2004): http://www.lexpress.fr/concours/100mots/
FADICE (*Federación de Asociaciones por el Derecho al Idioma Común Español*) (31.03.2005) http://www.ctv.es/USERS/fadice/fadice.htm
<u>*Acción Cultural Miguel de Cervantes*</u>: http://www.ctv.es/USERS/fadice/acmc.htm
FFI (*Forum francophone international*) (31.03.2005) http://www.voxlatina.com/
<u>Constitution</u>: http://www.imperatif-francais.org/articles2/statut.html
<u>Creation</u>: http://www.voxlatina.com/vox_dsp2.php3?art=910
<u>History</u>: http://www.voxlatina.com/vox_dsp2.php3?art=1034
<u>Villers-Cotterêts Appeal</u>: http://www.voxlatina.com/petition4.php3
Figaro, Le (2004) http://www.lefigaro.fr
<u>London Protocol</u> (accessible in archives of *Le Figaro*) http://www.langue-francaise.org/Articles_Dossiers/Dos_Brevet_figaro27_12_02.html
France bonapartiste (21.04.2006) http://francebonapartiste.free.fr/
France, Government of (31.03.2005)
<u>AIF</u> (*Agence intergouvernementale de la Francophonie*) http://agence.francophonie.org/
<u>European Union</u>: http://www.parlez-francais.com/
<u>French language</u>: http://www.agence.francophonie.org/actions/francais/index.cfm
<u>*Assemblée nationale*</u>:
Dauge Report: http://www.assembleenationale.fr/rap-info/i2924.asp
Résolution sur la diversité linguistique: http://www.assemblee-nat.fr/12/ta/ta0229.asp
Tavernier Report: http://www.assemblee-nationale.fr/rap-info/i2592.asp
Herbillon Report (7.02.2006) http://www.assemblee-nationale.fr/12/europe/rap-info/i0902.asp
Herbillon Resolution: http://www.assemblee-nationale.fr/12/europe/resolutions/ppe0907.asp

Conseil constitutionnel, Le: http://www.conseil-constitutionnel.fr
DGCCRF *(Direction générale de la concurrence, de la consommation et de la répression des fraudes)* http://www.finances.gouv.fr/DGCCRF/
DGLFLF *(Délégation générale à la langue française et aux langues de France)* http://www.culture.gouv.fr/culture/dglf/
Assises: (2.11.2006)http://www.culture.gouv.fr/culture/dglf/politique-langue/assises/compte_rendu_assises.htm
History: http://www.culture.gouv.fr/culture/dglf/lois/archives/histoire1.htm; http://www. culture.gouv.fr/culture/dglf/lois/archives/histoire2.htm
Reports: 2001–2006 :http://www.culture.gouv.fr/culture/dglf/publications/publications.htm
Francophonie: http://www.francophonie.org/
CIFDI *(Carrefour international francophone de documentation et d'information)*: http://cifdi.francophonie.org/
Charter: http://www.presse-francophone.org/francophonie/francophonie_charte. htm
Institutions: http://www.presse-francophone.org/francophonie/francophonie_institutions.htm
Laval: http://www.tlfq.ulaval.ca/axl/francophonie/francophonie.htm
Légifrance: http://www.legifrance.gouv.fr/
Loi Savary: http://www.legifrance.gouv.fr/Waspad/ImagesSarde.jsp?anee=1984&pageDebJO=0.431&pageFinJO=0+440&annexe
Legisnet: http://www.legisnet.com/france/marianne.html
MAE *Ministère des Affaires Étrangères:* http://www.france.diplomatie.fr
DGCID*(DirectiongénéraledelaCoopérationinternationaleetduDéveloppement)*http://www.diplomatie.gouv.fr/fr/ministere_817/missions-organisation_823/structure-administration-centrale_808/direction-generale-cooperation-internationale-du- developpement_3146/index.html
MCC *(Ministère de la Culture et de la Communication)* http://www.culture.fr
Carcassonne Study: http://www.culture.gouv.fr/culture/dglf/lang-reg/langreg7. htm
Cerquiglini Report: http://www.culture.gouv.fr/culture/dglf/lang-reg/rapport_cerquiglini/langues-france.html
Enrichissement:http://www.culture.gouv.fr/culture/dglf/terminologie/grand-ligne-dispo.html
Jospin Reports: http://www.culture.gouv.fr/culture/dglf/lang-reg/lang-reg7. htm
1998(a): http://www.culture.gouv.fr/culture/dglf/lang-reg/lang-reg8.htm
Loi Deixonne: http://www.tlfq.ulaval.ca/axl/Europe/France-loi_Deixonne-texte-1951.htm
Poignant Report: http://portalcat.univ-perp.fr/ftp/RapportPoignant.pdf
Raffarin Circular: http://www.culture.gouv.fr/culture/dglf/lois/circ–14–2–03. html
OIF *(Organisation internationale de la Francophonie)* http://www.francophonie. org/Diouf: http://www.francophonie.org/doc/dernieres/Discours_sg_2006_01_16.pdf (06.04.2006).
RIFAL *(Réseau international francophone d'aménagement linguistique)* http://www. rifal.org/index_f.html
Senate:
Grignon Report: http://www.senat.fr/presse/cp200110628a.html

London Protocol: http://www.senat.fr/presse/cp20010628a.html
Teaching: http://www.senat.fr/evenement/archives/scolaire.html
France politique (17.03.2005) http://francepolitique.free.fr/
Francophonie see France, Government of
French Government see France, Government of
Gesellschaft für deutsche Sprache (31.03.2005) http://www.gfds.de
Goethe Institut (31.03.2005) http://www.goethe-institut.de
Haut-Comité pour la défense et l'expansion de la langue française (17.03.2005) http://
    www.culture.gouv.fr/culture/dglf/lois/archives/31_03_66.htm
IEPF (*Institut de l'énergie et de l'environnement de la francophonie*) (31.03.2005) http://
    www.iepf.org/
INED (*Institut national des études démographiques*) (17.03.2005) http://www.ined.fr/
INSEE (*Institut national de la statistique et études économiques*) (17.03.2005) http://
    www.insee.fr/
Institut für deutsche Sprache (31.03.2005) http://www.ids-mannheim.de/
Instituto Cervantes (17.03.2005) http://www.cervantes.es/
    Centro Virtual Cervantes: http://cvc.cervantes.es/portada.htm
International Declaration of Linguistic Rights (31.03.2005) http://www.galernn.
    lautre.net/Francais/decldroitlingfr.htm
Italy, Government of (31.03.2005)
    1998 Proposal: http://www.camera.it/_dati/leg13/lavori/stampati/sk5000/
    articola/4649.htm
    Ministry of Foreign Affairs: http://www.esteri.it/
Jeune France (17.03.2005) http://www.jeune-france.org
Langue française (17.03.2005) http://www.languefrancaise.net/dossiers/dossiers.
    php?id_dossier=61
Légifrance see France, Government of
Legisnet see France, Government of
Libération: http://www.liberation.fr/
    Chefd'oeuvremasochiste(30.05.2005)http://www.liberation.fr/page.php?Article=
    300064
Liguria Independence League (31.03.2005) http://www.mil2002.org/
    Italian Radical Party: http://www.mil2002.org/stampa/030310em.htm
Linternaute (17.03.2005) http://www.linternaute.com/histoire/annee/1794/a/1/1/
    index.shtml
*Lire : le magazine littéraire. L'actualité de la littérature française et de la littérature
    étrangère.* (29.03.2005) http://www.lire.fr
Lombardy League (31.03.2005) http://www.legalombarda.net/
London Protocol (17.03.2005) http://www.aprobi.asso.fr/AccordLondres.html
Merriam-Webster Dictionary On-line (31.03.2005) http://www.m-w.com/
Ministère de la culture (MCC) see France, Government of
Ministère des affaires étrangères (MAE) see France, Government of
Northern Ireland (31.03.2005)
    Languages: http://www.dcalni.gov.uk/allpages/allpages.asp?pname=language
Office pour la langue et la culture d'Alsace (15.03.2006) http://www.olcalsace.org
Ordine dei giornalisti (31.03.2005) http://www.odg.it/
Organisation pour les Minorités Européennes (Organisation for European Minorities)
    (31.03.2005) http://www.eurominority.org/version/fra/index.asp
OVI (*Opera del Vocabulario Italiano*) (31.03.2005) http://www.eurfedling.org/ita/
    ovi.htm

Oxford English Dictionary (31.03.2005) http://www.oed.com/about/history.html
Página del Idioma español, La (17.03.2005) http://www.elcastellano.org/
Padania (31.03.2005) http://www.lapadania.com/
PDPE-ALE (*Parti démocratique des Peuples d'Europe – Alliance libre européenne*) See
   Europe politique.
Polemia (5.10.2006) http://www.polemia-com/contenu.php?cat_id=22&iddoc=398
Rassemblement Gaulliste (31.03.2005) http://www.gaulliste.com/
Real Academia Española (31.03.2005) http://www.rae.es/
   Dictionary: http://buscon.rae.es/diccionario/cabecera.htm
Réseau des femmes parlementaires (31.10.2006) http://apf.francophonie.org/
   -Le-reseau-des-femmes-.html
RIF (*Rassemblement pour l'Indépendance et la Souveraineté de la France*) (31.03.2005)
   http://www.souverainete.org
Royal Society of London (3.10.2006) http://www.royalsoc.ac.uk
Salva la lingua (31.03.2005) http://assente.altervista.org/?g+node/view/28
Scotland (31.03.2005)
   Languages: http://www.scottish.parliament.uk/home.htm
Senate see France, Government of
Senior Citizens (Nuremburg) (31.03.2005) http://www.rolandhegendoerfer.de/
Società Dante Alighieri (10.04.2006) http://www.ladante.it/index.asp
Société française des traducteurs (31.03.2005)
   Petition: http://www.voxlatina.com/petition2.php3
SOS République (2.11.2006) http://sosrepublique.free.fr/
Stop-Françafrique (31.03.2005) http://www.stop-francafrique.com/
Survie (31.03.2005) http://www.survie-france.org/
ThefreeDictionary (On-line dictionary/encyclopedia in English) (17.03.2005)
   http://www.encyclopedia.thefreedictionary.com/%20%20%20/
Universität Wien (31.03.2005) http://www.univie.ac.at/
   Rivarol text: http://homepage.univie.ac.at/manuel.chemineau/Texte/rivarol-
   univ-lf.htm
Université Laval (17.03.2005) http://www.tlfq.ulaval.ca/axl/
   Breton: http//www.tlfq.ulaval.ca/axl/francophonie/HIST_FR_s9.Fr-contem-
   porain.htm (accessed 30.03.2005).
   Francophonie: http://www.tlfq.ulaval.ca/axl/francophonie/francophonie.htm
   Germany: http://www.tlfq.ulaval.ca/axl/Europe/allemagne_pol-lng.htm
   Great Britain: http://www.tlfq.ulaval.ca/axl/europe/royaumeuni.htm
   History: http://www.tlfq.ulaval.ca/axl/francophonie/histlngfrn.htm
   Index: http://www.tlfq.ulaval.ca/axl/monde/index_alphabetique.htm
   Italy: http://www.tlfq.ulaval.ca/axl/europe/italieacc.htm
   Languages in the world: www.tlfq.ulaval.ca/axl/index.shtml
   Revolution: http://www.tlfq.ulaval.ca/axl/francophonie/HIST_FR_s8_Revo-
   lution1789.htm
   Spain: http://www.tlfq.ulaval.ca/axl/Europe/espagneetat.htm
   Catalonia: http://www.tlfq.ulaval.ca/axl/Europe/espagnecatalogne.htm
   Wales: http://www.tlfq.ulaval.ca/axl/europe/paysgalles.htm
Université Paris 2 Panthéon-Assas (31.03.2005) http://www.u-paris2.fr
UniversityofPennsylvania(31.03.2005)http://ccat.sas.upenn.edu/~haroldfs/540/
   handouts/french/ordVC.html
University of Toronto (30.03.2005)

Schlieben-Lange: http://www.chass.utoronto.ca/epc/langueXIX/naisphil/np_
4. htm
UPF (*Union internationale de la Presse Francophone*) (17.03.2005) http://www.presse-
francophone.org/
US English Foundation, Inc. (17.03.2005) http://www.us-english.org/foundation/
US Library of Congress (31.03.2005) http://lcweb2.loc.gov/
Verdammi (31.03.2005) http://www.verdammi.org/
Verein deutsche Sprache (31.03.2005) http://www.vds-ev.de
VIGILE (17.03.2005) http://www.vigile.net/99mai/AGQdurandsarre.html
Voix des Français, La (21.04.2006) http://www.vdfr95.com/index.htm
Voxlatina (30.03.2005) http://www.voxlatina.com/
  ALF (*Avenir de la langue française*) http://www.voxlatina.com.vox_dsp2.
  php3?art=1789
  Appel au redressement: http://www.voxlatina.com/vox_dsp2.php3?art=1737
  Bollmann: http://www.voxlatina.com/vox_dsp2.php3?art=1773
  Daguet: (7.12.2003) http://www.voxlatina.com/vox_dsp2.php3?art=1767
  Demonstration: http://www.voxlatina.com/vox_dsp2.php3?art=1761
  Dossier du Non [European Constitution] (9.12.2005): http://www.voxlatina.
  com/dossiers.php?dossier=7
  Entente souverainiste (5.10.2006). http://www.voxlatina.com/vox_dsp2.php3?art=
  1681
  Villers-Cotterêts Appeal: http://www.voxlatina.com/petition4.php3
Wales (31.03.2005) http://www.tlfq.ulaval.ca/axl/europe/paysgalles.htm
  Welsh Language Act: (2.11.2006) http://www.opsi.gov.uk/acts/acts1993/Ukpga_
  19930038_en_1.htm
Webster's Dictionary (17.03.2005)
  Brief History (1989): http://ling.kgw.tu-berlin.de/lexicography/data/B_HIST_
  EU.html
  Merriam-Webster: http://www.m-w.com/
Wikipedia (on-line encyclopedia in many languages) (31.03.2005)
  Deutsches Wörterbuch: http://de.wikipedia.org/wiki/Deutsches_W%C3%
  B6rterbuch
  English: http://en.wikipedia.org/wiki/Main_Page
  French: http://fr.wikipedia.org/
  Fruchtbringende Gesellschaft: http://de.wikipedia.org/wiki/Fruchtbringende_
  Gesellschaft
  German: http://de.wikipedia.org/
  Grimm: http://fixedreference.org/en/20040424/wikipedia/Jakob_Grimm
  Spain: http://es.wikipedia.org/wiki/Portada

Index

Note: Abbreviations are explained on p. viii

ABC de la langue française 1, 7, 11, 30, 31, 47, 86, 89, 91
Académie française 1, 4, 5, 10, 19, 24, 50-55, 82, 115, 119, 122, 129, 135, 139, 149, 161, 170
Accademia della crusca 110, 111, 119, 121-122
ACCT 15, 69, 139
acquisition planning *see* language planning
actors *see* language planning
AFAA 59
AFAL 16, 17, 29, 46, 68
AFP 9
Ager, Dennis 14, 44, 48, 49, 106, 125, 136, 156, 161, 163
AIF 16, 23, 70-73, 75
AIMF 21, 23, 68, 75
ALF 16, 17, 18, 29, 44, 46, 98, 101, 104, 165, 167, 168
Alliance française 10, 11, 50, 55-60, 122, 129, 134, 139, 140, 173
Alliance souverainiste 100, 102, 104
Alsace 82, 90, 94-98
Alsace d'abord 93, 94-98, 120
Anglo-saxons, les xvii, xix, 1, 58, 89, 143, 152, 160, 170, 172
APF 21, 23
APROBI 41
ASSELAF 16, 17, 29, 39, 46
Assemblée nationale 28, 31, 37, 42, 78, 79, 100, 151, 152, 162, 166, 167
Assises nationales des langues de France 17, 66, 67
AUF 21, 22, 24, 47, 68

Barère, Bertrand 7, 84, 85, 86
Berlusconi, Silvio 120, 121
bottom-up planning *see* language planning
Braudel, Fernand 154
breton 9, 30, 31, 86
British Commonwealth 22, 89, 136
British Council 58, 134, 139, 140
Bruézière, Maurice 55, 56, 58
Brussels 7, 20, 29, 34, 43, 44, 48, 104, 123, 140, 157, 162

Calvet, Jean-Louis xvi, xx, 3, 71, 109, 144, 145, 148, 149, 152, 155, 156, 159, 169, 170, 171
Canada 12, 15, 48, 88
Carcassonne, Guy 38
Carpette anglaise, Prix de la 17, 37, 173
Carrère d'Encausse, Hélène 54
Cassamarca Foundation 123
Castilian 125-130
Catalan 31, 93, 111 127-131
Catalonia 126-128, 130
Centro Virtual Cervantes 130
Cerquiglini, Bernard xvi, 1, 31, 39, 62, 65-66, 83, 84
– Report 31
Charlemagne 83
Chirac, Jacques 14, 26, 57, 59, 61
Citron, Suzanne xix, 1, 2, 87-88, 147, 154, 155, 158
CLIC 122
Clubs d'orthographe 174
colonies xviii, 10-11, 15, 56, 70, 73, 88-89, 90, 133
Comité Valmy xvii, xix, 17
Common European Framework of Reference 169
comparisons 107-142
Conseil constitutionnel 25, 27, 35, 38, 151
Constitution, European *see* European Constitution
Constitution (French) 27, 31, 35, 38, 39, 85
Convention, European *see* European Convention
Convention, la 7, 8, 9, 52, 82, 83, 85-86, 90
Cooper, Robert *see* language planning
corpus planning *see* language planning
Corsican 32, 33, 92
Council of Europe 34, 35, 36, 37, 38, 39, 65, 109, 117, 169
Courrier Sud 24
crisis xv, xvi, xx, 143, 153, 163, 166, 169, 171, 174

Crystal, David xviii, 169
CSA 66, 151
CSLF 14, 38, 140

Dante Alighieri Society 58, 122, 129, 139, 140
Daugé Report 60, 78
DCCF 59, 76
death of languages xviii, 145
Declaration of the Rights of Man 23, 36, 103
De Gaulle, Charles 14, 15, 57, 61, 104, 157
Denglish 118, 141
D'Estaing, Giscard 15, 26, 43, 158
Deutsche Sprachwelt 116
DGCCRF 28
DGCID 59, 74-76, 162
DGLF 14, 16, 34, 62, 64, 65, 66, 110, 139, 140
DGLFLF 16, 17, 28, 29, 34, 39, 47, 50, 53, 59, 60-67, 68, 70, 71, 73, 81, 89, 110, 139, 141, 151, 162, 163, 164, 167
diffusion planning *see* language planning
dirigisme xv, 143, 150
discourse xiii, xv, xviii, 16, 31, 158
DLF 16, 17, 24, 29, 47, 165, 167, 173
Droit de comprendre 17, 37
Druon, Maurice 7, 52, 55
du Bellay, Joachim xx, 2-3, 144, 170
Duruy Report 9, 93
Duteil, Yves 173
Dutourd, Jean 47
Duvernois Report 74, 78
DWB 115

ECML 109
education system (French) xiii, 3, 9-11, 19, 25, 30, 33, 58, 59, 68, 70, 87, 93, 95, 105, 155, 162 *see* also MEN
EFNIL 110-112, 116, 117, 121, 122, 123, 128, 131, 136, 139, 140
ends *see* language planning
élite xv, 19, 40, 44, 55, 68, 144, 148, 150, 158, 161, 165, 174
Engliano 124
English Academy 135
English-speaking Union 136
enlargement of the EU 36, 37, 38, 42, 43, 45, 62, 80, 163
Enlightenment 6-8
enrichissement de la langue française 12, 53, 64
Entente souverainiste 98-100, 104
Estienne, Henri 3
Etiemble 13, 60
European Charter for Regional or Minority
    Languages 36, 39, 43, 65, 95, 97, 117, 124, 131, 137, 139, 141, 150

European Constitution 36, 43-44, 48, 85, 96, 101, 140, 153, 157-158, 168
European Convention 43, 158
European Language Portfolio 169
European Union xv, xix, 7, 20, 27, 29, 34-45, 72, 73, 80, 86, 93, 96, 97, 107, 109, 116, 117, 122, 124, 136, 140, 142, 143, 153, 156-158, 163
– Committee of the Regions 131

fascism 92, 120, 123, 127, 152
Federal Republic of Germany *see* Germany
Félibrige 92
feminisation xviii, 63, 124, 131
Ferry, Jules 10, 11, 30, 87
FFI xvii, xix, 17, 41, 44, 47, 98-99, 101, 105, 116, 147, 158
fines/penalties (*Loi Toubon*) 17, 26, 28, 151
Fishman, Joshua xviii, 160, 168, 169
Forza Italia 120, 121
Franco, General 126, 127, 129
François 1er xvii, 2-3, 4, 5, 49, 77, 82-84, 138, 174
Francophonie, la 12, 14-16, 22, 23, 47, 50, 53-54, 57, 62, 63, 64, 67-74, 75, 76, 78, 79, 82, 87-90, 100, 139, 140, 162, 165, 166, 167, 170
franglais, le 13, 60, 138, 151,174
Front National, le 96, 105
Fruchtbringende Gesellschaft 115, 139

Germany 112-118
girondin 40
globalisation xviii, 29, 34, 44, 99, 101, 156, 158-160, 166
Goethe Institute 58, 116, 129, 134, 139, 140
Grégoire, *Abbé* 8, 30, 66, 85-87, 91
Grignon Report 41
Grimm brothers 115

Hagège, Claude xvi, xviii, xix, 1, 33, 153, 155, 156, 159, 168, 169, 172, 173
Haut comité de la langue française 14, 26, 61, 62, 139
*Haut comité pour la défense et l'expansion de la
    langue française* 14, 50, 61, 62
Héran, François 33, 66, 95
Holocaust 114

Identity 153-160
INED 33, 66, 95
INSEE 66
Institut für Deutsche Sprache 110, 116, 139
Instituto Cervantes 129-130, 139, 140

internet 45-49
Italy 118-124

jacobin 28, 40
Jeanne d'Arc 132
Johnson, Dr Samuel 135
Jospin, Lionel 26, 33, 38
Judge, Anne 1, 10, 28, 35, 83, 84, 100, 105, 163

Kessler, Marie-Christine xix, 56, 57, 59, 68, 70, 73, 77, 80, 83

Länder 112, 113, 114, 115, 117
language and politics 50-81, 150-153
language dominance xvii, xviii, 3, 11, 33, 45, 124, 131, 133, 134, 136, 145, 173
language planning xiv, 4,8
– acquisition planning xiv, 5, 10 ,13, 42, 45, 50, 71, 73, 76, 163
– actors 20, 27, 29, 50, 161, 163, 165, 167
– behaviours 25, 36, 37, 161, 163, 165, 166
– conditions 163, 167, 169, 170, 173
– Cooper, Robert xiv, xix, 4, 20, 32, 51, 62, 80, 161, 162, 165, 166
– corpus planning xiv, 4, 5, 6, 12, 14, 19, 50, 62
– decision-making process 21, 164
– diffusion planning xiv, 14, 45, 50, 63, 67, 76, 77, 163
– effect 32, 45, 80, 162, 164, 168
– ends: overt/latent 20, 24, 32, 36, 163, 166
– environmental influences 33, 45, 62, 67, 70, 81, 97, 167
– information 163, 167
– means 4, 20, 25, 26, 28, 29, 32, 45, 80, 163, 164, 167
– people 162, 165, 166
– processes 21, 32, 81, 162, 163, 164, 166, 167
– status planning xiv, 4, 5, 6, 7, 10, 14, 20, 27, 32, 45, 50, 60, 63, 71, 73, 76, 163
language policy xiv, xix, 8, 15, 20, 24, 29, 32, 36, 60, 66, 67, 70-79, 84, 86, 88, 91-93, 97, 105, 106, 107, 110, 112, 114, 117, 120, 121, 138, 144, 146, 151, 152, 161, 163-167
langue d'oc 84, 192
langue d'oïl 2
laws (language) 24-29
Légifrance 12, 13, 25, 28, 29, 33
Légisnet 25
Liberté, Égalité, Fraternité 7, 27, 85, 90, 151
linguists xv, xvi, xviii, 10, 24, 46, 54, 55, 56, 65, 92, 115, 116, 122, 125, 129, 138, 144, 145, 148, 149, 150, 174

Loi Bas–Lauriol 13, 25, 26, 27, 32, 139
Loi Deixonne 13, 15, 31-33, 139
Loi Toubon xiv, 12, 13, 16, 25, 27-29, 37, 38, 53, 63, 139, 140, 142, 151-152, 165, 168
Luther 113

MAE 74-81
Malherbe, François de 3, 84
Marso 173
MCC 62, 68, 70, 73, 162
MEN 59, 68
Mignot, Alfred xv, xix, 147
Mitterrand, François 14, 15, 32, 33, 57, 61, 67, 68
monolingualism 8, 32, 65, 72, 150
Montbret, Coquebert de 91
multilingualism 37, 160, 167
Mussolini 120, 126

Napoleon 9, 52, 112

occitan 30, 31, 131
official agencies 50-81
OIF 67-74
Orsenna, Eric 174
Ouagadougou 15, 22, 69, 74, 89
overt ends *see* language planning
OVF 12, 13
Oxford English Dictionary 110, 135-136, 139

patents 36, 40, 41
patois 7-8, 9, 11, 29, 86, 91, 92
penalties *see* fines
pilots 24
Pivot, Bernard 12, 17, 174
planning *see* language planning
plurilingualism 42, 63, 158, 171, 172
Poignant, Bernard 33, 38
politics *see* language and politics
Pompidou, Georges 12, 14, 61
Port-Royal 6
private associations xiii, xiv, xv, 7, 13, 16-19, 165-168
processses *see* language planning
Prodi, Romano 37
Protocole de Londres 40 ,168
provençal 30, 92
purity xvi, 3, 5, 6, 7, 91, 115, 119, 120, 129, 146, 149, 165, 166

Quebec xviii, 22, 69, 87, 88, 132, 166
questione della lingua 119

Raffarin circular 27, 42
rap 146, 172
Rastadt, Treaty of 6, 85
Real Academia Española 108, 110, 125,
  128-129, 131, 139
Reclus, Onésisme 10
Referendum (29.05.2005) 43-44, 157, 158
regional and minority languages xv, 8, 20,
  25, 29-34, 38-40, 65, 92, 95, 105, 125, 136,
  137, 143, 156, 157
Renan, Ernest 56, 146, 154
Republic, French xvi, 7, 8, 13, 18, 26, 27, 33,
  35-39, 48, 57, 82, 85-87, 91, 95, 96, 101,
  104, 109, 113, 141, 147, 156, 157, 166
Résistance, la xiii, xvii, 41, 99, 100, 143, 147
résistants xiii, xv, xvii, xviii, 6, 24, 40, 147,
  149, 150, 153, 170, 174
Révolution, la xiii, xvi, 6-8, 30, 82-90, 91-95,
  105, 106, 133
Richelieu, Cardinal 3-6, 51, 82, 84
RIF 44
riots (11.2005) 35, 105, 106, 147
Rivarol, Antoine de 6, 145

Salon, Albert xv, 45, 80, 89, 158, 159, 170
salons 4, 84
Scottish Parliament 133, 137
Senghor, Léopold Sédar 15, 21
Société française des traducteurs 25
Sommets de la Francophonie 13, 15, 23, 70, 75
Spain 124-132
Spanglish 131, 141
Spanish civil war 126-127
spelling reform xviii, 54, 63, 64, 65, 116, 118,
  124, 129
status planning *see* language planning
Statute of Pleading 133

Strategic Framework for Multilingualism
  169
symbols 51, 153, 154
syntax 54, 144

Talleyrand 9, 85
terminology 12, 13, 14, 26, 53, 54, 64, 123,
  144, 145, 162, 163, 165
Thermidor, decret du 2 8, 87
Toubon, Loi see Loi Toubon
Turkey 96, 97, 102, 157

UN xiv, xv, 21, 29, 34, 37, 72, 73, 105, 159,
  162, 163
UNESCO xiv, xv, 21, 29, 80, 162
United States xviii, 41, 80, 89, 99, 101, 108,
  125, 133, 134, 136, 146, 159, 160, 169
 – 'English Only' legislation 134
UPF 11, 12, 21
US English Foundation 109
USA *see* United States

Vaugelas, Claude Favre de 5-6, 84
Verein Deutsche Sprache 116, 117
*verlan*146, 155, 172, 173
Versailles, Treaty of 6
Villers-Cotterêts, Appel xvii, xix, 17, 41, 99
 – *Ordonnance* xvii, 2, 5, 41, 82, 83
Viot, Jacques 59
Voxlatina 25, 41, 42, 43, 47, 98-101, 144, 145,
  146, 147-148, 151, 158

Walter, Henriette xix, 1, 3, 4, 83, 84, 85, 86,
  113, 120, 125, 132, 135, 144, 149
Welsh Language Act 137
Welsh Language Society 133
World Trade Organisation 29, 80, 163